AF323396

SAUDI ARABIA

**Recent Titles in
Global Security Watch**

Global Security Watch—The Caucasus States
Houman A. Sadri

Global Security Watch—Kenya
Donovan C. Chau

Global Security Watch—Jordan
W. Andrew Terrill

Global Security Watch—Japan
Andrew L. Oros and Yuki Tatsumi

Global Security Watch—Sudan
Richard A. Lobban, Jr.

Global Security Watch—Central Asia
Reuel R. Hanks

Global Security Watch—Pakistan
Syed Farooq Hasnat

Global Security Watch—Venezuela
Daniel Charles Hellinger

Global Security Watch—India
Amit Gupta

Global Security Watch—Syria
Fred H. Lawson

Global Security Watch—The Maghreb: Algeria, Libya, Morocco, and Tunisia
Yahia H. Zoubir and Louisa Dris-Aït-Hamadouche

Global Security Watch—China
Richard Weitz

GLOBAL SECURITY WATCH
SAUDI ARABIA

Matthew Gray

 PRAEGER

AN IMPRINT OF ABC-CLIO, LLC
Santa Barbara, California • Denver, Colorado • Oxford, England

Copyright © 2014 by Matthew Gray

All rights reserved. No part of this publication may be reproduced, stored in a retrieval
system, or transmitted, in any form or by any means, electronic, mechanical, photocopying,
recording, or otherwise, except for the inclusion of brief quotations in a review, without
prior permission in writing from the publisher.

Library of Congress Cataloging-in-Publication Data

Gray, Matthew, 1970–
    Global security watch— Saudi Arabia / Matthew Gray.
      pages cm. — (Global security watch)
    Includes bibliographical references and index.
    ISBN 978–0–313–38699–2 (hard copy : alkaline paper) — ISBN 978–0–313–38700–5 (ebook)
1. Saudi Arabia—Foreign relations—1982– 2. National security—Saudi Arabia. 3. Saudi Arabia—
Military policy. 4. Saudi Arabia—Defenses. 5. Saudi Arabia—Politics and government—1982–
6. Economic security—Saudi Arabia. I. Title. II. Title: Saudi Arabia.
DS244.63.G74   2014
355′.0330538—dc23   2014021695

ISBN: 978–0–313–38699–2
EISBN: 978–0–313–38700–5

18 17 16 15 14   1 2 3 4 5

This book is also available on the World Wide Web as an eBook.
Visit www.abc-clio.com for details.

Praeger
An Imprint of ABC-CLIO, LLC

ABC-CLIO, LLC
130 Cremona Drive, P.O. Box 1911
Santa Barbara, California 93116-1911

This book is printed on acid-free paper ∞

Manufactured in the United States of America

Contents

A Note on Transliteration

There is no simple and universally accepted means of transliterating Arabic in English, and few translation systems are much help or use to nonspecialists. Whatever its shortcomings, I have adopted a fairly simple transliteration style here. For words that appear in English routinely, I have given them in their most common English format (thus, Emir, not 'Amīr; Qur'an not Qur'ān, etc.). This includes rendering the ruling dynasty's name as "Al Saud," since this is how it is most commonly seen in English sources, even though the scientific transliteration "Al Su'ūd" would be more accurate. At some points, however, I have been a little more precise, especially in including a ' for the Arabic letter 'ayn; this is sometimes important to distinguish the word from others or to make a meaning completely clear. While this may not be ideal for many specialists, it is the easiest and most appropriate format for an educated or interested lay audience.

To the frustration of some readers, perhaps, there are a few occasions when a person's name is presented with some or all of the person's lineage included. This may run to four, five, or more names. Take the example of King Abdullah, who is often referred to as King Abdullah bin Abd al-Aziz Al Saud, meaning Abdullah son of Abd al-Aziz, from the line of the Saud. This is to distinguish him from other Abdullahs from the same family line. His full name is Abdullah bin Abd al-Aziz bin Abd al-Rahman bin Faisal bin Turki bin Abdullah bin Muhammad bin Saud, which is almost never used in English materials because of its length, but is sometimes seen in Arabic sources. Here I have kept names as brief as possible, while ensuring that the person's lineage—which can be very important, politically or socially—is clear.

Dynastic references are presented with the word "Al." It is common, for example, to see the ruling family name in Saudi Arabia referred to as the "al-Saud," but in fact "Al Saud" or any such transliteration that keeps the "Al" as a separate word from the surname is more accurate. This distinguishes "Al" as a dynastic title (meaning something like "of the line of"), from "al-" as the Arabic definite article (which can appear in Arabic names too).

Preface

Few countries are as unique, enigmatic, or important as the Kingdom of Saudi Arabia. The only country in the world to be named after the family that rules it, Saudi Arabia grew out of tribal rivalries, especially between the Al Saud that came to dominate the Najd area around the center of the Arabian Peninsula and key tribes and families to the north and the east. Two Saudi dynasties rose and fell from the mid-eighteenth century until the late-nineteenth. In the twentieth century, it was only through a tripartite collaboration between Abd al-Aziz Al Saud (often referred to as Ibn Saud—the founding father of the modern, third Saudi state), the puritanical Wahhabi religious scholars, and the *Ikhwan*, a group of tribal religious fighters, that Ibn Saud was able to gain and consolidate control over the various territories that today constitute the modern state of Saudi Arabia.

Once Ibn Saud had consolidated power, however, and especially as the Kingdom's oil wealth grew as of the early 1950s, the Al Saud's rule has proven surprisingly durable, if not always popular or unchallenged. At various times both secular, modernizing forces and conservative, Islamist forces have challenged the legitimacy of the monarchy or the Al Saud family, sometimes even adopting violence against the state. The family has stared down several external threats, too. It has also had to manage divisions within Saudi society; those stemming from the spectrum of views on tradition and modernity or the role that religion should play in politics, but also those deriving from traditional social structures, modern institutional politics, and of course, sectarian identities. When all of these dynamics are put together, and when oil is understood as something that has been as much a curse as a blessing for the state's relationship with society, it becomes clear that the survival of the House of Saud was by no means assured when the modern state was proclaimed in 1932.

To some, the durability of the regime is a product of its nature; either of the traditional claims the Al Saud make of legitimacy or the result of their repressive capability. These, many argue, have been supported by the enormous influx of oil wealth into the country, which has provided the regime with cooptive and repressive means that it otherwise would not have had. When a ruling bargain with the clerical class and the (mostly Hijazi) business community is added to this cooptive and repressive capability, it is a potent conglomeration of political mechanisms that encourage and reinforce the status quo. Yet, another factor behind the Al Saud's durability—to some observers, the *key* dynamic—is the support of the United States. This relationship has helped the Al Saud by ensuring a supply of arms and other assistance, including an underwriting of the regime against regional external threats. Yet, important as it has been and remains, the Saudi-U.S. relationship has been a varied, often lukewarm one, and mostly a relationship of convenience, for much of the period since it was formalized in 1945.

The Saudi-U.S. relationship was also severely tested by the terrorist attacks against the United States on September 11, 2001, in which 15 of the 19 hijackers were Saudi nationals. This was, needless to say, part of Osama bin Laden's intention, targeting not only the United States but also Washington's support for the Saudi regime that bin Laden so detested. Regardless, the U.S.-led antiterrorism campaign since 2001, and the ongoing importance of Saudi Arabia as a source of Sunni extremism, has made Saudi Arabia all the more important to international security.

All of these dynamics are analyzed and assessed in the pages that follow. This is a book not just about Saudi politics and regime security in isolation, but also about how both internal and external Saudi security dynamics are shaped by and linked to wider Gulf and Middle Eastern forces and U.S. engagement with the region. Moreover, none of these dynamics can be properly assessed in isolation if the core issue at hand is security: Saudi domestic dynamics—whether they be the role of the state, rentier dynamics, the impact of history, or other aspects—all influence Riyadh's foreign policy and security perceptions, just as such external dynamics have a strong bearing on state-society relations and on the perspectives of Islamists and others in Saudi Arabia as well.

To give these arguments their due focus, while showing their inter-linkages and influences on each other as well, this book is laid out as six main chapters. The first is a history of Saudi Arabia, outlining the main events and figures that account for the emergence of modern Saudi Arabia and which explain why the country is as it is today. Chapter 2 is an outline of the Saudi political, military, and economic system. It provides details on the roles of various actors and institutions in the Kingdom, and discusses some of their perspectives and impacts on Saudi strategic culture and security settings. Chapter 3 examines the Saudi relationship with the United States in some depth, analyzing what sustains the relationship but also what tests, and at times undermines, it. Chapter 4 looks at the Saudi role in the region, including its relations with other key states in the Gulf, the security implications of the Gulf's sub-regional order and very limited security architecture, and some wider relationships and dynamics in the broader Middle East that link to Saudi security issues. Chapter 5 examines Islam, political Islamism, and Sunni extremism in Saudi Arabia. This is important in understanding the Al Saud bargain with the Wahhabi clerics, the role of Islam as a source of identity as well as of opposition in the country, and the degree to which Saudi religious figures and institutions have, wittingly or not, aided or contributed to the rise of Islamic extremism in the past couple of decades. The answers are not always simple: the Kingdom has been both a source and a victim of terrorism at various points; the reasons why are examined and explained in this chapter. Finally, Chapter 6 looks at some understudied, emerging, or potential security issues. These include both domestic and external issues, covering changes in the state-society relationship, emerging problems like climate change and water scarcity, and the rise of new powers in the Gulf. In its final pages, the chapter also provides a conclusion to the book as a whole, collating and encapsulating the core ideas and arguments.

Saudi Arabia is a complex and often opaque country to study and analyze. At times one feels like a Cold War Kremlinologist, looking for signs hidden in the public statements of the regime or the shifts in roles among key royals for signs of policy changes and new thinking, so rare are good quality research manuscripts with access to the Kingdom's inner workings. As with the Kremlinologists of the past, Saudiologists often find themselves dissecting not only what the regime says, but what its less-than-impartial opposition groups and figures— most of whom reside abroad—say about what is happening in the Kingdom. I hope that this book has sufficiently brought these various perspectives together, in the process offering both a solid summary of the key security dynamics in Saudi Arabia and some new ideas about Saudi history, politics, and political economy as they relate to security issues. The aim is to provide something which is readable for laypersons and students approaching the study of Saudi Arabia for the first time, but which will provide a good reference source for more seasoned observers of the Kingdom as well.

Several people have assisted me in the preparation of the book. I would particularly like to thank Raihan Ismail and Sebastian Klich, both of whom read the manuscript in its entirety at different stages of its finalization and who both provided very valuable advice that has improved its quality greatly. Raihan's deep expertise on Saudi Islamic politics, sectarianism, and state-cleric relations was invaluable, while Sebastian's eye for detail and ability to isolate the smallest of errors or imprecisions gave me a fresh perspective on the work and enhanced its flow and argument substantially. I would also like to thank Sean Foley, who provided me with considerable advice and encouragement on the project, as well as offering some fantastic ideas on its structure and some key points. Just as importantly, I am grateful as always to my colleagues at the Centre for Arab and Islamic

Studies at the Australian National University, for their friendship, support, and inspiration over nearly a decade now, and to my students, especially those in my graduate class on *The Gulf Strategic Environment*, who have engaged with many of the issues and dynamics discussed in this book, in the process helping me to test and refine many of the analyses that also appear in these pages. Finally, I thank my wife, Yasmine, and son Henry, for all their support. It must be hell at times, living with a writer always on a deadline of some sort, yet they not only put up with me, but give me an enormous amount of support as well.

For all the help and advice that I have received from others, the standard disclaimer applies: that any and all errors, omissions, and shortcomings are mine and mine alone.

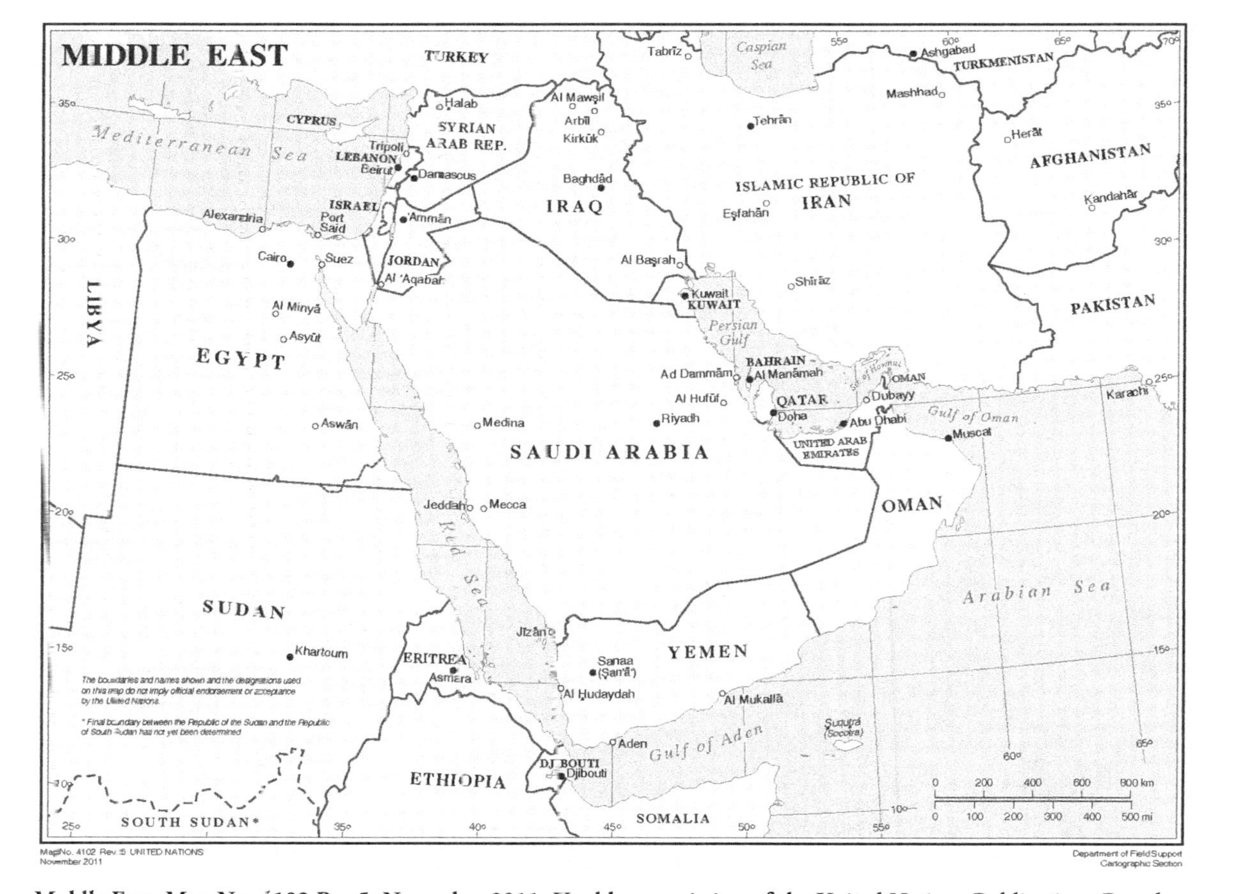

M_ddle East, Map No. 4102 Rev.5, November 2011. Used by permission of the United Nations Publications Board.

CHAPTER 1

The Creation and Development of Modern Saudi Arabia

The modern state of Saudi Arabia is a relatively new creation—it is one of the younger nation-states in the Middle East—and is an amalgamation of several distinct geographical areas, covering much of the Arabian Peninsula. Its formation and consolidation was the result of a history of family rivalry that culminated in the emergence of the Al Saud dynasty as its ruling family, and above all of the clever tactics adopted by the founding father of the current Saudi state, Abd al-Aziz bin Abd al-Rahman Al Saud (also commonly referred to as Ibn Saud) to consolidate his power across the various areas he conquered or subdued. The focus of this chapter is the history of Saudi Arabia, from the first Al Saud dynasty in the mid-eighteenth century to the creation and consolidation of the modern state over much of the twentieth. This history is important, both for the political order that it established and for the challenges that it created, which continue to pose challenges to Saudi security to the present day.

THE FIRST TWO SAUDI STATES

The Al Saud family was originally able to emerge as a political dynasty because of the fragmented and localized nature of power in the Arabian Peninsula over the sixteenth to eighteenth centuries,[1] combined with the astute political maneuvering of Muhammad Ibn Saud, the family patriarch and local ruler in the mid eighteenth century.

Beginning in the early 1500s, the Ottoman Empire began gaining control of parts of the peninsula, starting in 1517, when the conquest of Mamluk Egypt gave the Ottomans at least nominal control over the Hijaz and the Sharifian leadership there.[2] The Ottomans then expanded into what is now Iraq, taking Baghdad in 1534, which led to Hasa, in the eastern part of the Arabian Peninsula, submitting to them in 1550.[3] This arrangement lasted until 1670, when local rebellions in Hasa and other nearby towns saw the Ottomans pushed out of the area, only returning in the 1870s when they attempted to reassert control in the region by gaining the loyalty of the Rashidi emirate that controlled the northern part of the peninsula. At the same time, the Ottomans maintained an influence in the Hijaz, motivated more by the area's economic power than the religious importance of Mecca and Medina. The actual political power enjoyed by the Ottomans varied by both the level of interest they had in the area at different times, and beyond the main cities, by the relative power of tribal leaders vis-à-vis the Sharifian Sultan.[4]

The effect of all these dynamics was that the central Arabian area of Najd, from where the Al Saud emerged, was impacted by external events but never came under direct Ottoman control in the way that other areas, such as the western Hijaz area, did. The Najd area was not especially attractive to power holders elsewhere, such as those in Hijaz and Hasa, as it was sparsely populated, peppered with small towns and nomadic populations and producing little economic surplus that could be exploited through conquest and tribute. The Al Saud came out of the town of Dir'iyya, not far from what is now the Saudi capital, Riyadh. The town was significant enough to have a well-established population and to possess artisans, traders, and minor religious figures, but it was only a town, not a city like those to be found in the Hijaz. The Saudi emirs (rulers) in Dir'iyya probably originally gained power through the modest wealth they generated as a merchant family and as local landowners, which would have allowed them to finance trade undertaken by other families and, as a result, to gain political allegiance. It is widely assumed that the Al Saud emirs created a simple ruling bargain with the main local families, gaining tribute from them in exchange for protecting Dir'iyya and its surrounds and assisting with conflict resolution and other political tasks.[5]

At that time, it would have seemed unlikely that the Al Saud would ultimately rise to rule a modern nation-state. The Al Saud was not part of a major tribe or tribal confederation, compared with the rulers of the Rashidi emirate to the northwest, or the Bani Khalid rulers in Hasa, and they lacked the wealth of such dynasties as well. This meant that for a long time their rule was only a local one, never extending far from Dir'iyya. What ultimately launched their rise to greater power was the relationship that they formed with Muhammad Ibn Abd al-Wahhab (1703–1792),[6] a puritanical reformer within the Hanbali school of Sunni Islam. So crucial was this alliance that Saudi Arabia today is often described as following Wahhabi Islam—even if adherents reject this term—so named after Abd al-Wahhab. The religious profile of the country is more complex than what such a generalization would suggest,[7] but the Saudi-Wahhabi relationship has been central to the three Saudi states.

Abd al-Wahhab came from a family that produced several local religious scholars, and lived an austere life in the town of 'Uyayna, northwest of Dir'iyya, apart from periods traveling to study in Medina, Basra, and Hasa, until he was expelled from 'Uyayna by the emir there when local tribal opposition arose against his strict preaching. Pursued by the leaders of 'Uyayna, who feared that he would still be able to exert influence while in exile, he fled to Dir'iyya and sought protection with the Al Saud leader there, Muhammad Ibn Saud (?–1765, r. 1727–1765). What distinguished Abd al-Wahhab's teachings was his emphasis on a reversion to the fundamentals of Islam: he stressed the importance in Islam of *tawhid* ("monotheism"), *zakat* ("alms"), *jihad* ("holy war"), and simplicity in one's lifestyle. Too many people had, he believed, strayed from these principles. He rejected *bida'* ("innovation") in Islam, which to him included a range of cultural practices that had crept in to Islam over times, from the cults of saints to the veneration of holy men. He also ruled against other cultural practices such as tobacco smoking and the veneration of inanimate objects.

Abd al-Wahhab's arrival in Dir'iyya in 1744 led to a "religio-political" pact, a "union of political/military organization and religious ideology"[8] between him and Muhammad Ibn Saud. This marked the start of the first Saudi state (sometimes called the first Saudi *realm* or *emirate*), which lasted until 1818. Ibn Saud reportedly welcomed Abd al-Wahhab warmly and the pact between them was agreed quite quickly.[9] In effect, they established the symbiosis between the Al Saud and the *'ulema* (religious scholars) that in amended form still underlies the Saudi political order today.[10] The Al Saud received political endorsement and legitimacy from the *'ulema* in exchange for supporting the propagation of Islam, giving the *'ulema* authority on key religious matters,[11] and allowing them considerable control over the judicial system.[12] Abd al-Wahhab's insistence on the collection of *zakat* would have potentially bolstered Ibn Saud's coffers.[13]

The Saudi-Wahhabi pact marked the rise of the Al Saud as a power on the Arabian Peninsula. Although the geographical expansion of the dynasty began quite slowly, by the end of the eighteenth century it was extensive. Much of the mid-eighteenth century was spent consolidating power in southern Najd, as Ibn Saud's military forces were nascent and the Wahhabi tenets still faced considerable opposition from religious figures in surrounding areas.[14] It was under Ibn Saud's son Abd al-Aziz (r. 1765–1803) that the Saudi realm expanded more rapidly.[15] Small settlements near Dir'iyya were conquered in Abd al-Aziz's early years in power, often with Wahhabi clerics moving in first as a religious and cultural force that paved the way for Al Saud conquest. The first major victory of note was the conquest of Riyadh in 1773, which removed the nearest dynastic threat to the Al Saud. Beginning in 1784, the Al Saud then turned to conquering Hasa and its ruling Bani Khalid clan; this conquest started with border raids and small clashes, before the Al Saud won a key battle in 1789, gaining full control of the area only in 1795 once all Hasa's key settlements were subdued. This victory delivered the Al Saud an important and productive agricultural area, as well as control of a stretch of the Persian Gulf's southern coast.[16] It also, for the first time, brought a substantial number of Shiites under their rule.[17]

The Al Saud then turned to the area that is now southern Iraq, attacking various towns and promoting a counterattack by the Mamluk rulers. In 1801 the Saudis attacked Karbala, a city sacred to Shiite Muslims, massacring perhaps 5,000 people and looting the city. The attack was so nasty that it still poisons relations between Shiites and Wahhabis today.[18] More immediately, it led to the 1803 assassination of the Saudi leader Abd al-Aziz by a Shiite from what is now Iraq. The Saudi expansion went west across the Arabian Peninsula into the Hijaz. Ta'if fell in 1802, with the Saudis then gaining control of Mecca and Medina in 1803 and 1804, respectively. In these two holy cities, Mecca and Medina, the Saudis reintroduced more austere religious practices and public piety to the populations. To the east, the Al Saud gained control over much of the Gulf's southern coastline.

However, the Saudi expansion into the Hijaz and to the north did not last long. This was partly because, as a mobile raiding force, they often seized territory but did not or could not establish permanent control there. Their boundaries kept shifting, as their control waxed and waned and the loyalty and relative power of tribal groups fluctuated.[19] The Ottomans, using a common imperial tactic, encouraged their client Muhammad Ali Pasha of Egypt to use his forces for an expedition, which began in 1811, to recapture Mecca and Medina. He successfully did so in 1813, and then after a short lull, Muhammad Ali's son Ibrahim Pasha pushed on in 1815 to try to conquer the Saudis' Najd heartland. Saud ibn Abd al-Aziz died in 1814, and power passed to his son, Abdullah, who was ill equipped to face the Egyptian-Ottoman threat. By 1818, the Egyptian forces reached the Saudi capital of Dir'iyya. They laid siege, and when it fell in September that year it was largely destroyed by the Egyptians. The loss of the capital, the capture and later beheading of Abdullah, and the flight of most the key figures, signaled the end of the first Saudi state.

The second Saudi state, from 1824 to 1891, began when Abdullah's son Turki returned from exile and established himself at Riyadh, near the former capital of Dir'iyya. By this point the Egyptian forces mostly had pulled back from Najd, due to local opposition, although a few remained to keep the Egyptians technically in control. Turki reestablished a militia force and took control of Riyadh and surrounding areas relatively easily. By 1830, he had regained power over Hasa, although Ha'il to the north remained a much tougher area to subdue. The main problem for Turki—a recurring theme throughout the second Saudi state—was intra-family divisions. Turki was challenged by a cousin, Mishari, who succeeded in assassinating him in 1834. Turki's son Faysal managed to seize control of Riyadh back from Mishari, but Faysal ran into trouble when he failed to pay tribute to the Egyptian forces, then based in the Hijaz, leading them to imprison him in Cairo from 1837 to 1843 and interrupting his rule, which otherwise lasted until 1865.

After Faysal's death in 1865, his son Abdullah (r. 1865–1871) faced fierce rivalry from some of the extended family, including an uprising led by a half-brother, Sa'ud. Successive (brief) rulers found the same problem, having to stare down challenges from the family, keep the Rashidi emirate at bay, and placate the Egyptians. Some leaders managed this better than others, but none did it deftly, and the second Saudi state saw four more rulers in the two decades after Abdullah's reign. In 1887, two brothers Abdullah and Abd al-Rahman competed for power after the death of Sa'ud. Abdullah appealed to the Rashidi leader, Muhammad ibn Rashid, for support, but he instead took the opportunity to attack Riyadh and turn it, in effect, into a Rashidi vassal state. The Saudis fought back through an alliance with key tribes, especially the Qasim, which led Muhammad ibn Rashid to strengthen his own local coalitions. Ultimately, their rivalry was decided at Mulayda, on the southern edge of modern-day Riyadh, in 1891. Muhammad ibn Rashid's forces soundly defeated the Saudi ruler, Abd al-Rahman, who fled for his life pursued by the Rashidis. The routing of the Saudis as a political dynasty marked the end of the long-fragile second Saudi state.

After initially escaping into the southeastern Rub' al-Khali (Empty Quarter) desert and linking up with a tribe there, Abd al-Rahman then moved in 1893 to Kuwait, where he established himself and his family under the patronage of the Kuwaiti rulers, the Al Sabah, also gaining basic Ottoman support. This time in exile cemented the Al Saud-Al Sabah friendship that is still strong and important in Gulf regional relations. The Rashidi emirs, meanwhile, remained strong in this period.

It was ultimately the resurgence of the Saudi dynasty and their creation of the third Saudi state that destroyed the Rashidi emirate. In 1902, the founder of modern Saudi Arabia, Abd al-Aziz bin Abd al-Rahman Al Saud (as mentioned, also known as Ibn Saud), returned from the family exile in Kuwait, recaptured Riyadh, killed its Rashidi governor, and declared himself ruler. In so doing, he set off an almost 20-year conflict between the Saudis and the Rashidis for power in central Arabia. This period overlapped with the decline of the Ottoman Empire, the First World War, and the expansion of British influence. That the Rashidis aligned themselves with the Ottomans, and the Saudis with the British, helps accounts for the Rashidi demise, but also important was the increased rivalry within its extended dynasty in the early twentieth century,[20] allowing Ibn Saud to ultimately triumph and build the third Saudi state.

THE FORMATION AND EXPANSION OF SAUDI ARABIA

The start of the formation of the contemporary state of Saudi Arabia is typically dated to Ibn Saud's capture of Riyadh in 1902. Following this, however, it took some three decades for Ibn Saud to form and consolidate modern Saudi Arabia. The Kingdom of Saudi Arabia was formally proclaimed in 1932. This was the ultimate product of several dynamics, including the political and martial skill of Ibn Saud and the declining power at that time of other emirates such as the Rashidis and the Hijazis. Furthermore, the relationships that Ibn Saud built with the local clerics and the *Ikhwan* militia were important: the clerics remain symbiotically linked to the Al Saud to this day, while the *Ikhwan* were initially helpful but later proved problematic, and a rebellion by them had to be suppressed by Ibn Saud before he could fully stabilize his political realm.

The capture of Riyadh was achieved with a surprisingly modest force of some 40–60 warriors—the exact number is uncertain—largely through the element of surprise. After Riyadh fell on January 15, 1902, Ibn Saud then began further campaigns in Najd, pushing Rashidi forces out of key Najdi towns as he went. Through to 1906, there were several battles between the Ottoman-backed Rashidis and the Kuwaiti-backed (and British-endorsed) Saudis. As Al-Rasheed has noted, British and Ottoman involvement, reflecting the great power context of the time, were important components in the success of the third Saudi dynasty.[21] The Wasim area to the east of Najd fell to Ibn Saud in 1906, causing a Rashidi retreat to their Ha'il heartland and an Ottoman acknowledgment of the Saudi control of Qasim and much of Najd. Not long after this, Ibn Saud expanded his territories further, beginning with the 1913 conquest of Hasa in the east. Hasa remained technically Ottoman, but in reality Ibn Saud's reach, and later his full control, there was reflected in the 1913 Ottoman-Saudi Treaty and by an agreement between Ibn Saud and the local Shia leadership. Under the latter, the Saudis permitted the Shia some religious freedom in exchange for their political loyalty; a promise that was not kept by Ibn Saud, with the Wahhabi leadership quickly allowed to attack the Shia as rejectionists.[22] However, the agreement needed to work only for a short time and served its purpose.

Ibn Saud's domestic alliances were important in his ability to return to Najd, seize Riyadh, and undertake the territorial expansion that followed. The role of the British and mistakes and divisions among other dynasties in the area were important too, but the symbiotic relationship with the local religious force, the *Mutawwa'*, and the zeal of the Wahhabi *Ikhwan* militia, arguably were more important still. Without these, it is doubtful that modern Saudi Arabia would have come into being; Ibn Saud would have lacked both legitimacy and a highly dedicated military force.

The relationship with the *Mutawwa'* was a revivification of the arrangement that had been so politically crucial in the first Saudi state, where Abd al-Wahhab's pact with the Al Ibn Saud had been integral to Muhammad's ability to maintain power and spread his dominion. The *Mutawwa'* acted in a similar way in the twentieth century. They were useful allies for Ibn Saud because of the earlier alliance and because of their social, cultural, and political roles. They were usually sedentary Najdis who conducted local religious services and offered teaching. They were rarely formally educated in religion—such people became *'ulema* in larger towns and cities, or judges—but instead they spread Wahhabi ideas in a local area or village, helped people with rudimentary religious interpretation, and performed basic religio-cultural duties. Typically, they enforced Islamic law and religious practices in their area, too. They were important to Ibn Saud as a fifth column, moving ahead of Saudi forces into areas marked for expansion. After a conquest, they were then vital in raising taxes and troops, imposing order, and sustaining religious and political obedience in newly captured territories. At times, they were harsh in punishing what they determined to be transgressions against Islam, and most of them saw this as their main task. The *Mutawwa'* later formed the core of the Committee for the Propagation of Virtue and Prohibition of Vice, sometimes colloquially called the "religious police" (discussed later), who play a key role in maintaining public adherence to Islam in Saudi Arabia today.

Just as important to the spread of Ibn Saud's rule as the *Mutawwa'* were the *Ikhwan*. The *Ikhwan* were a tribal force, originally from 'Arid in southern Najd but later coming from a wider area, which began as a royal guard for Ibn Saud in the initial years after the capture of Riyadh. With ideological and recruitment assistance from some *Mutawwa'*, a tribal *Ikhwan* force was established and ideologically motivated to expand Ibn Saud's realm and that of Wahhabi ideology. They were important for their martial utility and religious zeal, but also because they reduced the divisions between urban dwellers and tribally based peoples. Nonetheless, like the *Mutawwa'*, they could be violent; their atrocities against the Shia in Hasa, after it fell in 1913, was one notorious example. The *Mutawwa'* lived and worked with the *Ikhwan*, and in so doing supported and influenced their thinking, and Ibn Saud dispensed resources to both groups as part of his political arrangement with them.

With the Al Saud-*Mutawwa'*-*Ikhwan* domestic political bargain in place, Ibn Saud was able to expand his realm more rapidly as of the mid-1910s. The outbreak of the First World War brought Ottoman-British rivalry into sharp relief and profited Ibn Saud. Through the 1915 Anglo-Saudi Treaty, London recognized Ibn Saud as leader of the territories that he controlled at that point, and also committed the British to arming and financing Ibn Saud.[23] In return, Ibn Saud agreed not to intervene in the politics of the littoral Gulf sheikhdoms of Kuwait, Bahrain, Qatar, and Oman, all of which already had agreements with the British for protection. Importantly, at the same time Ibn Rashid maintained his alliance with the Ottomans, which provided him some (modest) support, but which greatly weakened the Rashidi emirate after the Ottoman defeat in the war.

Ha'il ultimately fell to Ibn Saud's forces not during the First World War, even though he tried to capture it in 1917, but in 1921. Saudi-Rashidi conflict had persisted through the war years, but the Rashidi loss of their patron on the defeat of the Ottomans left them unable to compete with the British-supported Saudis. Rashidi decline also encouraged internal disputes over succession, and less support from the vitally important Shammar tribal confederacy, which lost access to trading centers that had fallen under Saudi control. The Rashidi capital Ha'il was besieged in August 1921 and surrendered on November 1. This removed the most prominent barrier to Ibn Saud, and so expanded his territory that he could then move on to capture areas to the west, especially the Hijaz, which he quickly did.

An Ibn Saud rivalry with King Hussein of the Hijaz had emerged after the First World War, but in military terms was localized for some time around the disputed village of Khurma, near their shared boundary, and then Turaba, nearby. There was an agreement, with British involvement, that brought about a brief ceasefire between the two sides until 1924. However the Saudi encroachment on Hijaz did not stop, and as scholars have noted, it was a *zahf* ("crawling") form of gradual conquest.[24] This gave Ibn Saud time to consolidate his position in Ha'il, to move into the southwestern region of 'Asir, and to work on ensuring that the British would accept his further expansion.[25] 'Asir was subjugated in 1922, in part because of the weak local ruler who governed the Idrisi Emirate there and the Saudi ability to gain tribal support in the area.

Saudi forces began the conquest of Hijaz in September 1924, when they seized the town of Ta'if in the southwestern mountains. Atrocities committed at this time are another example of the zealotry of the *Ikhwan* at times. The Hijazi ruler, Hussein, was forced by local elites to abdicate, handing power to his son Ali, which encouraged the Saudis to encroach further into the area by conquering Mecca, the holiest city in the Islamic world, in December that year. Ibn Saud claimed that his invasion was to guarantee access for pilgrims to the holy city, although his real intent had always been more ambitious and material. He captured the rest of the Hijaz in 1925, laying siege to the port city of Jedda from January to December that year while at the same time taking Medina, the second holiest city in Islam. When Jedda fell, Ali departed in a deal brokered by the British. With the major cities of Hijaz subjugated and the British seemingly acquiescent to Ibn Saud's conquest, the Hijazi emirate was doomed. The Saudi ruler could declare himself King of the Hijaz, backed by local elites swearing allegiance to him, in early January 1926. In a matter of months, Ibn Saud obtained recognition from the major European powers of his rule over most of what is modern-day Saudi Arabia.[26] He was Sultan of Najd, King of Hijaz, and ruler of other provinces and areas conquered in the previous quarter-century such as Hasa, parts of the southeast, Ha'il and other northern areas, and 'Asir.

The borders of today's Saudi Arabia were also set around this time in part because the British moved in this period to ensure the integrity of Iraq and Transjordan (the latter now Jordan). London made agreements with Ibn Saud on his border with Transjordan, and the Basra Agreement between Ibn Saud and Iraq created that border. As a result, further Saudi expansion into either of these realms was extremely unlikely. The 1927 Treaty of Jedda restated British agreement to the Saudi borders at the time and, quite unusually, explicitly stated that Ibn Saud was independent from Britain. The, only condition on the Saudi ruler was that he respect the independence of the other Gulf monarchs who had agreements in place with London, and that he maintain access to Islamic holy cities for Muslim pilgrims. This agreement was the backbone of Ibn Saud's unique Kingdom, which when formally proclaimed in 1932 was loosely under British influence but not London's authority. The only border still not finalized, that with Yemen, was set by the 1933–1934 Saudi-Yemeni War.

One challenge remained for Ibn Saud in the late 1920s, however: the *Ikhwan* rebellion. While the Al Saud-*Mutawwa'-Ikhwan* political bargain had served all three parties well from 1902 to 1926, after the fall of Hijaz, key *Ikhwan* leaders wanted to continue expanding into Iraq, Kuwait, Transjordan, and presumably even further. This was in defiance of Ibn Saud, and had the *Ikhwan* gotten their way, it would have constituted a direct challenge to the British that London would not have permitted. *Ikhwan* raids on Transjordan and then Kuwait, while not military successes, prompted the British to send air forces to Kuwait, sending a warning to Ibn Saud. When the *Ikhwan* did not back down on this issue, the *Ikhwan* rebellion was triggered. However, by this time Ibn Saud had a broader military force in place than just the *Ikhwan*, and also astutely gained endorsement from the religious elite in Riyadh that confirmed his sole authority, including in matters of war. This was a key step in Ibn Saud cementing his relationship with the Najdi *'ulema*, which remains a foundation of Saudi rule to this day. The *Ikhwan* rebellion included several key battles. The largest, the Battle of Sabilla on March 30–31, 1929, saw around 500 *Ikhwan* killed by a far more technologically advanced and well-equipped Saudi army. There were then some further skirmishes, but in January 1930 the main *Ikhwan* leaders surrendered to the British in Kuwait. By this time most of their leaders were dead or captured, and the remaining rank and file of the *Ikhwan* were incorporated into regular forces. This was not their last gasp, however, and *Ikhwan* grievances reappear later in Saudi history, with powerful impacts.

IBN SAUD'S RULE AND POLITICAL LEGACY

Saudi Arabia came into being on September 22, 1932, when Ibn Saud declared the creation of the Kingdom of Saudi Arabia (*al-mamlaka al-'arabiyya al-su'udiyya*). The creation of modern Saudi Arabia was a landmark event, not least of all because of its distinctiveness in the Arab world. But it was not the end of the process of establishing modern Saudi Arabia; if anything, it was the start of a new, lengthy, and complex phase in Ibn Saud's legitimization and consolidation of power. It took many years for him to fully solidify his elite relationships, and to achieve the broader state-building and nation-building needed to give the new Kingdom a strong chance of survival. It was after 1932 that the key, often symbiotic, relationships with the clergy, the merchants, the main tribal leaders, and the United States were strengthened, and in some cases formalized, into political bargains appropriate to a twentieth-century nation-state. Ibn Saud also needed to consolidate his own position, not just within the growing Saudi polity but within the royal dynasty itself.

This was an issue because Ibn Saud faced potential competition for power from his own line in the family, including from a set of cousins known as the 'Ara'if, as well as potential challenges to his authority and legitimacy from other branches of the family. In what is a common practice in the Arab world, but a particular feature of Ibn Saud's tactics, groups like the 'Ara'if were brought into the political fold in a controlled way through marriage; in this case, one between Ibn Saud's sister and a key 'Ara'if figure was important.[27] The wider risks from other branches of the Al Saud dynasty were sometimes handled in the same way. Ibn Saud had at least 22 wives during his lifetime—by some accounts a great many more than that[28]—some for brief periods and others for much longer. Several of these were strategic or political marriages designed to shore up or guarantee support from particular tribal figures, notables, or others who might otherwise be inclined or able to challenge Ibn Saud. Beyond strategic marriages, in some other cases cooptation was used to pacify or control potential rivals. In the pre-oil era, this was most commonly through small financial payments, or by appointment to government positions such as governorships and administrative appointments. Later, the oil-driven expansion of the state made commercial opportunities more prominent tools of cooptation too.

Another strategy for Al Saud consolidation was the expansion of the royal line. Ibn Saud's many marriages were not only political because they linked other key families to the Al Saud, but were important in creating a large group of successors to Ibn Saud. His marriages led to the births of some 44 sons and over 50 daughters. The former would become the future monarchs of Saudi Arabia into the twenty-first century; all kings subsequent to Ibn Saud, from Saud (r. 1953–1964) to Abdullah (crowned in 2005), have been sons of Ibn Saud. This did not preclude marriages themselves being a method for dividing potential opposition groups or reminding conquered groups of the new political order, as Al-Rasheed has noted,[29] but at the same time, in many cases marriages did solidify allegiance to the Al Saud or provide for sons in the inner core of the monarchy who possessed different social origins.

Beyond family dynamics, the consolidation of the political order was also achieved through other mechanisms, arguably more important to the longer-term durability of the Al Saud dynasty, even if they were reliant on a large and cohesive royal circle being first established. These included regular gatherings, called a *majlis* (literally a "sitting"), typically chaired by the king; the creation of a small and nascent bureaucracy to implement and enforce the monarch's decisions (and, through jobs, as a way to distribute wealth and favors); and the creation of symbiotic relationships with key sociopolitical groups and forces, especially the clerics and the merchants, to ensure their support for the King in exchange for resources and input into decisions relevant to them. Such tactics are routine in patrimonial political systems, such as Ibn Saud's early Saudi Arabia was, and have been retained and developed into still informal, but very powerful, relationships in the more neo-patrimonial system that characterizes the modern state.[30] In a patrimonial system, a leader manages the political system through a web of often-divided key elites, who themselves maintain elite links down into the social groups and institutions necessary for the maintenance of the political system. Resources and opportunities flow down from the leader through these networks, while information and loyalty flow up. Neopatrimonialism is similar, but adds a modern state apparatus and bureaucracy to the process, which attends to the more specialized and complex tasks of state as well as assisting the image-building and mythologizing of the leader.

As a core element of (neo-)patrimonial rule, the *majlis* concept is a practice long used by leaders in the Arab world, especially in the Arabian Peninsula, and was extensively used by Ibn Saud. It was a visual reminder of where power ultimately lay, of course, and in poorer societies such as pre-oil Saudi Arabia, even a modest *majlis* probably looked pompous and generous by ordinary people's standards. Just as important was the role they played.[31] They were the usual route for dispute resolution, reinforcing the ultimate authority of a leader or monarch while also contributing to social stability. They were also an opportunity for communication between the ruler and the ruled, an opportunity for people to confirm their allegiance to the ruler, or in this case the king, while also giving the king insights into the issues that mattered to people or the chance to take suggestions and ideas from local elites. Financial support or largesse was often distributed too, in something of a precursor to the rentier bargain that underpins the state-society relationship in states like Saudi Arabia today. That these sittings were held in regional areas and involved local elites sitting alongside the king added to all of these roles they played. More private meetings might also constitute a *majlis*, or have the effect of one, say where participation was limited to an inner circle of advisers, or where the king would hold a religious gathering to reinforce his authority to clerics while at the same time reminding them of his piety and humility.

The early financial arrangements of the royal household, and the spending that occurred, was also important in sustaining and consolidating Al Saud rule. Money most often came from the informal collections from pilgrims and by their local spending on necessities. Important too was *zakat*, since the Saudi monarchy centralized the collection of alms and redistributed the funds through the nascent state. Lastly, income from merchants and wealthy notables was important. At first, it was often presented as being a donation, but in actuality was expected and understood to constitute informal taxation. After the 1930s, Ibn Saud expanded and increasingly formalized this taxation by imposing customs duties on trade in and out of Hasa and Hijaz, the two key trading areas of Saudi Arabia, located on the Gulf coast and Red Sea coast, respectively. Taxes on agricultural produce and people's holdings of precious metals were also introduced, too, along with a levy on pilgrims.[32] The money raised in such ways was partly spent on the family, but mostly was used to sustain the small bureaucracy and, above all, was redistributed to key figures and society more widely to strengthen Ibn Saud's legitimacy. To achieve this, Ibn Saud worked closely with his trusted financial adviser, and later finance minister, Abdullah ibn Sulayman, who helped develop revenue collection and managed the royal finances. He served Ibn Saud until the latter's death.

It was also in this period around and after 1932 that the basic state apparatus was established. Under ibn Sulayman, a rudimentary finance ministry came into being. Even before 1932, a foreign ministry had been established in 1930 both to represent the Ibn Saud and then the state to external parties, and to handle visas and otherwise regulate foreign visitors to Saudi Arabia. The foreign ministry became larger and more sophisticated in the 1930s and 1940s, as their duties expanded. Military matters were initially handled by the palace and the finance minister. However, a ministry of defense was established in 1944, once the need for a more formal military became evident: previously there had been only a national guard and the separate *Ikhwan*, the remnants of the latter being folded into the former after the suppression of the *Ikhwan* rebellion in 1930. Other small institutions were created at this early stage, including a Political Committee in 1930 to handle some affairs of state, chaired by Faisal, one of Ibn Saud's sons.

It was not until the oil era—technically beginning as of 1933, but only sizeable and export driven as of the 1940s—that the state greatly expanded in size and reach. It was in 1933 that ibn Sulayman signed Saudi Arabia's first oil concession, with the U.S. firm Standard Oil of California (SOCAL), giving them oil exploration rights. This was the start of a transformation of the Saudi political economy that subsequently has been integral to Al Saud rule, the Saudi–U.S. relationship, and Saudi Arabia's position in the world. The SOCAL concession was the product partly of the U.S. firm looking for new oil fields in the region not already grabbed by the British, and Ibn Saud's agreement to it reflected the financial pressures he was under given his limited resources at the time and the cost of mounting the fight against the *Ikhwan* rebellion. At the time, Ibn Saud was in enormous debt to a range of lenders, including the Indian government, several firms, and some local figures. Income from the concession provided him with a loan and a guaranteed annual income, at a juncture when pilgrimage numbers were dramatically lower as a result of the onset of the Great Depression around 1930.

Still, it was to be some years before oil began being extracted and sold in large commercial quantities. The first extraction of commercial quantities was not until 1938, and the first oil for export was dispatched in 1939. The effects of the Second World War soon reached Saudi Arabia, however, delaying further oil exploration and production, even though total production still increased in the war years. This first decade of commercial oil production also saw the start of the oil-driven modernization of Saudi Arabia. The latter-1940s was a period of expansion and development in Riyadh—its population almost doubled in the decade of the 1940s[33]—while from the late 1930s onward, oil income paid for new palaces and public buildings. The first railway line was constructed in the latter part of the 1940s. The 1940s was still, however, a time of austerity in general. While Saudi Arabia was to become incredibly wealthy as a result of oil, in the war years there were food shortages at times, and usually problems finding skilled personnel to work in oil and resulting areas such as construction. These economic and social conditions were only eased by aid from the United States, which did not come until Saudi Arabia ended its technical neutrality and declared war on Germany in the dying days of the war in Europe.

The central event at this time was the meeting between Ibn Saud and U.S. president Franklin D. Roosevelt. This signified the decline of British influence in Saudi Arabia, which had supplied some military equipment to the Saudi monarch during the 1930s but had not provided aid to him in those lean war years. Ibn Saud had been unhappy anyway at the lack of British support in his 1933–1934 war with Yemen, and later seems to have been nervous that the British were partial toward other monarchs in the region, such as the Hashemites who ruled Transjordan and (at the time) Iraq. Thus, a relationship with the United States probably appealed for several reasons. The Americans sent their first diplomat to Jedda in 1942, whose emphasis—like the relationship overall—was on oil. The Arabian–American Oil Company (ARAMCO), formed in 1944 from a subsidiary of SOCAL that managed Saudi operations after the 1933 concession was granted, had become the central pillar and driver of the U.S.–Saudi relationship. Most importantly, it was ARAMCO that had pushed for and then arranged the meeting between Ibn Saud and Roosevelt, which took place on the USS *Quincy*, on the Great Bitter Lake in the Suez Canal, on February 14, 1945.

The meeting was impressive in its outcomes, firmly displacing the British in Saudi Arabia and replacing them with the United States. The two leaders decided on much. For his part, Ibn Saud agreed to allow the U.S. Navy to visit Saudi ports, and to the United States constructing the Dhahran Air Field, which operated from 1945 through to 1962 as the key U.S. military installation in the Kingdom. Ibn Saud also reaffirmed the oil concession with the Americans and agreed to the construction of the Trans-Arabian Pipeline (TAP), which was constructed between Qaisumah in northeastern Saudi Arabia and Sidon in southern Lebanon over 1947–1950, and operated from 1950 until 1976, and then continued pumping oil into Jordan until 1990. For the United States, the agreement was a strategic gain that helped ensure the supply of, and protection of U.S. interests in, Saudi oil. Arguably not accidentally, the agreement and new U.S. role in the Kingdom signaled the rise of the United States as a major power in the Middle East. The first U.S. military adviser arrived in Saudi Arabia in 1949, and in subsequent years the U.S.-Saudi Mutual Defense Assistance Agreement and then the U.S. Military Training Mission supported extensive U.S. training of Saudi military personnel. Still-deeper strategic and arms relationships followed. The relationship with the United States would underpin Saudi national security policy from the late-1940s to the present day, even if the relationship has fluctuated in strength and has predominantly been one of mutual convenience rather than shared values. That said, for Ibn Saud the new relationship with Washington helped the security of the state and of the regime in the critical final years of his rule and as the post-Second World War international order was becoming established.

As Al Saud rule grew stronger, two of Ibn Saud's sons, Saud and Faisal, were given greater responsibility in the affairs of state, and oil production was, by the early 1950s, expanding rapidly. From a tiny output of around 1,500 barrels a day in 1938, production expanded to about 58,000 barrels per day in 1945, then to half a million barrels per day in 1949 and to over one million barrels per day in 1954.[34] After the Saudis threatened to nationalize ARAMCO unless profits were split evenly, the revenue from oil increased dramatically, too, from US$113 million in 1950 to US$212 million in 1952.[35] This allowed for a massive increase in royal patronage to society and to key domestic allies, and some large public works and infrastructure projects, even if the Kingdom was yet to experience the massive oil booms that would come in the 1960s and especially in the 1970s, early 1980s, and again over much of the 2000s. Still, oil wealth at this time at least began the process of state-building and helped, if only at a simple level, in the building of national identity and the consolidation of it under the Al Saud banner.

STASIS UNDER SAUD, MODERNIZATION UNDER FAISAL

The most significant transitional challenge for the relatively new Saudi state came with the death of Ibn Saud on November 9, 1953. Ibn Saud's leadership had been integral in starting the processes of state-building and nation-building. Furthermore, the decade that followed Ibn Saud's death was a politically complex and contested one, in large part for three reasons. First, fierce competition emerged between the two sons, Saud and Faisal, over who should rule and how much power should lay with each. Second, while Saud briefly dominated that struggle, and was first to succeed Ibn Saud, he ultimately proved a weak, even incompetent, leader, which complicated politics during his rule. Finally, new political ideologies in the Arab world, through the 1950s and into the 1960s, amassed into a serious threat to the Al Saud's claims of legitimacy, presenting challenges that simply had not been present earlier.

The Saud-Faisal rivalry was not surprising given the number of descendants that Ibn Saud left behind and the natural competition within the family for power and opportunity. On Ibn Saud's death, Saud became King and Faisal crown prince, but tensions arose almost immediately because of the competition between them.[36] Both sought to build power bases through government appointments, and in Saud's case, by placing his own descendants into key positions, as his father had done. This worsened the problem of factionalism,[37] which then shaped many aspects of politics during Saud's rule. Saud's rule was not exclusively negative—a number of ministries and institutions were created during this period, and new projects inaugurated—but overall his rule was ineffectual and unimpressive. His profligate lifestyle saw considerable wealth squandered and an increase in the country's debt level, and his personal style was capricious and unpredictable. He was inefficient and lethargic at times, with rumor holding that this was due to alcoholism.

The rise of Egypt's Gamal Abdul Nasser after 1952 created a new, international set of problems quickly inherited by Ibn Saud's successors. It caused a rift in the Arab world between a "radical" republican movement, exemplified and led by Nasser, and a conservative, mostly monarchical group, in which Saudi Arabia was prominent. Saud had to face down the immense popularity of Nasser in the Arab world, which he did by strengthening the U.S.-Saudi relationship and by engaging in a cold war with Nasser. This did not preclude domestic opposition from emerging against Saud from new pan-Arabist and reformist circles, including some within the Saudi military and other institutions, while the feuding between Saud and Faisal made addressing such challenges all the more difficult.[38]

In 1958, Faisal gained considerable new authority relative to Saud, after the family intervened and, in conjunction with key clerics and tribal figures, agreed that most key responsibilities of government would be transferred to Faisal, even though Saud retained the title of King. Faisal countered domestic opposition forces by initiating some political liberalization and better managing government spending, and also proved adept at maintaining links with key tribal and clerical elites. As Saud struggled with ill-health and weaker political nous, Faisal strengthened his own base. By 1964, Saud's reputation and Faisal's astuteness combined to allow Faisal, with the agreement of the family, key tribes, merchants, and clerics, to force Saud to abdicate.[39] Faisal became king on November 2, 1964, and Saud went into exile until his death in 1969.

The development of Saudi Arabia under Faisal—in effect from 1960 or so, and as king from 1964, through to 1975 and continuing then under King

Khalid—was dramatic. Despite some formidable challenges, especially from regional political dynamics, Faisal substantially centralized the Saudi state, spent enormous sums on developing government and infrastructure, and stabilized elite and social dynamics in the Kingdom. In this he was aided by the influx of oil wealth: oil income roughly tripled in the 1960s,[40] and then quadrupled again after the massive oil price rises after 1973. Yet, Faisal's success was also the result of his effective leadership and a strategic approach to development.

In 1962, when he was still prime minster rather than king, Faisal had introduced his Ten-Point Program for Saudi economic and social development. Although broadly worded, it promised among other things a basic law (in effect a constitution); public and private sector development; new infrastructure projects; initiatives to widen the country's economic base; banking and finance reforms; and various socioeconomic strategies.[41] It was an ambitious new policy methodology, similar to the five-year plans that later were so central to the state's socioeconomic strategies. It played a central role in how Faisal ruled after 1964 and on what he focused; as Niblock has observed, "the manner in which expenditure was allocated in the national budgets between 1962 and 1970 indicates a reasonably coherent development strategy,"[42] which largely reflected the goals of the original program. Still, it was only a first step in the process of "trial and error" that characterized Saudi development planning in the oil era.[43]

Oil always remained dominant in the economy in this period, accounting for just under half of gross domestic product for most of the 1960s, then rising above the 50 percent mark when prices skyrocketed in the early 1970s.[44] Yet the economy both grew and diversified under Faisal. Sectors such as utilities, construction, and transport roughly tripled in value over 1962–1970, while others such as retail, banking, and government services roughly doubled in the same period.[45] Even within the energy sector most broadly, there was greater vertical integration and associated diversification, as the state moved from purely earning crude oil royalties into areas such as refining and petrochemicals.

Three other trends in this period with an implication for politics are worth noting. One is the rise of welfarism. The number of people receiving direct welfare transfer payments over this period almost tripled, from 25,197 in 1962–1963 to 72,681 in 1970–1971.[46] Oil rents also found their way to society through other means, including the expansion of public sector employment, the growth of publicly funded education, and new infrastructure and services. Such spending linked an increasing number of people to the state and gave them reasons to think positively about the state's allocative role, as well as improving living standards in general. Another related trend in this period was that the 1960s saw migrant labor first start moving to Saudi Arabia. This was crucial to the state's economic bargain with society because it gave the state control over the (foreign, short term) working class, removed the prospect of a working class becoming politicized. It also relieved most Saudis from having to work in mundane or low-status jobs.[47] At the same time, the growth of state employment and the expansion of the private sector created a much larger middle class, which extended the reach and capacity of the state while placating what otherwise could be a potential oppositional or reformist force.[48] Finally, the third trend in this period was the expansion of the private sector and the development of the indigenous business community. Large merchant families had always existed, especially in the trading centers of the Hijaz, but the increase in state spending as of the 1960s created new opportunities for these families, and funded the rise of new business families that, through connections or reputation, won government contracts or found other opportunities from the circulation of oil wealth. Often a firm or family gained a monopoly in a particular sub-sector or over a particular product through state concessions, and such patronage was dispensed by the royal family, through the state, with very deliberate political goals in mind.

At the political level, Faisal consolidated and stabilized Al Saud rule in a way that King Saud had failed to do. His infrastructural development and support of education, including the introduction of female education, gave him a reputation as a modernizer. He forcefully countered opposition to some changes, including female education and the introduction of television, while also supporting the religious elite and avoiding wider political liberalization. In fact, in politics he was not a modernizer. He had promised in 1962 to introduce a legislature, but never did so. He also gained a firm control over the cabinet, by being both king and prime minister, and placed loyal family members in key ministerial posts such as interior, oil, and defense.[49] He also—arguably very wisely—pushed most of Saud's line out of the positions in which the former king had placed them, which followed his broader tactic of downplaying the Saud period of rule. He made his half-brother Khalid the crown prince, keeping the sons of Ibn Saud in the direct line to the throne but at the same time neutralizing any remaining threats from the remnants of the pro-Saud faction within the family.

Faisal still faced considerable challenges. As late as 1969 a serious coup attempt was uncovered,[50] prominently involving army and police officers and stemming from the pan-Arabism and republicanism still very popular in the Arab world at the time. Indeed, throughout the 1960s Saudi foreign policy was dominated by the cold war with Egypt, especially Saudi support for royalist forces, against Egyptian support for republican ones, in the 1962–1970 Yemeni Civil War. The Arab-Israeli conflict also shaped this period; while Faisal was sympathetic to the Palestinian cause, it created new pressures on his rule. The 1967 Six Day War arguably was a double-edged sword, enhancing Faisal's position and prestige relative to the recently defeated Egyptian leader, but also further radicalizing parts of the Arab world and challenging the Saudis' conservative foreign policy.[51] The British withdrawal from the Gulf in 1971 was also a watershed moment. It increased U.S. attention on Saudi Arabia, and prompted greater U.S. military assistance to Faisal in recognition of the Kingdom's regional role and conservative strategic worldview.[52]

The 1973 Arab-Israeli War and the oil price booms that followed it was a key moment for Saudi Arabia in several respects. By then, the Kingdom had witnessed almost a decade of economic development under Faisal, had its first Five-Year Plan (1970–1975) in place, and was shifting closer, if cautiously, to the United States. One of the tests for Faisal was to balance his need for a strong relationship with the United States, against his requirement, for both regional standing and domestic legitimacy at home, to support the Palestinian cause. Thus, as he had warned, he wielded oil as a political tool when the 1973 Arab-Israeli War broke out, joining the other Arab oil-exporting states in an embargo on oil shipments to countries, including the United States, that backed Israel. However, he delayed joining it as long as he could, but eventually he had little choice but to join it. Even then, while the price impacts of the embargo were dramatic, the Saudis only partially enforced it and then ended it after only about six months.[53] Between the flood of rents into Saudi Arabia and the boost the embargo gave to Faisal's standing in the Arab world, Faisal's balancing act on the embargo was not surprising. Importantly, he ensured that it had little long-term impact on the relationship with the United States, which was too important and mutually convenient for Faisal to let Arab-Israeli pressures impact. The United States recognized the Saudi economic and religious influence in the region, its vulnerability given Soviet support for most of the republican Arab states, and the domestic imperatives faced by Faisal, while the Saudis continued to need American military support and hardware, as well as the implicit security guarantee in the relationship. At the same time the relationship broadened into new areas, such as a boom in Saudi investment in the United States and a U.S.-assisted modernization of the Saudi military.[54]

A longer-term outcome of the 1973 war for the Middle East was that it led to Egypt shifting away from the Soviets and toward the U.S. camp, and then after the 1978–1979 Egyptian-Israeli peace, Egypt was ostracized from the Arab world. Both of these created significant strategic and political benefits for the Saudis, and gave them a larger role in regional affairs. More widely, including in the West, Saudi Arabia came to be seen at both elite and popular levels as a regional power; coupled with its massive oil wealth, its image evolved into that of a somewhat shy and conservative, yet very powerful, Arab state. Faisal was central in that happening, while also putting much of his still-growing economic wealth to use in modernizing and developing the economy and in expanding and consolidating the state's cooptive mechanisms. In his final years, Faisal delivered yet-higher rent wealth to society, imported still more foreign workers, and created enormous and generous opportunities for Saudis in tertiary education and state employment. This all outlasted Faisal's rule, only challenged when the price of oil plummeted in the mid-1980s.

Faisal's rule ended on March 25, 1975, when a cousin assassinated him during one of his regular *majlis* sessions. Despite being painted by the Saudi government at the time as the act of a madman, the assassination is now widely assessed as being an act of revenge: during protests against the introduction of television into the Kingdom in 1965, police had shot and killed the assassin's brother.[55] However, the two events point to a wider issue in modern Saudi history. The transformation of the country under Faisal masked the fact that opposition to him remained significant, and in fact there was an underlying discord between the socioeconomic modernization that Faisal delivered and the conservative religious values that he promoted and regularly spoke about. While he probably never would have expected the introduction of television to eventually lead to his own assassination, the fact that it probably did highlights the contested nature of economic and social modernization and change in the Kingdom.

FROM KING KHALID TO KING ABDULLAH

As crown prince, Khalid (r. 1975–1982) assumed the throne after Faisal's assassination. His rule, and then that of Fahd (r. 1982–2005) after him, would see changing internal and external dynamics, with attendant risks and threats for the Al Saud. In effect, Faisal had embarked on a massive socioeconomic development program and shifted Saudi Arabia closer to the United States, while also increasing the use of Islamic rhetoric and sending conservative signals to society at the broader political levels. Khalid largely continued this trend, for all its benefits and risks.

Khalid's brief reign witnessed several regional events of momentous impact for Saudi security. The first was the 1979 siege at the Grand Mosque in Mecca. This began on November 20, 1979, when Juhayman ibn Muhammad al-'Utaybi and Muhammad ibn Abdullah al-Qahtani, together with several hundred followers, took control of the Grand Mosque during the annual Hajj pilgrimage month.[56] Juhayman was a self-anointed leader and preacher who had been highly critical of what he saw as a corrupt, materialistic, and immoral Saudi royal family. He argued that Muhammad al-Qahtani was the true, awaited *mahdi*, or "guided one," a prophesized figure who it is claimed will take power, rid the world of evil, and rule until judgment day. Juhayman's group took some hostages (although most were released quickly), barricaded themselves up in the holy building, and repelled an attempt to retake the mosque. To recapture the mosque, the Saudi government sought approval to use military force from the leader of the Saudi *ulema*, Abd al-Aziz bin Baz, given that the shedding of blood within the mosque's precincts has traditionally been forbidden. Bin Baz granted approval for an operation to recapture the mosque, on the condition that some of the social changes of recent years were rolled back, such as the appearance of women announcers on television, the employment of women in mixed workplaces, and the black markets for alcohol that had been allowed to emerge.[57] Far stricter religious education within the Kingdom was also demanded by bin Baz and granted by the Saudi leadership.

The Grand Mosque was successfully retaken after a lengthy operation, and in due course, Juhayman and the other figures in the siege were beheaded, but the event had shaken the royal family and the Saudi elite. The siege was another reminder of the risks and threats inherent in the rapid social and economic modernization of the 1960s and 1970s, while religion and traditional values were at the same time being rhetorically articulated by Kings Faisal and then Khalid. Juhayman had actually studied under bin Baz, demonstrating the murky boundaries between the established *ulema* and more extremist Islamism. He was also a descendent of *Ikhwan* figures and was born in a former *Ikhwan* stronghold,[58] again noteworthy as it demonstrated that the suppression of the 1927–1930 *Ikhwan* rebellion had never been completely achieved. The event also passed into the memory and mythology of other Islamists: it has been suggested that Osama bin Laden was detained by police in Mecca in December 1979 on the (false) suspicion of belonging to Juhayman's group and that, some years later, the future leader of al-Qa'eda spoke of Juhayman's actions in glowing terms and as being reflective of a "true Muslim."[59]

Another event that marked the momentous year of 1979 was a Shia uprising in the east of the Kingdom. The Shia had long been discriminated against by the Saudi state and the *ulema* on religious grounds, and were looked down on because of their poor, peasant origins, even though most of them lived above the oil fields that were making that same state rich.[60] The Shia were given only lowly positions in the oil sector, while oil wealth was disproportionately going to Sunnis living elsewhere in the Kingdom. During Faisal's rule, little was done to curtail either *ulema* condemnation of the Shia or the secular discrimination that they faced. Given these dynamics, and encouraged by the 1978–1979 Iranian revolution, the Shia began taken to the streets in the east during the Shia *ashura* festival, and then demonstrated again in large numbers in Qatif in early 1980. The Saudi National Guard was used to put down the protests, which had developed into rioting, and a number of people were killed in the process. Again, this event has gone into popular memory and mythology among many Shia, and despite government attempts to placate the Shia by offering them more opportunity and better infrastructure and facilities, a sense remains among them, to the present day, that they are second-class citizens.

Finally, 1979 marked the climax of the 1978–1979 Iranian revolution, which not only emboldened the Saudi Shia, but also created a new Saudi-Iranian dynamic, which, in varying ways, has been a salient feature of the strategic environment of the Gulf ever since. As "twin pillars" in the U.S. policy toward the Gulf since the Nixon administration, the two states had shared some strategic and security perspectives when Iran's Shah had been in power, if still being something of strategic rivals as well. However, protests against the Shah gained momentum in 1978, culminating in his departure on January 16, 1979. With the return from exile of Ayatollah Ruhollah Khomeini on February 1, both Iranian politics and the Gulf strategic environment were dramatically reorganized. By then, Khomeini was the de facto leader of the revolution, and was able to parlay this into permanent political power. A referendum was held on March 30–31, 1979, on whether Iran should become an "Islamic republic," which was overwhelmingly endorsed despite the concept remaining undefined, and then a new constitution was developed, with both theocratic and Western-style institutions and processes, which made Khomeini the Supreme Leader of the country in late 1979 and, in effect, the overarching power in its complex new political system. Although it took some time for Khomeini to solidify his position, as of late 1979 Iran was in effect under his control and its foreign policy now largely a product of Khomeini's thinking and his strong Persian, Shia nationalism. This was also a new dynamic in the region because the goals of states such as Saudi Arabia and Iraq were so at odds with Khomeini's worldview and interests. The revolution also removed Iran's Shah as a conservative monarch who shared many interests and goals with the Saudi royals. Quickly thereafter, Gulf dynamics were further rearranged by impacts of the 1980–1988 Iran-Iraq War, post-revolutionary Iranian-U.S. hostility, and Iranian rhetoric about the "export of the revolution" that deeply unnerved the Saudi leadership.

By this time, King Khalid was in poor health, having had numerous operations and other medical treatment throughout the 1970s and into the 1980s, and the crown prince, Fahd, was given considerable control over the day-to-day government matters. He also served as first deputy prime minister, which gave him more power than previous crown princes. He was thus well-prepared for power when Khalid died on June 13, 1982. Fahd inherited a complex security environment, as well as domestic political challenges, but he maintained certain trends set by the previous two monarchs. He continued the emphasis on public religiosity and piety, and the support for the propagation of Islam, that Faisal had begun and Khalid had continued. At the same time, his own personal conduct, especially abroad, had been luxurious and at times less than Islamic; a mostly unspoken allegation was that he was a gambler and womanizer, especially when he traveled in Europe. Despite his lip service to Islamic piety, he tried to limit the influence of the *ulema* by increasing the royal family's role in religious decision making and propagation, such as with the creation of the Supreme Council of Islamic Affairs to decide on and vet the role of religion in education, social, and cultural matters. Fahd also continued to avoid political liberalization, even as he increasingly opened up the economy and sought to diversify it. As two examples, a 1991 letter from key moderate figures calling for reform[61] was ignored, despite being widely circulated, while in 1991 and 1992, a petition from Islamists attacking corruption and seeking a greater public voice and fairer distribution of wealth was at first ignored and then emphatically blocked.[62]

Fahd was not a reformer, but he faced both a formidable set of external challenges and a strong opposition to the Al Saud. The 1990s were, broadly speaking, a time of considerable pressure from what Niblock categorizes as both "Islamists" and "modernizers."[63] At the same time, oil prices were for most of the decade very low, inhibiting the state's (still considerable) ability to spend and, through this, to co-opt societal forces and potential opposition. The 1990s witnessed the creation and high point of the Committee for the Defense of Legitimate Rights (CDLR), the first serious attempt to build a formal opposition group to the Al Saud and something that was firmly repressed.[64] The CDLR was forced into exile in London, and eventually were superseded by other groups, while the more radical Advice and Reformation Committee (ARC), also operating in exile, was suppressed and eventually extinguished, largely because it was a more extreme group with links to Osama bin Laden, among others.[65] This opposition was a reflection of underlying political disenchantment in society, but also reflected the economic challenges and limitations faced by the Saudi state. From about 1984 onward, oil prices plummeted, reaching a nadir of US$8 per barrel in 1986. This placed a severe, almost existential, strain on the regime's ability to maintain its governing bargain with society. Although much spending was cut as revenue plunged, the state could not withdraw spending on the main social benefits such as health care, education, or even state employment.[66] Nor could the government introduce taxation to its citizens, who were used to a standard of living now under threat. All the state could do was increase fees, charges, and costs for some state-delivered services such as utilities—and even that caused considerable popular resentment[67]—while running large budget deficits. Other initiatives such as "Saudization," which sought to replace expatriate workers with local Saudi ones, and a greater role for Saudi women in the workforce, were both born at this time, even though they have struggled ever since to become as effective as originally hoped.[68] Instead, social divisions and youth disenchantment became stronger, as a sense of relative deprivation and intergenerational unfairness grew greater.

At the same time, Fahd also faced considerable regional challenges. The 1980s were dominated by the 1980–1988 Iran-Iraq War, which itself threatened the security environment and thus the economic potential of the Gulf. Importantly, the 1979–1989 Soviet war in Afghanistan would turn out to be a crucial factor in Saudi Arabia's future, too. The Kingdom became a key sponsor of the Afghan *mujahideen*; the conglomeration of militias that fought the Soviet occupation. While the United States came to supply funding and arms through Pakistan to the *mujahideen*, the Saudi role was also important, roughly matching the U.S. financial contribution.[69] This Saudi support stemmed in part from a sense of Muslim solidarity with the Afghans, but at a more practical level, the Saudi leadership was motivated by a desire to enhance its domestic and regional image and to offset Iranian influence by enhancing Sunni influence in the region.[70] Yet the

Afghan war also had a strong negative impact on the Kingdom, creating a generation of radicalized Saudi *mujahideen*, famous among the ranks of which were Osama bin Laden. More broadly, however, the war created, radicalized, and legitimized a sizable number of Saudis who would later become a force for Islamization in the Kingdom and some of whom, in the early-mid-2000s, encouraged the extremist insurgency against the Saudi state or the international Islamist insurgency against the Iraqi government and U.S. forces in Iraq after 2003. That the Soviets eventually withdrew from Afghanistan, in effect defeated by the insurgency, added to the sense among Islamists that even a superpower could be defeated by a pious, committed Muslim opposition.

On the back of Afghanistan, Fahd quickly faced one of the most critical security challenges ever posed for the modern Saudi state, the 1990–1991 Gulf War. The August 2, 1990, Iraqi invasion of Kuwait was the first great security challenge of the post-Cold War international environment, but even more important for Saudi Arabia, it redrew the lines of Gulf international relations. It disproved the regional notion that Arab states do not conquer each other, and within the Gulf it showed that Iraqi president Saddam Hussein was an unpredictable threat. It also questioned the wisdom of wealthy Gulf states focusing on their qualitative military capability as a counter to the quantitative capability of Iran and Iraq. The Saudis had invested heavily in such an approach to defense modernization in the 1970s and 1980s, only to find that even after this vast, often-profligate spending, U.S. military intervention was still needed to guarantee Kuwait's liberation from, and Saudi Arabia's security against, Iraq.

The 1990–1991 Gulf War also presented a set of domestic challenges for Fahd. Saddam became a potential existential threat to Saudi Arabia, assuming Saddam had designs on the Kingdom as many Saudi figures feared. The crisis came at a time when domestic opposition and resentment toward the Saudi royal family was especially strong, the result of the economic strains of the latter-1980s and because Fahd himself was not especially popular or inspiring to many Saudis. Above all, the Saudi desire for U.S. military support in case Saddam continued on to Saudi Arabia, and the need for a U.S. military presence in the Kingdom to deter Saddam and, later, to launch the January–February 1991 war against him, was especially delicate. It required the Al Saud to again bring the *ulema* into the decision-making process and to endorse the U.S. military presence on Saudi soil that was being proposed—something they would not normally look favorably on. Many younger scholars opposed any U.S. presence, and indeed were unhappy at the Saudi-U.S. security relationship more generally, but key senior scholars eventually accepted the need for a U.S. deployment. As in 1979, *ulema* endorsement came at a cost for the monarchy. Fahd had to give the clerics greater social influence and allow a crackdown on reformist trends in Saudi society; it was during the U.S. military build-up in late 1990, for example, that societal calls for greater openness, and an attempt by women to defy the ban on them driving, were both suppressed. The calls for reform from both reformist and more Islamist or traditionalist social forces that the regime subsequently faced in the early- and mid-1990s were the product, in part, of this U.S. presence in the Kingdom during and then after the Gulf War, and of the trade-offs made by the royal family in 1990.

The Afghanistan conflict in the 1980s and the 1990–1991 Gulf War were both contributing factors, along with the rising coherence and attraction of Islamism in Saudi Arabia, to the emergence of al-Qa'eda and the events of September 11, 2001. The precursor organizations to al-Qa'eda were established in the early-mid-1990s. Bin Laden had been linked to the ARC and shared its fundamental views, and his networks built in the 1980s during the Afghanistan war were the origins of al-Qa'eda. The Gulf War greatly infuriated bin Laden, above all the presence of U.S. forces on Saudi soil, and was probably the most important issue setting him against the Saudi monarchy.[71] When he then moved via Pakistan to Sudan, where he set himself up in opposition to the Al Saud and in effect the United States, he was stripped of his citizenship by the Saudi government in 1994. From there he built links with other Islamists, and after his expulsion from Sudan in 1996, moved on to Afghanistan, which by this point was largely under the control of the medievalist Taliban that ruled the country until their removal from power in late 2001 by U.S.-led military action after the September 11, 2001 terrorist attacks.

Moreover and perhaps of most immediate security concern to the Saudi regime, there were a series of terrorist attacks in the Kingdom in the mid-1990s, including the 1995 Riyadh bombing and the 1996 bombing of a U.S.-run facility in al-Khobar. These reflected a greater radical stream among Saudi Islamists. While the exact details of what bin Laden did during the 1990s and the degree to which he was in operational control of al-Qa'eda is somewhat unclear, he probably did not directly manage such attacks but certainly encouraged them with his ideological pronouncements against the Al Saud.[72] More attention is given to this issue later, but the important point here is that a small but important Islamic extremist element emerged in Saudi Arabia and began to engage in violence, motivated by domestic grievances and the reinvigorated and expanded U.S-Saudi relationship after the Gulf War.

The decade of the 2000s would see even greater extremist challenges to the Al Saud, although the dynamics of this changed after the ascension to power of King Abdullah in 2005. Abdullah, like Fahd before him, gained considerable experience as a crown prince because of the ill-health of his predecessor. In Fahd's case, he was drastically weakened by a stroke in 1996, after which time Abdullah became crown regent. Fahd died on August 1, 2005, and Abdullah was formally anointed two days later. Abdullah has been a reformist leader of some substance, especially with judicial, educational, and some social reforms. He also steered the Kingdom through significant economic reforms as crown regent, which he has sustained during his own rule. In this he has been helped by a period of (mostly) sustained high average oil prices, which allowed the Saudi government budget to run surpluses for much of the 2000s. His main challenges, which are discussed later, are in managing internal tensions between traditionalism and reformism; confronting the enduring extremist threat to the Saudi regime itself and from Saudi extremists operating elsewhere; and ensuring stability in the face of the post-2011 Arab uprisings. In many of these, he has been confronted with the same dynamics as his predecessors. As a son of Ibn Saud, like all Saudi kings to date, he has inherited the patronage system and state capacity that has long supported Al Saud rulers, but he has also had to retain most of the obligations of that regime maintenance strategy. He has needed the same bargains with the *ulema*, tribes, businesspeople, and the United States as did previous monarchs, and these have usually set the context, climate, or processes for Saudi politics and security under Abdullah, just as they did under his predecessors. It is to these dynamics that this book now turns.

NOTES

1. Much of the history here is drawn from Madawi Al-Rasheed, *A History of Saudi Arabia*, 2nd ed. (Cambridge: Cambridge University Press, 2010), 13–68.

2. On the Ottoman role in the Arabian Peninsula and the creation of the Arab Gulf states, see Frederick F. Anscombe, *The Ottoman Gulf: The Creation of Kuwait, Saudi Arabia, and Qatar* (New York: Columbia University Press, 1997).

3. Ibid., 12–13.

4. On the Hijaz in the later 1800s and early 1900s, see Joshua Teitelbaum, *The Rise and Fall of the Hashemite Kingdom of Arabia* (London: Hurst, 2001), 11–36.

5. Al-Rasheed, *A History of Saudi Arabia*, 14–15.

6. On Abd al Wahhab and the emergence of what is sometimes called Wahhabism, see for example, Natana J. DeLong-Bas, *Wahhabi Islam: From Revival and Reform to Global Jihad* (Oxford: Oxford University Press, 2004), 7–40; and Charles Allen, *God's Terrorists: The Wahhabi Cult and the Hidden Roots of Modern Jihad* (London: Little, Brown, 2006), 42–68.

7. The term is contentious, not least of all because it displeases many adherents. See Tim Niblock, *Saudi Arabia: Power, Legitimacy and Survival* (London: Routledge, 2006), 23; and David Commins, *The Gulf States: A Modern History* (London: I. B. Taurus, 2012), 62.

8. Christine Moss Helms, *The Cohesion of Saudi Arabia: Evolution of Political Identity* (London: Croom Helm, 1981), 77, quoted in Daryl Champion, *The Paradoxical Kingdom: Saudi Arabia and the Momentum of Reform* (New York: Columbia University Press, 2003), 22–23.

9. David Commins, *The Wahhabi Mission and Saudi Arabia* (London: I. B. Taurus, 2009), 18–19.

10. Joseph Nevo, "Religion and National Identity in Saudi Arabia," *Middle Eastern Studies*, 34:3 (1998), 38.

11. Champion, *The Paradoxical Kingdom*, 22–23, Andrew Hammond, *The Islamic Utopia: The Illusion of Reform in Saudi Arabia* (London: Pluto Press, 2012), 20–21.

12. Andrew Hammond argues that this is the core principle defining modern Saudi Arabia as an "Islamic state." See Hammond, *The Islamic Utopia*, 20–21.

13. Al-Rasheed, *A History of Saudi Arabia*, 17.

14. Commins, *The Gulf States*, 63.

15. Ibid., 64.

16. Ibid., 64.

17. Al-Rasheed, *A History of Saudi Arabia*, 20.

18. Commins, *The Gulf States*, 64.

19. Al-Rasheed, *A History of Saudi Arabia*, 20–21.

20. Ibid., 27–29; also see Anscombe, *The Ottoman Gulf,* 153–159.

21. Al-Rasheed, *A History of Saudi Arabia*, 2–3, 40–41, 44–45, and elsewhere.

22. Ibid., 39.

23. Ibid., 40.

24. Joseph Kostiner, *The Making of Saudi Arabia, 1916–1936: From Chieftaincy to Monarchical State* (New York: Oxford University Press, 1993), 62, cited in Teitelbaum, *The Rise and Fall of the Hashemite Kingdom of Arabia*, 271.

25. Teitelbaum, *The Rise and Fall of the Hashemite Kingdom of Arabia*, 271–272.

26. Al-Rasheed, *A History of Saudi Arabia*, 44.

27. Ibid., 69–70.

28. The figure is certainly more than 22, but the exact number is uncertain. Al-Rasheed quotes St. John Philby claiming that Ibn Saud admitted to him having had a total of over 235 wives. See Harry St. John Philby, *Arabian Jubilee* (London: Hale, 1952), 111, quoted in Al-Rasheed, *A History of Saudi Arabia*, 72. The fact that even key tribal figures, who were almost always polygamous, were surprised at the number of Ibn Saud's wives suggests that the number was large.

29. Al-Rasheed, *A History of Saudi Arabia*, 73–77.

30. On patrimonialism and neopatrimonialism in the Middle East, a good overview source is James A. Bill and Robert Springborg, *Politics in the Middle East*, 3rd Ed. (Glenview, IL: Scott, Foresman and Company, 1990), 137–176.

31. What follows is drawn in large part from Al-Rasheed, *A History of Saudi Arabia*, 77–83.

32. Ibid., 84–85.

33. Ibid., 90.

34. Ibid., 90; see also the Saudi Aramco Web site, http://www.saudiaramco.com/en/home.html#our-company%257C%252Fen%252Fhome%252Four-company%252Four-history0.baseajax.html, accessed March 1, 2013.

35. Al-Rasheed, *A History of Saudi Arabia*, 90.

36. On the Saud-Faisal struggle and the challenges of the time, see Ibid., 102–110.

37. Sarah Yizraeli, *Politics and Society in Saudi Arabia: The Crucial Years of Development, 1960–1982* (New York: Columbia University Press, 2012), 20–24.

38. Niblock, *Saudi Arabia: Power, Legitimacy and Survival*, 40–45.

39. Ibid., 44–45; also Al-Rasheed, *A History of Saudi Arabia*, 110.

40. Oil royalties increased from SR564 million in 1961–1962 to SR1,573 million in 1970–197; see Tim Niblock with Monica Malik, *The Political Economy of Saudi Arabia* (London: Routledge, 2007), 40 (Table 2.2).

41. On the Ten-Point Program see Yizraeli, *Politics and Society in Saudi Arabia*, 98–117.

42. Niblock with Malik, *The Political Economy of Saudi Arabia*, 41.

43. Ylzraeli, *Politics and Society in Saudi Arabia*, 98.

44. Niblock with Malik, *The Political Economy of Saudi Arabia*, 44.

45. For the specific figures and the relative contributions of sectors to GDP over 1962–1970, see Niblock with Malik, *The Political Economy of Saudi Arabia*, 45–46 (Table 2.4).

46. Ibid., 47.

47. Niblock, *Saudi Arabia: Power, Legitimacy and Survival*, 54–55.

48. Ibid., 56.

49. Al-Rasheed, *A History of Saudi Arabia*, 118.

50. Ibid., 126.

51. Niblock, *Saudi Arabia: Power, Legitimacy and Survival*, 59–60.

52. Ibid., 60–62.

53. Al-Rasheed, *A History of Saudi Arabia*, 131–134.

54. Ibid., 136–137.

55. Ibid., 137–138.

56. A good recent work on the Grand Mosque siege is Yuroslav Trofimov, *The Siege of Mecca: The Forgotten Uprising in Islam's Holiest Shrine* (London: Allen Lane, 2007).

57. Ibid., 98–101, 241–243.

58. Al-Rasheed, *A History of Saudi Arabia*, 139–140.

59. Trofimov, *The Siege of Mecca*, 246–247.

60. Al-Rasheed, *A History of Saudi Arabia*, 141–143.

61. Champion, *The Paradoxical Kingdom*, 219–220

62. Ibid., 220–225; also Niblock, *Saudi Arabia: Power, Legitimacy and Survival*, 90–95.

63. Niblock, *Saudi Arabia: Power, Legitimacy and Survival*, 91.

64. Champion, *The Paradoxical Kingdom*, 226–229.

65. Ibid., 229.

66. Al-Rasheed, *A History of Saudi Arabia*, 143–145.

67. Ibid., 145.

68. Ibid., 146–148.

69. William Maley, *The Afghanistan Wars* (Basingstoke: Palgrave Macmillian, 2002), 81–82.

70. A similar point is made in Ibid., 82.

71. Niblock, *Saudi Arabia: Power, Legitimacy and Survival*, 153.

72. Ibid., 154–155.

CHAPTER 2

The Saudi Political, Economic, and Military System

It is often stated, too simplistically, that Saudi Arabia has an autocratic and centralized political system with a simple polity dominated by the king and some key royals. Certainly, the inner circle of the royal family is especially powerful, and they possess disproportionate decision-making power in most important areas and ministerial portfolios. However, like any ruling elite, the Al Saud relies on a web of elite networks across and also beyond the royal family, and it needs a wider legitimacy to maintain its rule. The Saudi system of politics—dominated though it is by the Al Saud—therefore encompasses a broad set of cooptive and repressive mechanisms and incorporates an enormous variety of actors and forces. Although royal power may appear to be unobstructed, in fact it is negotiated and regulated by complex elite and state-society dynamics. The durability of the Saudi regime can be understood only with an assessment of these actors, forces, and mechanisms of control. Moreover, these determinants of power will likely only increase in their importance in future, as society becomes increasingly well educated and sophisticated, and globalization changes many tools of politics. This chapter lays out how the Saudi political system operates, including the nature of its political economy, the roles of various actors and forces, and some background on key institutions, especially the military and others in the security realm.

THE ROYAL FAMILY

The complexities of Saudi politics notwithstanding, the royal family is at the center of power in Saudi Arabia. Indeed, Saudi Arabia is the only country in the world named after the family that created and rules it. Since the creation of the third (current) Saudi state, the royals have used cooptation, repression, elite bargains, and claims to popular legitimacy to maintain power. Cooptation has always been preferred, of course: it is the favored method of control in any authoritarian system, and the vast oil wealth that has flowed into the Kingdom since the 1950s has allowed for a level of cooptation unimaginable to Ibn Saud in his early decades of rule. That said, the other methods have had their place and still do. Elite bargains are important in stifling or controlling those who might challenge the royals grasp on power or who may have the financial means or wider support to do so. Repression serves to neutralize more dedicated opposition, while narratives of legitimacy can improve the support, or at least gain the acquiescence, of wider segments of society.

The king is, of course, at the center of the political system, and has enormous influence over the strategic direction of policy as well as making many day-to-day decisions. He is the head of the Al Saud family and dynasty, the head of state, and the prime minister of the cabinet (thus, the crown prince, or heir apparent, is deputy prime minister and, since Faisal's reign, a second heir has also been identified informally by appointment as second deputy prime minister). As both head of state and head of government, the king possesses enormous power. Yet, his power is not absolute, and cases such as King Saud's forced abdication are a reminder that a king must still maintain harmony in the family and be seen as competent by key actors.

The Saudi kings thus far have all been chosen according to agnatic primogeniture; that is, all have been the sons of Ibn Saud, and power has passed to them by age rather than following a single line of intergenerational descent. Some potential successors to the throne have been bypassed, such as Prince Muhammad bin Abdulaziz (1910–1988), who stepped aside as crown prince in 1965, allowing Khalid to take his place, probably because of pressure from the family to help stabilize the family and reduce the tension between some of its wings. Historically, a king would appoint a crown prince, although this was not formalized until the Saudi Basic Law in 1992,[1] and in 2007 was superseded by the creation of the Allegiance Council. Historically, the crown prince would be endorsed through an oath of loyalty (*al-bay'a*) by key family members and notables in a council (called *ahl al-'aqd wa al-hall*).[2] This endorsement of the proposed heir helped ensure elite solidarity when the time came for him to take power. It also provided an impression of royal consultation beyond the family, important in itself for political stability and legitimacy. As mentioned, the further appointment of a prince as deputy prime minister has in effect indicated the next in line to the throne.

King Abdullah amended the succession process first with a succession decree in October 2006 that gave princes a vote on future heirs to the throne, and then as mentioned when the Allegiance Council (*al-hay'a al-bay'a*) was established in

October 2007. The Allegiance Council formalized the mechanism for endorsing successors, in particular by approving a crown prince soon after a new monarch had assumed power. The creation of the council was probably prompted by divisions among key princes over succession; it had been rumored that key princes from the Sudairi line within the Al Saud had been unhappy about Abdullah's ascension to the throne rather than one of their own such as Prince Sultan. However, the council performed other political roles. Crucially, it creates a mechanism for succession in the longer term, when Ibn Saud's sons have all died and kings will have to be chosen from grandsons.

The council endorsed crown princes in October 2011, when it sanctioned Prince Nayef as crown prince, and again in June 2012 after Nayef's death when it endorsed Prince Salman for the role. The practice has been that the council endorses a crown prince from a list supplied by the king, or that the king asks the council to nominate a specific person. The council can also, when a king is incapacitated, declare a crown prince to be monarch. However, there have been questions raised as to whether or not the council is given a sufficiently wide choice of candidates, especially in the case of Salman's appointment in 2012, and it remains unclear whether the council actively voted on these crown prince appointments or rather "rubber stamped" a prearranged candidate.[3] The council's efficacy was challenged by Prince Talal bin Abdulaziz, a senior but liberal prince, when in 2011 he openly expressed concern when Nayef was appointed crown prince.[4]

The Allegiance Council is a senior royal body. The broader Al Saud dynasty is large and politically diverse, including princes born to lines from across the Kingdom. The royal family is typically described as consisting of some "5,000 to 8,000 adults,"[5] with some estimates reaching 10,000 or more adults.[6] Once children and very distant parts of the family are included—remembering that the family consists not only of Ibn Saud's line, but all the lines from his brothers and the cadet branches of the dynasty—the final figure is probably in excess of 20,000 and is perhaps much more.[7] A 1996 U.S. diplomatic cable published by *Wikileaks* in 2011 implies that back in the mid-1990s some 5,300 royals were receiving stipends from the government (payable from birth, but only to certain royals in the Ibn Saud line), implying an extended royal family ultimately of such size. Regardless, the royal family consists of "circles" of power[8]; in effect metaphorical concentric circles of royals surrounding the king and the first, most inner circle of key royals.

Of these, and beyond the handful of most senior royals, some 2,000 or so key people from the main lines of the dynasty are most important, including an inner circle of a few hundred, often holding key appointments, and hundreds more who are prominent in cultural or business circles. Traditionally, the most powerful core of the family were the main sons of Ibn Saud, especially those holding cabinet portfolios, senior institutional appointments, or with the largest business interests. Among these were the so-called *Sudairi Seven* or *Sudairi clan*, a group of Ibn Saud's sons all from Ibn Saud's marriage to Hassa bint Ahmad Al Sudairi (1900–1969), from the powerful Sudairi dynasty in the central Najd district. Hassa was reportedly the favorite wife among Ibn Saud's many, perhaps because of her reported beauty, although she was also very astute in creating a sense of solidarity and cohesion among her children. The Sudairi Seven—of which only four remain alive as at early 2014—includes the former king Fahd (1921–2005, r. 1982–2005); former defense minister and former crown prince Sultan (1929–2011); former deputy defense minister Abd al-Rahman (1931–); former interior minister and former crown prince Nayef (1934–2012); former deputy defense minister Turki (1934–); former governor of Riyadh and crown prince, as of December 2013, Salman (1935–); and former deputy interior minister Ahmad (1942–).[9] These were the Seven, all males, although there were also four daughters born to Hassa.

The influence of the Sudairi sons grew greatly during Faisal's rule, when he promoted several of them to cabinet positions and relied upon them as a key, cohesive sub-group; it was in 1962, when Faisal was seeking to outmaneuver Saud, that Fahd was appointed interior minister, Sultan defense minister, and Salman governor of Riyadh. After becoming king in 1964, Faisal strengthened his ties with the Sudairis. Their influence remained strong under King Khalid, when Fahd was crown prince, and of course then when Fahd was king. Nayef was not appointed interior minister until 1975, but he immediately appointed his brother Ahmad as his deputy, and he ultimately became perhaps the most powerful of the Seven who did not reach the throne, given his ministry's central role in domestic affairs and internal security. Despite the fact that observers often describe him simplistically as a conservative, he also instituted reforms within his portfolio and was a power broker beyond simply one part of the family.[10]

That the Seven were closely bound and loyal to each other helped them enjoy considerable informal power throughout this period, including through the promotion of their sons into key positions as well. As an example of this, one of Sultan's sons, Bandar, served as Saudi Ambassador to the United States for over two decades (1982–2005), and in this time exerted enormous influence over Saudi foreign policy as well as amassing huge wealth.[11] After this time in Washington, Bandar returned to Saudi Arabia reportedly to boost his political credentials and opportunities. He became Director General of the National Security Council, and after almost two terms in that role, was appointed Director General of Saudi Intelligence Agency from July 2012 to April 2014, and was then appointed a special envoy for the king. He is now the only figure from the Sultan wing of the Sudairi Seven still holding considerable political power.[12]

However, the power of the Sudairi Seven and their descendants remains checked by King Abdullah and the growing institutionalization of Saudi politics. It is often assumed, for example, that the Allegiance Council was intended by Abdullah to counter some of the power of the Sudairi, not least because they were reportedly unhappy with Abdullah's ascension to the throne ahead of a Sudairi such as Sultan. Certainly, the Sudairis' power has been waning under Abdullah, but it remains a powerful part of the family.

Other groupings of full brothers have been important from time to time, such as the sons of another wife, Shahida, who as Kéchechian notes occupied the defense and deputy defense portfolios in the 1950s and early 1960s.[13] Even more important for the stability of the Al Saud is the broad unity that is maintained among most key members of the family. There is overwhelming agreement on the need for discretion, stability, and durability of the family's rule. Only very occasionally, such as Prince Talal's public querying of Nayef's appointment as crown prince, do divisions become public. That incident was more indicative of a broad divergence among Ibn Saud's sons into comparative liberal and comparative conservative types, although any "liberal" or "conservative" appellations are misleading to the extent that they imply there are only two, relatively cohesive groupings in the family. Just as important as ideological orientation are the political and administrative fiefdoms that develop when key princes retain portfolios for as long as many inner royals do. These have often allowed the formation of particular power centers dominated by one part of the Al Saud.

Other royals are less central to the political order, but powerful or influential in other spheres. Some of Ibn Saud's sons have considerable commercial power by virtue of their business interests. Talal, mentioned above, enhances his influence in the family by promoting his more liberal views, by his activism and nongovernmental organizations, through his philanthropy, and through business interests. Prince Nawwaf, too, has held various political positions since 1961 and been active in various international engagement roles, but also is a wealthy individual with business interests in real estate, tourism, banking, energy, and other areas. The grandsons of Ibn Saud are increasingly cutting their political teeth as governors or deputy governors, or sometimes as deputy ministers, military officers, or diplomats. Perhaps the most famous of them is Prince Al-Waleed bin Talal; with a net worth of about US$20 billion, he is the richest person in Saudi Arabia and ranked 26th richest in the world by *Forbes*.[14] He owns 95 percent of Kingdom Holding Company, which holds stakes in real estate, equities, and other investments in both Saudi Arabia and abroad. Al-Waleed began investing in 1979, and by the 1990s was a powerful business actor. He derives some influence from his wealth, of course, but his power also comes from his family connections and through informal roles such as donations to international development activities and bequests to foreign universities.

Princes derive some influence from being royals, more if they are from Ibn Saud's direct line. Their business roles become symbols of the family's power and reach, but can also provide a means for the family to gauge wider opinion from, in this case, the business community. The inner royals are only a core of a much larger and broader dynasty. The descendants of Ibn Saud are described here as the "inner" royals because they are in the royal line. The Al Saud also has five other main cadet branches, which are part of the dynasty but are not royal branches of it, even where some members of these branches may play active (if comparatively less important) political roles or occupy important positions in state institutions. It is important to remember that some parts of the family have nothing to do with politics and the Ibn Saud line: some broke away from the royal line in disagreements over succession, access to resources, or their political loyalty.

When they support the royal branch of the Al Saud, other parts of the dynasty are important in several ways. At the most basic level, their support helps the legitimacy and durability of Al Saud rule. The family tries to build an image in society that one observer described as being like a "super-tribe,"[15] where the Al Saud represents the dominant tribe in a nation-state highly defined by tribal affiliation. The dynasty is also important in the mechanics of patronage. Wealth is distributed not only through state spending but also through allowances paid to all princes and princesses—something that promotes loyalty to the dynasty, of course, but since allowances are paid from birth, this also encourages Al Saud parents to have large families. Beyond monthly allowances are additional gifts, such as land grants at the time of marriage. In some cases, these allowances are large enough to live comfortably on, and in such situations, networks of favor strengthen patron and link them to their clients, thereby binding various wings of the family to the core of it. For more distant members of the dynasty, allowances can be supplemented by state employment or business opportunities, often coming from their royal affiliation and again part of the inner royals' tactic of maintaining family cohesion and support for the political status quo.

These dynamics of Al Saud rule all reinforce and sustain the dynasty's dominance of Saudi politics. The dynasty sits at the summit of the neopatrimonial system, with control over an array of institutions and processes, which not only permits the wider political relationships that support the royal family but also is important in ensuring the stability of that ruling dynasty itself. Yet, much more than just the Al Saud dynasty is needed to maintain the political status quo, and state institutions have become increasingly important over the decades in maintaining the political order.

THE BUREAUCRACY AND STATE INSTITUTIONS

Despite the centrality of the royal family to both formal and informal politics, political institutions are also important and powerful. These are not so much a check on Al Saud power—which is constrained much more by its symbiotic elite relationships than by formal process—but rather, these institutions are important because they provide seemingly formal mechanisms for otherwise quite informal political processes. Various institutions help allocate oil wealth, in some cases dispensing it as cash, in other cases as jobs or business opportunities. Some institutions support the consultation or information gathering that the Saudis need to rule smoothly and securely. Still other institutions are apparatuses of state repression, used by the royals to exert political control or neutralize threats. In varying ways, therefore, institutions still matter in Saudi Arabia.

The Saudi executive is, as noted, dominated by the king himself, who is head of state and prime minister. He has near-complete control over ministers, and a significant amount of authority in the judicial sphere as well, given the absence of an elected legislative body and the importance of royal decrees in implementing changes and decisions. Monarchs may take other roles. The current king, for example, held onto the position of head of the Saudi National Guard until 2010, and also held or holds other chairs of various government councils. The primacy of the king does not mean that ministers are meaningless; the deputy prime minister (crown prince), 23 ministers with portfolios, and 7 ministers of state exert their own power based on their access to and esteem with the king, the importance of their portfolio, and typically, how long they have held their appointment and the extent to which they have mastered the portfolio and have their own power bases within it. Many key ministers are Al Saud family members, but there are also others, especially technocratic managers often found in more complex or technologically driven portfolios, such as agriculture, finance, and petroleum. The Minister of Islamic Affairs, Endowments, Call and Guidance usually comes out of a prominent clerical family.

The only legislative body in the Kingdom is the Consultative Assembly, or Shura Council (*majlis al-shura*). It is not a law-making parliament, but rather a body of 150 members, appointed by the king to advise him and to propose legislation. It has some of the pomp and positions of a parliament such as a speaker, but it cannot initiate its own laws nor pass motions of no confidence against ministers. Its (limited) power comes from its role in developing the Kingdom's Five Year Plans, its ability to debate issues, and a limited ability to question ministers. It presumably exerts some influence over the king's views of a minister's performance, too, but only informally. Still, its informal activities and advisory role are important nonetheless. While it cannot pass laws, it can offer advice on the interpretation of them. It can comment on treaties, plans, and state initiatives. Its greatest influence is probably drawn from the informal advice it can offer a king when a matter is still under consideration, making it is a genuinely consultative body, if not one with many formal powers.

It is also worth recalling that some sort of consultative politics has long been part of Saudi politics. Kings have always included a degree of consultation (*shura*) in their decision making, and Ibn Saud created the first *shura* body in 1924.[16] Consultative politics went through various experiments under Ibn Saud, including a body in 1925 that briefly had the unwritten authority to draft legislation, and later models that varied in the size of their membership or the exact emphases of its roles. It was also a period when the institutions of government were nascent and underdeveloped, and so these bodies acted as government-by-consensus more than as a voice for loyal opposition. If anything, Ibn Saud used these bodies to build consultative networks with the areas he conquered and to ensure mechanisms for the informal resolution of grievances or concerns, while at the same time not ceding any actual authority or sovereignty to such an institution. After Ibn Saud's death in 1953, as politics was more institutionalized, many such roles shifted to ministers and the cabinet, although there continued to be both a *shura* type of consultation and *majlis* meetings after that time. The promulgation of the Basic Law in 1992 included a modernization of the laws surrounding a consultative council, and over the 1990s and 2000s the Assembly was expanded, by 30 members each four-year term, from 60 members in 1993 to 150 members in its fourth term over 2005–2009.[17]

Where there is a modicum of representative government is at the local level. In 2003, it was decided by the cabinet to increase popular participation, and the decision was taken to allow voting for municipal councils, perhaps in response to opposition calls for more significant reform at the national level. Over February–April 2005, polls were held for half the positions on local councils. Some 608 people were eventually elected to 178 councils, out of 9,330 candidates.[18] The polls excluded women—as both voters and candidates—as well as military personnel and people under 21 years, and so ultimately the number of voters as a proportion of the population was small: slightly less than 793,432 registered voters.[19] The outcome of the polls was somewhat predictable. Islamists won a sizable number of the positions, and Shiites won only in some areas of the northeast, and even then not in major eastern cities. Yet, the polls were important as an initial but notable political reform providing a new link between (local) political institutions and society. Even though they have been limited in scope and probably are an attempt by the regime at calculated political decompression and top-down, limited political modernization,[20] they have symbolic value and suggest further reform might come in the future. A sign of this was that in the delayed 2011 polls, there was an even greater controversy about women not being able to run and vote, prompting King Abdullah to declare that women would be able to run and vote in the planned 2015 polls.[21]

Many political institutions have been either weak or based on informal power, or in some cases both. This was the case with the legislative bodies and to a lesser extent local authorities, but is true of some ministries and state-owned firms as well. Ministries vary greatly in their autonomy, quality, and performance in large part because of the impacts of rents; as Hertog has explained well, the various mixes of clientelism, based on rents, means that even within an institution, good quality processes may exist, but often are side by side with or overlapping other far less effective or very out-of-date ones.[22] This may be the product of regime dynamics and power variations between elites, or of institutions playing wider roles as, say, employers or political systems, rather than existing only to efficiently deliver government services or to implement policy. Still other institutions are relatively weak, often so because of the fiefdoms and corruption that exists in the system. Thus, the bureaucracy is hierarchical and vertically divided at the institutional level, with the main central authority being, of course, the Saudi political elite, while within organizations a similar dynamic occurs, in which units and institutions are weak because of the clientelism and patronage that bureaucrats enjoy and the motivations inherent in the system to avoid decision making and accountability.[23] It is for this reason that fiefdoms emerge so easily from ministers or senior officials keen on establishing such power, and this bureaucratic structure also makes genuine reform and economic diversification difficult. As a result, when true reform is needed, a new agency is usually created to bypass the existing process. This is one way in which oil often has negative impacts on political development, because it affords informal patronage and co-optation to those at the top, undermining rational-legal processes.

State-owned firms are somewhat better than ministries in this regard, probably because such firms recycle and reproduce rents, and so there is a political motivation to make them efficient and profitable, in contrast with ministries and agencies that often have as at least one of their goals the cooptation of citizens through state employment. Thus, the bureaucracy serves the role of employer and coopter in the kingdom, whereas state-owned firms are part of the regime's allocation strategy and therefore are kept relatively efficient and profitable. As an example, the state-owned national oil company, Saudi Arabian Oil Company (usually referred to as Saudi ARAMCO), is world class in its capabilities, efficient, and far more accomplished at training and developing Saudis for positions at the firm than most private sector businesses, while it continually revises and reforms its processes to lower costs and increase profits.[24] It is not the politicized, inefficient behemoth so common in republican, nonoil states. Similarly, the main petro-chemicals firm, Saudi Basic Industries Corporation, which is floated on the stock market but has 70 percent of shares held by the state, is also highly efficient and profitable. So too are other state-owned firms. In fact, state-linked listed firms seem to outperform private listed firms in many respects, including in their profitability.[25] This is probably because they have never been politicized in the way that most were in more radical republican Arab states. In contrast, the Saudi leadership has been willing to give state-owned firms' managers considerable autonomy and unobtrusive support.[26]

The other exception to the inefficiency rule in recent times has been the judiciary, which underwent massive reform under Abdullah after 2005. Again, such reform is from a very modest starting point, given the enormous power of the king in the judicial realm and the lack of transparency with many court outcomes. However, changes in the legal framework have been significant, starting with Fahd's 1992 Basic Law. More recently, on October 1, 2007, King Abdullah announced the creation of a Supreme Court and new first-degree courts, plus reforms to the appeals court system.[27] Some US$2.8 billion was also allocated to legal training and judicial infrastructure. Some of these reforms were primarily about modernizing the commercial and business realm, but many were broader and more significant than that.[28]

Relatively weak, in contrast, are state and state-controlled sectors such as education and media. There has been talk of educational reform, especially under Prince Faisal bin Abdullah, the education minister since 2009. He has attempted to negotiate reforms of the schooling system with parents and teachers, including more focus on mathematics and the sciences, sports instruction for girls, and more opportunities for training in areas most needed in the economy.[29] Despite these economically important goals, the education system is hampered not only by conservatism among some families and educators but also by the enormous sums spent on the education bureaucracy. Moreover, religion still has a dominant place in education, despite the attempt to increase the time and resources spent on more marketable and technical skills. Amazingly, "in 2002, religious instruction took up 31 per cent of course load in the primary system, compared with 20 per cent for mathematics and sciences."[30] Crucial as it is for political change and economic development, education is a very political undertaking.

Equally political, and equally tightly controlled by the state, are media institutions and actors. It is a highly regulated field, such that even private sector actors are characterized by self-censorship among journalists and editors, and an understood threat that the state has the power to silence any attempts at substantive debate anyway.[31] The debates that do appear in the media are, therefore, usually sponsored by the state or are known to be acceptable to it. This may still give the media some influence, say in hosting debates that encourage a discussion of important issues or give a veneer of political openness, but the media is by no means a fifth estate. The Internet is a little freer than traditional media, but it too is monitored and regulated.[32] Where it matters, in other words—in the institutions and organizations that have the potential to influence opinion or mount opposition to the government or the royals—state control is very stringent and inflexible.

THE MILITARY AND STATE SECURITY SERVICES

Institutionally, the military, security, and intelligence services are all important for the maintenance of Al Saud rule. The family and political elite are equally concerned about internal and external security, facing as they do both the threats and risks of regional rivalry and conflict, and internal threats from terrorism and social unrest. At times, the two may even seem interrelated, as when perceived rivalry with Iran is translated into problems with the Shiite community in the east, and Shiite disquiet assumed to have been stoked or supported by Tehran.

Such dynamics are the focus of later chapters. The important point here is that the heads of these institutions are chosen carefully, given above all the central role they play in regime maintenance, as well as their significance in shaping Saudi strategic culture and security posture.

While the king enjoys enormous executive power, the Saudi national security structure and decision-making apparatus technically is run through the Saudi National Security Council (SNSC). The SNSC was established by King Abdullah in 2005 as the peak national security body. It is chaired by the king, with the crown prince and minister of defense sitting as deputy chairman and also includes the ministers of interior and foreign affairs, as well as Prince Bandar bin Sultan, the head of the Saudi intelligence service, who is the body's Secretary General. On paper the SNSC has enormous power, including to declare war and to undertake investigations into the armed forces and the security and intelligence agencies. In reality, the most critical decisions are still made more informally, through consultation by the king with key senior royals.

The Saudi armed forces as a whole consist of some 233,500 personnel.[33] This is a complex amalgam of those from the army, or Royal Saudi Land Force (some 75,000 personnel), the Royal Saudi Air Force (20,000) and a separate Air Defense Forces (16,000), the Royal Saudi Navy (13,500), plus the domestically focused Saudi Arabian National Guard of some 75,000 personnel—closer to 100,000 once tribal militia attached to it are included as well[34]—and paramilitary forces such as a Border Guard of some 10,500, and an Industrial Security Force (of at least 9,000), and a Coast Guard of 4,500. The size and complexity of these services and forces contribute to a contrast in Saudi security: it has one of the best-equipped militaries in the region but its coordination and decision making are poor,[35] which undermines its potential. The Saudi military capacity overall is arguably sufficient for internal regime security, and able to exert influence and through qualitative advantages deter some external actors from acting hostilely toward Riyadh, but for existential security against a major threat, the capacity of the Kingdom's military is less certain. The 1990–1991 Gulf War—when the Saudis agreed to U.S. basing in the Kingdom under fears that Iraq would push on from its invasion of Kuwait into Saudi Arabia as well—was a reminder that the United States still is the ultimate guarantor of the Saudi regime's survival when external threats are sufficiently large or credible.[36] Modernization efforts since that time have included attempts at addressing this matter and improving the qualitative capacity of the military, while domestic concerns remain a key driver of the security and intelligence services nonetheless. Ultimately, however, if Iraq were to threaten Saudi Arabia again the way it did in the summer of 1990, or the Kingdom were to face a comparable military threat from elsewhere, Riyadh would probably still rely on U.S. support to ensure its protection.

Still, the Saudis possess considerable military capacity. The Army dates in effect to the early 1920s and Ibn Saud's expansion into the east and southeast of the peninsula, and it gained later combat experience in the 1948 Arab-Israeli War, in the Yemeni civil war in the 1960s, and later, fighting alongside U.S. and allied forces in the 1990–1991 Gulf War against Iraq. The oil boom of 1973–1984 saw a considerable modernization of the military, including the army, with plans announced in 1974 to expand army manpower by around 50 percent over the decade ahead. Critical too was the development of capability, with the purchase of new platforms that Saudi Arabia's new oil wealth suddenly afforded. The same 1974 survey envisaged the purchase of some 440 helicopters, new M-60A1 tanks, howitzers, TOW missiles systems, and other equipment.[37] Despite the ambition of this transformation and some periods of pause, often because of oil price fluctuations, the army was eventually modernized along such lines, and again in the 1990s and 2000s, while there was no real increase in personnel numbers, the army still improved its capabilities, especially its facilities and its mobility.[38] By the early 2010s, the army's combat capability consisted of four armored brigades, five mechanized brigades, an airborne brigade, an artillery brigade, and other light units, with the major equipment and platforms, including some 600 main battle tanks, 1,423 armored personnel carriers, 909 artillery pieces, MANPADs, and various helicopters.[39] While impressive on paper, many of these are thought to be under-strength, given the problems in recruitment, retention, and absenteeism.[40]

The Royal Saudi Air Force is a technologically advanced air force with considerable defensive and offensive capability. It too dates back to the 1920s, when an air capability was developed with British assistance, but Saudi air power increased most markedly once U.S. military assistance began after the Dhahran air field opened in 1952. Again, it was the oil wealth after about 1973 that allowed for the most impressive expansion of Saudi air capability. The Kingdom had purchased 55 F-5B/E aircraft in 1971, but as of the mid-1970s it enhanced its military capability with the purchase of additional F-5s with greater offensive capability and also purchased C-130 transport aircraft from Lockheed.[41] In 1978, despite fierce lobbying against the sale in Washington, the Saudis were given approval to purchase 60 F-15 aircraft.[42] Later upgrades kept the F-15 capability world-class, and in the 1980s the Saudis also purchased other equipment, including (controversially) five E-3A AWACs aircraft and eight KE-3A tanker aircraft in 1981,[43] and the 1985 *Al-Yamamah* deal had at its center the purchase of 72 Panavia Tornado jets, in two variants, from the United Kingdom.[44] As of the early 2010s, the air force still had the F-15 and Tornado as the backbone of their power, but had placed an order in 2007 with BAE Systems for 72 Eurofighter Typhoon aircraft, and in 2011 agreed a purchase from the United States of 84 new, more advanced F-15s and upgrades to bring 70 older F-15s up to the same standard.[45] Separate to the Air Force, the Air Defense Forces operates Saudi Arabia's extensive radar defenses—among the most advanced in the world—and its anti-aircraft capabilities.

The Royal Saudi Navy is a smaller service than the army or air force, and arguably receives less attention and prestige in Saudi security thinking, but nonetheless it is a sizable force and a well-equipped one. It is headquartered in Riyadh but operates a western fleet out of Jeddah, on the Red Sea, and an eastern fleet based at Jubail, on the coast of the Gulf. Created in 1960, it emerged later than the other services, but was given similar attention in the defense modernizations from the 1970s onward; in the early 1970s, in fact, the Navy had barely 1,000 personnel and was little more than a basic coast guard service. Its acquisition in the 1970s and 1980s of missile patrol vessels, mine sweepers, landing craft, and a dramatic improvement in infrastructure,[46] which was in part linked to the modernization of the other services but was also intended to create a viable maritime force in the face of a rising Iranian one. In the 1980s it also improved its command, control, and communication, and bought corvettes from the United States early that decade. Later that decade, French-built frigates were added to the fleet, and then in the 1990s and 2000s, further additions were made to the fleet, including the addition of three destroyers in the early 2000s and various other vessels throughout this period. The Navy also has a sizable fleet of naval helicopters, including 12 Super Pumas with an anti-ship missile attack capability.[47]

An interesting and quite unique part of the Saudi military, with crucial political and strategic roles to play, is the Saudi Arabian National Guard (SANG). Although part of the Saudi land forces, it is very separate from the army in both its history and roles. Unlike most national guard forces elsewhere in the world, the SANG is not a part-time or reserve force for predominantly or exclusively home defense, but rather is an important ground force in its own right. It serves partly as a praetorian guard for the royal family, as a counter to the main army and thus a type of anti-coup force, but also it is both a loyal service against external attack and crucially also serves as a military force to protect against domestic threats and uprisings. It was SANG troops, for example, which entered Bahrain in March 2011, as the Arab Spring was unfolding, to suppress the popular uprising there against the Sunni and closely Saudi-aligned Al Khalifa dynasty, and it had previously served in other important and substantial conflicts, most notably the 1990–1991 Gulf War.

The SANG emerged out of the remnants of the *Ikhwan*.[48] Originally called the "White Army,"[49] and incorporating some remaining *Ikhwan* foot soldiers after the 1927–1930 *Ikhwan* rebellion, it became the National Guard in 1954. A crucial force for the consolidation of Ibn Saud's rule, and then later as the SANG, it played an important role in supporting the Saudi royals. As the army was modernized and expanded in the 1960s and especially from the mid 1970s onward, it became more powerful in relation to the Guard, but in the late 1970s the SANG underwent a modernization as well. Starting in 1973, and lasting through the 1980s, U.S. advisers helped refurbish and transform the Guard into a quite-effective light mechanized force.[50] Increasingly, the tribal elements

Table 2.1 Saudi Arabian and Gulf Military Forces and Platforms (2013)

	KSA	Bahrain	Kuwait	Qatar	Oman	UAE	Iran
Total defense budget (US$)*	59.6 bn	1.39 bn	4.43 bn	~13.6 bn	9.25 bn	9.32 bn	17.7 bn
Total armed forces personnel	204,500	~19,460	~22,600	11,800	45,000	~51,000	523,000
Army	*75,000*	*6,000*	*11,000*	*8,500*	*25,000*	*44,000*	*350,000*
Navy	*13,500*	*700*	*~2,000*	*1,800*	*4,200*	*~2,500*	*18,000*
Air Force	*16,000*	*1,500*	*2,500*	*1,500*	*5,000*	*4,500*	*30,000*
National Guard or similar	*100,000*	*~11,260*	*~7,100*	*0*	*10,800*	*0*	*125,000*
Main battle tanks	600	180	293	30	117	471	1,663+
Armored personnel carriers	1,423	375	260	226	206	1,642	640+
Artillery pieces	771	151	218	89	233	561+	8,798+
Principal naval surface vessels	7	1	0	0	1	0	0
Submarines	0	0	0	0	2**	10**	29**
Patrol / coastal vessels	69	12	17	12	13	25	69
Combat aircraft	305	39	66	18	52	201	334
Helicopters	91***	61	42	43	51+	61	~114

*Based on official exchange rates; Qatar and UAE figures are for 2012; others for 2013.

**All Omani and UAE submarines, and eight of Iran's, are swimmer delivery vehicles rather than tactical combat submarines.

***Includes both Air Force and Navy helicopters.

Source: Derived from figures and data provided in International Institute for Strategic Studies, *The Military Balance 2014* (London: International Institute for Strategic Studies), 114:1 (2014), especially 313350 and Anthony H. Cordesman and Bryan Gold, *The Gulf Military Balance. Volume I: The Conventional and Asymmetric Dimensions* (Washington: Center for Strategic & International Studies, 2013), draft of May 22, 2013, online https://csis.org/files/publication/1305022_Gulf_Mil_Bal_Volume_I_1.pdf, accessed February 28, 2014.

within the SANG have provided infantry capacity, and although not very well trained or equipped compared to the Army in particular, they are important both by their numbers and because of their political allegiance. They are a critical institutional bond between the royal family and several key tribes.[51] Today, the SANG has some 75,000 troops, as well as another 25,000 or so tribal militia troops affiliated to it, making it larger than the standing army.

The SANG is also kept politically distinct from the rest of the armed forces. In the past, it was a separate organization that bypassed the defense ministry and reported directly to the king. It was commanded by King Abdullah from 1962 until 2010. Since the ministry of defense was commanded by a Sudairi, Prince Sultan, around the same time—1963–2011 to be precise—the SANG was also a counterbalance to the power of the Sudairi brothers within the inner royal circle. It perhaps still serves this role, given how tightly Abdullah has retained his control over it. When he finally relinquished command of the SANG, he handed command to one of his sons, Prince Mutaib bin Abdullah, a Sandhurst-educated career Guardsman.[52] Several other sons hold key senior appointments in the Guard too. On May 27, 2013, the Guard was transformed from a military service into a full ministry, with Prince Mutaib taking the title of Minister of the National Guard.[53] This gave the Guard new power, on top of that which it already derived from its tribal linkages and, given its regime protection role, from being predominantly urban based (rather than located mostly at borders or in strategic regional areas).[54] It is thus a powerful organization, more politically significant than the other armed services, with a central role in both external defense and if necessary internal security.

This power offsets that of the mainstream defense ministry, which is still a strong political actor nonetheless. Controlled by the Sudairi clan, the minister from 1962 to 2011 was Prince (later Crown Prince) Sultan. After his death, Sultan was replaced by his full brother Prince Salman, formerly the long-serving governor of Riyadh over 1963–2011. Salman later became crown prince and deputy prime minister in June 2012, but retained the defense minister position as well. The Sudairis thus retain considerable power within the defense establishment, although the power of Sultan's line was diminished by the curtailing and then dismissal of his son Khalid as deputy defense minister.[55]

Sultan's line still retains some power. This is the case, for example, with Prince Bandar bin Sultan, the former long-serving ambassador to the United States, and then head of the Saudi General Intelligence Agency, the kingdom's main intelligence service, over 2012–2014. The appointment was probably intended to make use of a key royal with especially good international ties and connections, especially in the United States and the West—something important given the increased rivalry with Iran and the continued uprisings, mostly by Shiites in eastern Saudi Arabia, which had been very violent in 2011 and into 2012—or his appointment may have been a sign that reform or development of the Agency was being planned.

The Agency is charged with foreign security, anti-terrorism, liaison, analysis, and coordinating foreign operations, including covert activities overseas.[56] Its budget is estimated to be the highest in the Arab world,[57] suggesting considerable capacity and a breadth of operations. On paper at least, it is also a key institution because it is charged with coordination and oversight of all the intelligence agencies, such as those within the Ministry of the Interior, the armed forces, and the National Guard.[58] Technically, therefore, the head of the General Intelligence Agency holds an extremely powerful position, and some of the General Intelligence Agency's capabilities and activities are quite impressive,[59] even though the other Saudi intelligence agencies are not especially coordinated or collaborative.

The General Intelligence Agency dates to 1957, and established some offices overseas in its initial years, but its size and importance increased markedly after the 1979 Grand Mosque siege at Mecca, when the Al Saud were given a nasty reminder of the risks of internal opposition to regime stability. It has a strong reputation for effectiveness and professionalism compared to most Arab intelligence agencies, as one observer noted: "In the Saudi model [of intelligence-gathering], the [terrorist] network is left preserved so that it can be monitored or one of its members can be turned. In this way, the Saudis not only neutralize that one cell, but any other cells or individuals it comes into contact with. This is how Saudi General Intelligence may have been able . . . [to] infiltrate al-Qaeda itself."[60]

Other intelligence and security agencies fall under the extensive structure of the ministry of the interior. This was the source of Prince Nayef's enormous power from the early-mid-1970s through until his death in 2012, and the portfolio remains no less diverse or powerful now. Prince Ahmad bin Abd al-Aziz was briefly the replacement for Nayef, himself replaced as minister in November 2012 by the now very powerful Muhammad bin Nayef. The ministry includes, albeit under different chains of command, defense-related institutions such as the Coast Guard, Civil Defense Administration, and the Border Guard, plus security services such as the General Security Service (GSS), or Mubahith,[61] which is the main internal intelligence or secret police agency, along with the police, emergency services, passports and immigration, and other such homeland security bodies and institutions. Not surprisingly, the ministry gained greater attention and resources after September 11, 2011, and in the late-2000s the ministry and many of its institutions were reformed to improve their capacity and coordination. The Saudi government has also sought external advice from the United States, Britain, France, and other countries, both when initially improving its internal security capabilities in the 1970s and 1980s and again in the 2000s.[62]

Of the bodies under the ministry of the interior, the paramount intelligence agency is the GSS. It is the key domestic security intelligence service and also performs counterintelligence and special investigations. The GSS runs prisons and has considerable rights to detain and interrogate people; in this regard, it has been accused of human rights abuses by international nongovernmental organizations such as Amnesty International, which noted for example that torture and attempts to forcefully extract confessions from detained people occurs, as do inhumane and degrading treatment of such people.[63]

Another important group is the Public Security Police (PSP). The PSP is staffed by around 4,000 personnel—essentially paramilitary police officers—assigned either to a centrally controlled office or to a regional governor.[64] There is also a Special Emergency Forces, which have been the main institution to tackle al-Qa'eda and related extremism within the kingdom; the expertise of the 10,000 or so personnel includes counterterrorism and counterinsurgency operations, and their capabilities have recently been improved and modernized in large part because of the continued threat posed by Sunni extremists to domestic stability.[65] In their roles, these various security and police forces are assisted by the armed forces, including within the army a special forces capability, and they provide an extensive security and law enforcement capacity in all the urban areas of the Kingdom. In some more remote or tribal areas, however, some security and policing functions are still performed by tribal militia or forces, and the state provides some financing to key tribal leaders for such purposes.[66]

Finally, the *Mutawwa'* are a group worth noting, especially given the attention and controversy they have attracted. The *Mutawwa'* (plural *Mutawwa'een*)—their proper title in Saudi Arabia is the Committee for the Promotion of Virtue and the Prevention of Vice (CPVPV)—are a state-run religious "police"; some have argued, especially in the past and prior to the reforms of the 2000s, that the term *vigilante* group applies better.[67] There are around 3,500 *Mutawwa'een* plus additional volunteers, located mostly in the major cities. They are charged with promoting Islam and ensuring public adherence to Islamic law (*shari'a*) and practices: this can include intervening in male–female fraternization; ensuring that people pray and shops close at prayer times; acting against unlawful or un-Islamic conduct such as prostitution, drug and alcohol use, and nonadherence to fasting during Ramadan; and ensuring that men and women (especially women) are dressed modestly and that women do not drive motor vehicles. The *Mutawwa'* that acted as a supporting religious force in the expansion of Ibn Saud's realm were a crucially important force. It is worth stressing, in contrast, that the *Mutawwa'* of today are much less so. Ibn Saud gained control over them as he expanded his power in the 1920s and then later they, along with a range of locals in various towns, were brought together institutionally and formalized as the Committee for the Propagation of Virtue and the Elimination of Sin and later as the CPVPV.

Throughout the second half of the twentieth century, they were renowned for harassment, arrests, floggings, and other aggressive or nasty tactics; indeed, until 2007, they carried canes and would often be accompanied by police officers.

Even then, however, they carried little weight among the clerical class, and were a socio-religious group with little importance in a security sense. Reforms were introduced after King Abdullah took power, beginning in 2006 with a curtailment of some of their powers of arrest and interrogation, followed in 2007 by greater regulation of their actions, and in effect, less autonomy for them in undertaking their activities. These reforms partly reflected Abdullah's relative moderation compared to previous monarchs, but were also a response to several controversies, the most famous of which was the 2002 fire at a girls' school in Mecca. As the fire spread, the CPVPV at the scene barred the girls from leaving the building as the flames spread, reportedly because of a fear that the girls were not properly covered and that they might come into physical contact with firefighters. Some 15 girls died and another 50 were injured.[68]

To more liberal Saudis, the CPVPV had long been resented, but even among more traditional Saudis there was a concern that the power of the CPVPV reflected a state intervention into gender issues that previously had been the preserve of the family and tribe and the responsibility of senior males in those social groups. In recent years, the CPVPV has been greatly curtailed. It continues to patrol public areas, telephone male relatives to criticize a woman's conduct, or reports more serious misconduct to the police, but has less power to intervene directly and less authority to punish people its members deem to have misbehaved. Perhaps above all, it is important to note that the CPVPV members are religious figures of comparatively weak standing within the religious establishment.[69] They are mostly very minor *'ulema*, not directly controlled by the clerical elite, and whose views typically gain little attention in religious debates among senior *'ulema*. They remain important as symbols of Wahhabism and as a reminder of state authority in the religious and social spheres, but have little influence over the Saudi religious and political elite.

THE CLERICAL ELITE AND BUSINESS COMMUNITY

Important as political and security institutions are to the maintenance of Al Saud rule, crucial too are the informal symbiotic bargains that the royal family has made with key actors who might otherwise undermine or challenge their rule. The Saudi-U.S. relationship is important as existential insurance for the kingdom, and will be discussed in the next chapter. Here, two key groups are of interest: the cleric elite and the business elite. Gaining and maintaining the support of both is important for the monarchy. In the case of the clerics, their endorsement is central to a wider support or tolerance by society. The merchants, meanwhile, are important both because of their economic power and because the most important ones come from the more cosmopolitan Hijaz region where they possess their own local base and links. With both of these groups, Ibn Saud made a mutual bargain for support, where these groups ceded any political aspirations they had in exchange for Saudi support and some autonomy over matters of most interest to them.

Of the two, the longest royal relationship has been with the *ulema*, dating back to the formation of the first Saudi state in 1744. This relationship has always been a symbiotic one, where "the Saudi state has relied on the religious legitimacy" provided by the clerics, in exchange letting the clerics implement their "vision of an Islamic society" supported by the royals and, especially in the current Saudi state, backed by state institutions and mechanisms.[70] That noted, the relative power of the *ulema* has declined as the Al Saud has gained fuller control of the institutions and cooptive apparatus of the state. Furthermore, they are not a cohesive or consolidated political actor: while the top "establishment clerics"[71] work closely together and with the state, and a large number draw a salary from the state, the views of various *wahhabiyya* figures can be at variance. Some are more radical and rejectionist, resisting Al Saud dominance or oppose the royal family outright.[72] This variation in views is in large part contained by establishment clerics, who are an integral link between the state and wider religious actors and interests and are part of what Niblock calls a Saudi religious "constituency."[73]

A key cleric from the latter part of Ibn Saud's reign until his death was Abd al-Aziz bin Baz (1912–1999). In many ways bin Baz represented both the fundamental tenets of Wahhabism and also the flexibility of the clerical elite in bending to the wishes of Ibn Saud.[74] Bin Baz came to prominence in the 1940s as a vocal opponent of U.S. business involvement and technical advice to Ibn Saud. He was called to the palace, where Ibn Saud challenged his views by arguing that there was nothing precluding assistance being sought by a ruler from non-Muslims, and asking for a wider clerical endorsement of this position. The *ulema* endorsed this argument, even though it took some debate for bin Baz to eventually concur; the courage of his convictions and his fidelity to Wahhabism gave him considerable legitimacy among other clerics (and more widely), letting him become a key cleric, and then the Saudi Grand Mufti (the highest legal-religious authority in the country), from 1992 until his death in 1999.[75] He is the only Grand Mufti to have not come from the Al al-Sheikh family, which is descended from Muhammad Ibn Abd al-Wahhab and so has particular religious pedigree. Bin Baz had an important career both as a teacher of clerics and in providing clerical endorsement for several key royal decisions.

The clerics faced somewhat diminished power under King Saud, but their political role resurged under Faisal, Khalid and later, given Faisal's focus on building religious legitimacy and, later, because of external events that required clerical endorsement of the monarchy's position. A pivotal case of the latter was the siege at the Grand Mosque in Mecca in 1979, outlined in the previous chapter. As noted, to recapture the mosque from Juhayman and the others, the Saudi government sought from the *ulema* approval to use military force within the mosque's grounds, something traditionally strictly forbidden. That bin Baz granted such approval reflected the seriousness of the situation, but also demonstrated his pragmatism and his ability to gain concessions from the king in return. Notably, Juhayman had studied under bin Baz, which is perhaps why the latter condemned the revolt but refused to declare Juhayman an infidel or non-Muslim for his actions.[76]

An even more critical event was the 1990–1991 Gulf War, which was potentially the first existential challenge to the Kingdom and Al Saud rule. Again, *ulema* endorsement was needed for the positioning of U.S. troops in Saudi Arabia, something that would be deeply unpopular among the clerics and indeed with wider society. The U.S. military presence in the Kingdom had previously been very discreet, but Operations *Desert Shield* and *Desert Storm* brought the U.S.-Saudi strategic alliance into the open, and suggested that the royals were incapable of protecting the kingdom. When the clerics finally issued a fatwa, or religious edict, it reportedly came only after considerable negotiation, including direct, detailed discussions between King Fahd and bin Baz. Moreover, the decision created considerable disquiet, and would harden some of the more severe opposition to the royals and to what was seen by many as a conspicuous submission by the establishment clerics to the political wishes of the royals.[77] What the clerical endorsement most did, however, was give the *ulema* a short-term leverage with the monarchy, but at the longer-term cost of cementing their position as the junior partner in the royal-*ulema* relationship. While important in many ways, the clerics have since come to be seen as more submissive, and as they have become more institutionalized and bureaucratized, they have been drafted into the regime's attempts at royal power consolidation.[78] They have considerable autonomy over religious matters, but are consulted more widely only when their imprimatur is needed.

The other group with potential financial autonomy and a separate power base to the royals, and thus which are coopted by the Al Saud, are the merchants. The term *merchants* refers not to the wider private sector, which, while large and at times politically active, varies from the much more powerful key business families that form the "merchant" echelon. Business in general exerts influence through collective activity such as the work of chambers of commerce and through the business media,[79] but this power is offset to a significant degree by the rentier power of the state and the ability of the Saudi elite to buy business support, distribute commercial opportunities, and the like. The key merchants, in contrast, have enormous wealth and often connections or family ties with the Al Saud and other political elites. These merchants enjoy the fruits of rents too, of course, but they benefit most from very close informal relationships they have with each other and the royals.

In the past, the most powerful merchants were the large commercial families from the Hijaz, especially from Jedda.[80] The Najdi merchants were important in supporting Ibn Saud after 1902, lending him both political support and money[81]; however, once the modern Kingdom came into being, the much wealthier Hijazi merchants became equally or more important. They held their wealth in land and assets within the Hijaz, and most had trading networks and assets abroad as well.[82] They then supplemented this wealth with the patronage dispensed by Ibn Saud, often through concessions in certain areas of the economy that favored those merchants who agreed to be politically loyal. Often a concession made an already-affluent merchant exceedingly wealthy.[83] The bin Laden family initially made their money this way, through state contracts in construction, after Mohamed bin Laden gained a reputation with the royals for reliability and skill in road building and construction.[84] Although they surrendered political power to the royals, key merchants were consulted on important matters, an example being when the inner royal elite wanted to remove King Saud in 1964.

However, the power of the traditional merchants—those whose wealth predates 1902 or who built their family wealth under Ibn Saud or King Saud[85]—has declined relative to other economic actors in later decades. This is because of the transformation of the political economy, which has created new economic elites and restructured some of the kingdom's economic dynamics. The most dramatic change was from the exploitation of oil, first in the 1940s and 1950s but especially after its nationalization in the 1970s. This gave the state greater rentier power over business, as well as creating state capitalists at the summit of state-owned firms such as Saudi ARAMCO. These were mostly senior public servants, some of them Al Saud, who controlled but did not own key economic assets, and who had considerable power because of their position within the state structure. Further, new private sector actors emerged because of oil, too, including some firms that serviced the oil sector and others that benefitted from oil-funded state expenditure. Finally, other businesspeople arose because of the expansion of the state. Both large, wealthy families and an assortment of professionals established themselves after the 1950s by being reliable business partners of the state or able technical experts or professionals. Some then developed their commercial interests further, gained new opportunities, and evolved into wealthy actors. Thus, there is a paradox in the private sector's political role: it has become larger and wealthier over time, but not more politically powerful, since it has also become more fragmented and remained highly reliant on state wealth. The merchants have influence, formal and informal, but "there is no evidence of this affecting overall economic policy."[86] They need to be kept happy, and the wider private sector will be essential for the future economic diversification that the royals continue to seek, but business is not a true alternative power center, much less a counter-balance, to the royals.

WIDER SOCIAL DYNAMICS: REGION, SECT, TRIBE, AND SOCIAL CHANGE

Finally, broad societal structures and dynamics play a role in Saudi political economy, shaping political identity and views toward the state. As an expansive collection of regions, there are varying social groupings and hierarchies in the Kingdom and within its regions. There are also tribal, sectarian, and other identities that claim people's loyalties. Overlaying this has been the social impact of foreign workers moving into the economy as oil has been exploited, and later, a range of further social and cultural impacts from globalization.

Nation-state identity has become more powerful, as the idea of holding Saudi nationality has grown and the benefits of citizenship become obvious. To this extent, people in Saudi Arabia do talk about being "Saudi," and most attach' meaning and value to that tags. However, this does not preclude strong local identities from coexisting with national identity. Regional and local identity, indeed, is more closely linked to family, tribe, and sect, which are the key basic units of primordial identity. Thus, when Saudis note the district or region from which they derive, there is often an implied tribal affiliation or dynastic membership implied as well. This can be important as a class statement, a claim of social standing, or a reminder of someone's descent from a notable family or key tribe or *fakhdh* (a branch of a tribe). Tribe is especially crucial to Saudi identity because, until very recently, society was organized predominantly around tribal structures, and relations between tribes and confederacies often determined political outcomes.[87] It was no accident that tribes were the main grouping through which Ibn Saud organized politics and expanded his realm, using political alliances, agreements, and even marriages.

As Saudi Arabia has modernized in the oil era, tribes have been increasingly incorporated into the political system and rent distribution networks through informal patron-client linkages, and in settled areas, also through associations and institutions that formalize tribal affiliations.[88] Thus, as with clerics and businesspeople, while tribes have lost a lot of power as the state has grown wealthier, they remain important as a unit of identity and a means of representing and coordinating large groups of people. Therefore, the state continues to support tribal identity as a shared value across the kingdom and as something that shapes political worldviews.[89] At elite levels, moreover, tribal affiliation can be a more direct mechanism of patronage and control, as key tribal figures are often brought into Saudi rulers' (neo)patrimonial networks, with the expectation that tribal networks will be used by these actors, in return, to provide political loyalty.

Religion, if even more socially amorphous than tribalism, is also fundamental to Saudi identity. The original Saudi–Wahhabi arrangement in 1744 was essentially a religion-driven (quasi-)nationalism experiment, after all. The construction and articulation of narratives of identity by Ibn Saud and other elites included religious aspects, with Saudi identity presented as inseparable from Islamic values. Moreover, the nature of *wahhabiyya*, supported by a modern state setting, also links Islam to nationalism, insofar as it tries to link culture and values to Saudi legitimacy.[90] The main establishment clerics continue to play a central role in legitimizing the Saudi state and royal family, but religion is also important in shaping less formal political outcomes such as how people view the state's relationship with society. Even more cosmopolitan or secular-oriented Saudis often profess some piety or a respect for religion, when discussing their political values.

Separately, opposition forces have also arranged along religious lines at times. The main opposition *al-sahwa* (meaning "awakening") activists promoted their ideas in Islamist terms, loosely along the lines of a hybrid Muslim Brotherhood–Wahhabist philosophy.[91] Some have been coopted by the state through official appointments, but even then, the importance of religion to their political perspectives should not be ignored. Another opposition force, the much more puritanical neo-Salafists, are even more religiously driven,[92] with their dogmatic views often being their highest consideration in political matters. The dynamics of this is explored in Chapter 5, which reiterates the prominence of Islam in many Saudis' political and social opinions.

Religion is also important beyond the *wahhabiyya* tradition, as Saudi Arabia possesses a minority Shia population of some 10 to 15 percent of the population[93]—no official figure is published—mostly located in the north of the eastern province, but with small numbers in Medina and in Najran near the Yemeni border. Shia identity is sustained and reinforced by this "othering" from the Saudi mainstream and by the Shias own sense of particularity, as well as by their clerics by the solidarity built through intra-Shia family and social linkages.[94] Beginning with the uprisings in 1979, the Eastern Province has been the scene of considerable Shia unrest. Certainly, there historically has been a pattern of political and economic discrimination and exclusion against the Shia,[95] tolerated and sometimes nurtured by the state and often driven by the strong anti-Shia view inherent in Wahhabism. When the Arab Spring commenced in early 2011, the Saudi Shia were emboldened to express their grievances toward the state,[96] and rallies, protests, and even armed clashes began in the Eastern Province. The regime's firm response to this dissent has not succeeded in ending it.[97]

This does not mean that secular forces are unimportant. After 2001, a constitutional reform movement[98] emerged. It included Islamists and figures linked to religious movements, but also secular figures from the old Nasserist and Ba'athist movements, plus a range of un-affiliated secular professionals and intellectuals.[99] This movement did not challenge the legitimacy or the Islamic basis of the state, but still called for significant political reform such as the creation of a legislature and, at one point, even called for constitutional-based royal rule.[100] Some of these calls were addressed—at least partly—by the reforms undertaken by Abdullah after 2005, although such reforms have not fundamentally altered the Saudi power structure. Yet, the fact that oppositional forces have rallied across religious and social lines, and often incorporated secular figures, shows that secular opposition forces remain significant in Saudi politics.

The modernization of Saudi society and the effects of globalization have also shaped Saudi politics and society since the 1990s. Whether this is a boon for secularists or Islamists remains debatable, but as much as globalization has become clichéd in the past couple of decades, its impacts have nonetheless been real. Young Saudis do have much greater connection to the outside world than their parents; even though their parents may have studied abroad or will travel overseas regularly, Saudis today have a communications capability far beyond that of their parents' generation. While not automatically equating to Westernization or democratization, globalization nevertheless has had an impact on Saudi identity, culture, and politics. Satellite television, online communications, and cheaper and easier travel all have influenced people's perspectives, including their sense of self and the state. The profile of young Saudis seems to reflect some of this, for although still relatively conservative on many matters, many young people and some connected adults are increasingly well informed about the rest of the world, arguably even becoming gradually more cosmopolitan. At the same time, the state cannot hide unpleasant facts or disguise poor government performance as easily as in the past, necessitating a more complex discussion with society on issues and policies that, previously, the state often had a virtual autonomy to decide upon.

Complicating these social dynamics, however, is the fact that economic change has brought an enormous foreign workforce into the Kingdom. Of the country's estimated 2013 population of 26,939,583, some 5,576,076 were non-citizens.[101] They dominate in the private sector, where almost all lower-level positions, especially those in the service sector or involving manual labor, are held by foreigners.[102] Saudis are usually only found at more senior levels, in the professions, managerial ranks, and as business owners. In the public sector, Saudis are much more strongly featured, but significant numbers of foreigners are employed by the government, too, above all at the lower ranks. The government has had a scheme in place since 1985 to boost the employment of Saudis.[103] This Saudi-ization has remained a strong feature of policy since then, but its success has been limited. Too many employers prefer foreign workers, whether for their skills, the cost of their labor, or for the fact that, unlike Saudis, they can be easily dismissed. Saudi-ization has only become more urgent with the rise in unemployment and underemployment among Saudi youth, but as it stands, the policy is not achieving what was intended from it.

POLITICS, LEGITIMACY, AND IDENTITY

All of the dynamics above mean that the Saudi political system is not as straightforward as it is sometimes presented as being. While enormous power resides with the king and the inner royals, this power is not absolute. Most decisions require either consultation with key elites (usually those representative of wider institutions or social forces), or are the result of broad, if informally expressed, societal pressure. A simple generalization about autocracy does not sufficiently capture the complexity of Saudi political dynamics.

Thus, the sources of legitimacy for the royals are several, and the distinctions between them frequently blurred. As Niblock has noted, the Al Saud draw their legitimacy from religiously-derived ideology, tradition, personality, state spending and welfare, and legal and political structure and process.[104] Some texts on Saudi Arabia continue to paint its politics in simple terms, say as a basic "rentier" state. Important as rents and expenditure are to what Niblock called "eudemonic" legitimacy, and central as distributed wealth has become to society's expectations of the state, rentierism *alone* is insufficient to explain the state-society relationship. Rentierism is a *dynamic* of politics, but it is not a structural explanation for the Saudi political economy.[105] Similarly, the religious basis of the regime and its relationship with the clerics is important, but again, inadequate alone in explaining the regime's endurance. While the establishment *'ulema* have become so entrenched in the Saudi system that they are no longer a counter to the Al Saud, there are both oppositional religious figures and a wider role played by religion in society that makes Islam a complex force in the shaping of Saudi politics. Important as the royal–*'ulema* bargain is, therefore, as a tool of legitimization and stability, its role in setting and maintaining the state-society arrangement should not be overstated, either.

In fact, the Saudi leadership must draw on a range of political strategies and arrangements to ensure its survival, given the diversity of society and the complex array of risks that the royals potentially face. Society is far more diverse, dynamic, and politically cognizant than merely a collection of tribes meekly obeying a repressive regime in exchange for a share of oil rents. Tribe is important, but so too is family, so too is regional identity, and so too are other units of identity such as youth, gender, and class. Saudi social actors may indeed often be rent seeking, but this is only one aspect of their relationship with the state. For the Saudi regime to survive, it has to deal with society at more complex levels, too, addressing (or encouraging) the competition between various groups and, indeed, the competition that the state faces from religion, tribe, family, and other targets of political loyalty. This means that it needs to communicate with society, which it does directly, say through the media, as well as through information mechanisms such as neopatrimonial networks. At times, it needs to deal with unrest, too, which can come from an array of social forces. While books predicting the coming fall of the Al Saud are plentiful, and the pressures they face are significant, the Saudi regime has thus far been quite successful at managing many of these competing demands. They have outlived substantial domestic and regional challenges to their rule, using a combination of rentierism, state capitalism, neopatrimonial linkages, a consideration of societal views, and strong messages claiming legitimacy.

NOTES

1. A reprint of some of the *Basic Law*, translated into English, is provided in Joseph A. Kéchechian, *Power and Succession in Arab Monarchies: A Reference Handbook* (Boulder: Lynne Rienner, 2008), 461 (Appendix 15).

2. This literally translates as "those who bind and loosen," but is more accurately given as "those who resolve and contract."

3. On the Allegiance Council see Joseph A. Kéchechian, *Legal and Political Reforms in Sa'udi Arabia* (Abingdon: Routledge, 2013), 137–158.

4. On this see Kéchechian, *Legal and Political Reforms in Sa'udi Arabia*, 150–154.

5. Kéchechian, *Power and Succession in Arab Monarchies*, 245.

6. The debate and uncertainty over the number of royals is covered briefly if well in Daryl Champion, *The Paradoxical Kingdom: Saudi Arabia and the Momentum of Reform* (New York: Columbia University Press, 2003), 71.

7. Cable: "Saudi Royal Wealth: Where Do They Get All That Money?," Reference 96RIYADH4784, dated November 30, 1996, published by *Wikileaks*, September 1, 2011, http://wikileaks.org/cable/1996/11/96RIYADH4784.html, accessed June 17, 2013.

8. Madawi Al-Rasheed, "Circles of Power: Royals and Society in Saudi Arabia," in Paul Aarts and Gerd Nonneman (eds.), *Saudi Arabia in the Balance: Political Economy, Society, Foreign Affairs* (London, Hurst & Company, 2005), especially 199–208.

9. If current crown prince Salman outlives King Abdullah and becomes monarch, some observers argue that it is likely he would seek to make Ahmad crown prince. Given his age, he would have every chance of surviving to reach the throne. See as an example David B. Ottway, "The Struggle for Power in Saudi Arabia," *Foreign Policy*, June 19, 2013, http://www.foreignpolicy.com/articles/2013/06/19/the_struggle_for_power_in_saudi_arabia_abdullah?page=0,1, accessed June 24, 2013.

10. Kéchechian, *Legal and Political Reforms in Sa'udi Arabia*, 147.

11. By some accounts Bandar built his wealth through kickbacks and corruption; he was implicated in corruption allegations made about the BAe/Al-Yamamah arms deal, although the investigation into this by the UK Serious Fraud Office was stopped in 2006 and the details of it remain opaque. See on it Andrew Feinstein, *The Shadow World: Inside the Global Arms Trade* (New York: Picador, 2011), especially the references passim pp. 35–55 and 74–97.

12. Ottway, "The Struggle for Power in Saudi Arabia," n.p.

13. Kéchechian, *Power and Succession in Arab Monarchies*, 248.

14. "Profile: Prince Alwaleed Bin Talal Alsaud," *Forbes* "List of the World's Billionaires," effective March 2013, http://www.forbes.com/profile/prince-alwaleed-bin-talal-alsaud/, accessed June 25, 2013.

15. Champion, *The Paradoxical Kingdom*, 78.

16. Much of what follows in this paragraph is from Kéchechian, *Legal and Political Reforms in Sa'udi Arabia*, 116–118.

17. Ibid., 120–121.

18. Ibid., 123.

19. Ibid.

20. Ibid.; also Madawi Al-Rasheed, *A History of Saudi Arabia*, 2nd ed. (Cambridge: Cambridge University Press, 2010), 250.

21. "Women in Saudi Arabia to Vote and Run in Elections," *BBC News*, September 25, 2011, http://www.bbc.co.uk/news/world-us-canada-15052030, accessed June 25, 2013.

22. Steffen Hertog, *Princes, Brokers, and Bureaucrats: Oil and the State in Saudi Arabia* (Ithaca: Cornell University Press, 2010), 5.

23. Ibid., 10–11.

24. Yoshikazu Kobayashi, *Corporate Strategies of Saudi Aramco* (Houston: James A. Baker III Institute for Public Policy and Japan Petroleum Energy Center, 2007).

25. See for example Abuzar M. A. Eljelly, "Ownership and Firm Performance: The Experience of Saudi Arabia's Emerging Economy," *International Business & Economics Research Journal*, 8(8), August 2009, 25–34. The article is focused on a slightly different argument, but makes the point about the relative efficiency of state-linked listed firms.

26. Steffen Hertog, "Defying the Resource Curse: Explaining Successful State-Owned Enterprises in Rentier States," *World Politics*, 62 (2), April 2010, 261–301.

27. Kéchechian, *Legal and Political Reforms in Sa'udi Arabia*, 19–20, 27.

28. Ibid., 29.

29. Abeer Allam, "Saudi Education Reforms Face Resistance," *FT.com*, April 25, 2011, http://www.ft.com/intl/cms/s/0/07607fb0-6f5d-11e0-952c-00144feabdc0.html#axzz2XBK29Ud7, accessed June 25, 2013.

30. Allam, "Saudi Education Reforms Face Resistance," n.p.

31. "Saudi Arabia," *Freedom of the Press 2012* (Washington DC: Freedom House, 2012), http://www.freedomhouse.org/report/freedom-press/2012/saudi-arabia, accessed June 25, 2013.

32. Ibid.

33. The personnel numbers for the services and forces vary slightly by some sources. I have chosen here to use those from the very reputable International Institute for Strategic Studies (IISS), *The Military Balance 2013* (London: Routledge, 2013), 400–403.

34. Ibid., 402.

35. Ibid., 400.

36. See for example Al-Rasheed, *A History of Saudi Arabia*, 158–163; Peter W. Wilson and Douglas F. Graham, *Saudi Arabia: The Coming Storm* (New York: M. E. Sharpe, 1994), 108–117; and Dilip Hiro, *Desert Shield to Desert Storm: The Second Gulf War* (London: Paladin, 1992), 108–112, 119–121, 177–179.

37. Nadav Safran, *Saudi Arabia: The Ceaseless Quest for Security* (Ithaca: Cornell University Press, 1988), 207.

38. "Royal Saudi Land Forces," *GlobalSecurity.org*, n.d., http://www.globalsecurity.org/military/world/gulf/rslf.htm, accessed June 26, 2013.

39. IISS, *The Military Balance 2013*, 401.

40. "Royal Saudi Land Forces," n.p.

41. Safran, *Saudi Arabia*, 207–208.

42. Ibid., 299.

43. See the full list of arms purchases made over 1975–1982 in Ibid., 434–435 (Table 19).

44. Anthony Cordesman, *Saudi Arabia Enters the Twenty-First Century: The Military and International Security Dimensions* (Westport: Praeger, 2003), 217–220.

45. "US sells $30bn in F-15 jets to Saudi Arabia," *BBC News*, December 29, 2011, http://www.bbc.co.uk/news/world-us-canada-16358068, accessed June 26, 2013.

46. Safran, *Saudi Arabia*, 208.

47. IISS, *The Military Balance 2013*, 401.

48. Al-Rasheed, *A History of Saudi Arabia*, 87, 109; and Wilson and Graham, *Saudi Arabia*, 146.

49. Wilson and Graham, *Saudi Arabia*, 146.

50. On the U.S. role in modernizing the SANG over 1973 into the 1980s, see Safran, *Saudi Arabia*, 142–143, 154–155, 172–175, 208–209.

51. Sandra Mackey, *The Saudis: Inside the Desert Kingdom*, 2nd Edn (New York: Norton, 2002), 207.

52. See the short biography of him on the "About Saudi Arabia" page of the Web site of the Royal Embassy of Saudi Arabia in Washington DC, http://www.saudiembassy.net/about/Biographies-of-Ministers.aspx, accessed June 28, 2013.

53. Ottway, "The Struggle for Power in Saudi Arabia," n.p.; "Saudi King Turns National Guard into Ministry Run by Son," *Reuters*, May 27, 2013, http://www.reuters.com/article/2013/05/27/us-saudi-nationalguard-idUSBRE94Q0C220130527, accessed June 28, 2013.

54. This point about the benefits of basing and positioning is made in Stephanie Cronin, "Tribes, Coups and Princes: Building a Modern Army in Saudi Arabia," *Middle Eastern Studies*, 49(1), 2013, 22.

55. Ottway, "The Struggle for Power in Saudi Arabia," n.p.

56. Anthony H. Cordesman and Nawaf Obaid, *Saudi Internal Security: A Risk Assessment* (Washington: Center for Strategic and International Studies, 2009), 19.

57. Ibid.

58. Ibid.

59. Ibid.

60. Max Fisher, "What We Can Learn from Saudi Intelligence," *The Atlantic*, November 2010, also http://www.theatlantic.com/international/archive/2010/11/what-we-can-learn-from-saudi-intelligence/65518/, accessed June 28, 2013.

61. Cordesman and Obaid, *Saudi Internal Security*, 17.

62. Ibid.

63. See "Saudi Arabia," in the *Amnesty International Annual Report 2012*, http://www.amnesty.org/en/region/saudi-arabia/report-2012#section-31-8, accessed June 28, 2013.

64. Cordesman and Obaid, *Saudi Internal Security*, 18.

65. Ibid.

66. Ibid., 19.

67. Robert Lacey, *The Kingdom* (London: Fontana, 1982), 178.

68. Robert Lacey, *Inside the Kingdom: Kings, Clerics, Modernists, Terrorists and the Struggle for Saudi Arabia* (London: Hutchinson, 2009), 237–238.

69. Shmuel Bachar, Shmuel Bar, Rachel Machtiger, and Yair Minzili, "Establishment Ulama and Radicalism in Egypt, Saudi Arabia, and Jordan," *Center on Islam, Democracy, and the Future of the Muslim World, Research Monographs on the Muslim World, Series No. 1, Paper No. 4* (Washington: Hudson Institute December 2006), 15–16.

70. Guido Steinberg, "The Wahhabi Ulema and the Saudi State: 1745 to the Present," in Paul Aarts and Gerd Nonneman (eds.), *Saudi Arabia in the Balance: Political Economy, Society, Foreign Affairs* (London, Hurst & Company, 2005), 12.

71. Bachar et al., "Establishment Ulama and Radicalism," 15.

72. Steinberg, "The Wahhabi Ulema and the Saudi State," 11–12.

73. Tim Niblock, *Saudi Arabia: Power, Legitimacy and Survival* (London: Routledge, 2006), 14–15.

74. Steinberg, "The Wahhabi Ulema and the Saudi State," 26.

75. The Grant Mufti is a position that exists in some states, in effect as the highest religious authority in the nation-state. The position was created by Ibn Saud in 1953, then unfilled over

1969–1993 after the first Grand Mufti's death, and then restored in 1993 with Bin Baz's appointment. The current Grand Mufti (as at mid-2014) is Abdul Aziz al ash-Shaikh.

76. Steinberg, "The Wahhabi Ulema and the Saudi State," 28.

77. Champion, *The Paradoxical Kingdom*, 217–237; Thomas Hegghammer, *Jihad in Saudi Arabia: Violence and Pan-Islamism since 1979* (Cambridge: Cambridge University Press, 2010), 30–37; Niblock, *Saudi Arabia*, 87–104; and Steinberg, "The Wahhabi Ulema and the Saudi State," 30–33.

78. Gwenn Okruhlik, "State Power, Religious Privilege, and Myths about Political Reform," in Mohammed Ayoob and Hasan Kosebalaban (eds.), *Religion and Politics in Saudi Arabia: Wahhabism and the State* (Boulder, Lynne Rienner, 2009), 91–107.

79. Tim Niblock with Monica Malik, *The Political Economy of Saudi Arabia* (London: Routledge, 2007), 21–25.

80. Ibid., 23, 49–50.

81. Lacey, *The Kingdom*, 66.

82. Niblock with Malik, *The Political Economy of Saudi Arabia*, 48–49.

83. Ibid., 49.

84. See Steve Coll, *The Bin Ladens: Oil, Money, Terrorism and the Secret Saudi World* (London: Penguin, 2008), especially 46–79 on Mohamed's rise and business expansion.

85. Niblock with Malik, *The Political Economy of Saudi Arabia*, 49.

86. Ibid., 50.

87. Joseph Kostiner, "Transforming Dualities: Tribe and State Formation in Saudi Arabia," in Philip S. Khoury and Joseph Kostiner (eds.), *Tribes and State Formation in the Middle East* (Berkeley: University of California Press, 1990), 226.

88. Ibid., 246.

89. Ibid.

90. This point is made in Madawi Al-Rasheed, *A Most Masculine State: Gender, Politics, and Religion in Saudi Arabia* (Cambridge: Cambridge University Press, 2013), 14–15.

91. Stéphane Lacroix, "Islamo-Liberal Politics in Saudi Arabia," in Paul Aarts and Gerd Nonneman (eds.), *Saudi Arabia in the Balance: Political Economy, Society, Foreign Affairs* (London, Hurst & Company, 2005), 38–39.

92. Ibid., 39.

93. Frederic Wehrey, *The Forgotten Uprising in Eastern Saudi Arabia* (Washington: Carnegie Endowment for International Peace, 2013), 3.

94. Fouad Ibrahim, *The Shi'is of Saudi Arabia* (London: Saqi Books, 2006), 45–55.

95. Ibrahim, *The Shi'is of Saudi Arabia*, 30–44.

96. Wehrey, *The Forgotten Uprising in Eastern Saudi Arabia*, 4–12, 16–18.

97. Ibid., 12–16.

98. This movement, or collection of movements, became known literally as the "advocates of constitutional reform," or in Arabic, *du'at al-islah al-dusturi*; noted in Al-Rasheed, *A History of Saudi Arabia*, 261.

99. Ibid.

100. Ibid., 261–262.

101. Population figures are July 2013 estimates from the Central Intelligence Agency, published in the *CIA World Fact Book*, https://www.cia.gov/library/publications/the-world-factbook/geos/sa.html, accessed July 19, 2013.

102. See the discussion, and Tables 9.3 and 9.4, in Abbas J. Ali, *Business and Management Environment in Saudi Arabia* (Abingdon: Routledge, 2009), 143–148.

103. Niblock with Malik, *The Political Economy of Saudi Arabia*, 139.

104. Niblock, *Saudi Arabia*, 9–13.

105. Matthew Gray, *A Theory of "Late Rentierism" in the Arab States of the Gulf* (Doha: Center for International and Regional Studies, Georgetown University, School of Foreign Service in Qatar, 2011), 18, 36–37.

CHAPTER 3

The Saudi-U.S. Relationship

As important as various domestic political arrangements are to the survival of the Al Saud regime, the ruling family also needs an external security bargain both to guarantee its protection against external attack and to ensure it can purchase a qualitative defense capability. The strategic relationship with the United States performs this role. It is the Al Saud's most important strategic and diplomatic relationship, even if fundamentally it is a relationship of convenience for both parties and one that has been tested since 1945, above all by the September 11, 2001, terrorist attacks on the United States as well as by the Palestinian issue and other regional controversies. The relationship is also important because of the overlap of internal and external dynamics in Saudi security. The U.S. relationship provides the Al Saud a security guarantee and supplier of arms, but is also a source of opposition within the Kingdom, from clerics suspicious of external influences on society and from social forces that resent the Al Saud cozying up to a foreign, non-Muslim power largely for the sake of regime maintenance. Thus, Saudi and U.S. priorities, Middle Eastern regional dynamics, oil, religion, and Saudi state-society relations all influence each other, making the Saudi-U.S. relationship an important, complex, and oftentimes opaque security dynamic.

THE EVOLUTION OF THE RELATIONSHIP

As previously discussed, the Saudi-U.S. relationship is usually dated to the Roosevelt-Ibn Saud meeting on the USS *Quincy* on February 14, 1945.[1] Prior to that time, the relationship was less formal and much shallower than it became after 1945. In the early decades of the twentieth century, some U.S. missionaries traveled to Saudi Arabia, along with other occasional visitors, but Ibn Saud's main focuses had been on regional threats such as the Ottomans, until their empire came to an end after the First World War, and on the relationship with the British. After the U.S. recognition of Saudi Arabia in 1931, however, the foundations for a more substantial relationship were quickly built, boosted by the oil concession as of 1933. The oil concession saw the number of Americans in the Kingdom rise sharply, and the economic potential of the Saudi-U.S. relationship become more evident to both parties. That potential was strengthened still further once oil was produced in commercial quantities after 1938, when it became obvious that the Kingdom would ultimately become a major oil producer. The first commercially viable well, Dammam No. 7, was quickly producing more than most U.S. wells at the time,[2] and then the Second World War reinforced the strategic importance of oil for military power and capability. The war impacted the Saudi oil sector, slowing rather than halting it, and there was enough oil production during the war for Ibn Saud to take some (very basic) steps in oil-funded development. Other events at the time, including the worsening of Arab-Jewish relations in Palestine, entered into the relationship, though only superficially at first; the relationship was yet to be truly tested by the issue. The U.S. inclusion of Saudi Arabia in Washington's Lend-Lease program and U.S. (and other Western) aid were both important in the relationship, coming at a time of shortages and financial hardship for Ibn Saud.[3]

The Roosevelt-Ibn Saud meeting established a relationship that would run through the Cold War, including agreement on military ties such as U.S. ship visits and air power collaboration, a reiteration of the core U.S. role in the Saudi oil sector, and other initiatives that built strong strategic and security arrangements. Issues such as the Palestinian cause sometimes were thorns in the relationship, if ultimately not something that would break it. Yet, all the while, the relationship remained primarily one of convenience. Only the Iraqi invasion of Kuwait in 1990 brought the two sides together more profoundly, being the first regional threat that could genuinely be considered a potentially existential one for the modern Saudi state. Even then, Saudi-U.S. ties were soon tested again, by the 9/11 attacks, especially the prominence of Saudis in them.

In the immediate post-1945 period through the remainder of Ibn Saud's rule, the U.S. relationship was deliberately kept discreet by the king. For many Saudis, there was suspicion about the U.S. basing at Dhahran, established not long after the Roosevelt-Ibn Saud meeting, and a concern about a permanent American—that is, non-Muslim and external—military presence in the Kingdom. This suspicion and concern remained thereafter. Yet, Ibn Saud and the inner core of the royal family understood the need for, and possible benefits of, a relationship with the United States. At this time, the Saudis were still developing their economy and their military capability. By the late 1940s and early 1950s there was a strong fear in the Saudi regime of communism, which the United States was also keen to oppose in the region. More urgent still was the perceived threat to the Saudi system from anti-monarchical Arab nationalism and from Arab variations on socialism, both of which were gaining popularity and momentum in the Middle East. This, along with a benign political neglect, was probably why Ibn Saud made such a modest contribution to the 1948 Arab-Israeli war, sending only a single battalion to operate with the Egyptian army.[4] At any rate, the Saudis' military capabilities at the time were modest and mediocre.

As a result, defense and security ties were enhanced at the time and the U.S. role in the Kingdom increased, but both discreetly so. Ibn Saud made clear to the Americans his fear of Arab nationalism, petitioning them for arms and other support to counter what he saw as an intention by King Abdullah in Transjordan (as it then was called) to create a Greater Syria in the eastern Mediterranean, and in case Abdullah sought to recapture the Hijaz.[5] In 1951, Washington agreed to train 10,000 airborne troops for Ibn Saud in exchange for a renewal of the Dhahran Air Field agreement.[6] Under a mutual defense agreement the United States provided the Saudis with advisers, training, and a significant increase in air capability.[7] For a relationship in its infancy and lacking a formal alliance, this support was substantial, perhaps demonstrating that the United States already recognized the strategic potential of Saudi Arabia in the Cold War.

Saud's reign (1953–1964) continued this trend. There was an important strategic relationship developing, but with both sides, and especially the Saudis, hesitant and apprehensive about it. For the United States, its containment policy toward the Soviet Union focused it on Europe and, elsewhere, on allies closest to the Soviet border. In the Middle East, therefore, important as Saudi Arabia was, the United States had stronger strategic ties with Turkey and, after the reinstatement of the Shah in 1953, Iran. Relations improved slightly after the 1956 Suez crisis, when the Saudis viewed the U.S. role more positively, and when some states moved away from the United States, as Iraq did after their 1958 revolution. Early in Saud's reign, the Kingdom received further U.S. (and British) military assistance and arms, including B-26 bombers, F-86 Sabre jet fighters, and light and medium tanks, all arriving over 1954–1958.[8] Yet, straight after this, the Saudis pursued a policy of neutrality toward Egypt, led by Faisal (especially as prime minister over 1958–1960 and 1962–1964), and so toned down the U.S. relationship for a time. The king and top royals mistrusted many of the senior officers, who they feared were Nasserists or Arab nationalists at heart. This may have driven the changed approach toward the United States at the time, but the Saudis were, at any rate, focusing on the development of personnel rather than new platforms[9] at the time, and so needed the United States less than might be assumed.

The cooling of relations was significant. During the Kennedy administration, the relationship reached arguably its lowest point since 1945 and until the 1973 oil crisis, or even 9/11. Critically, in 1960, King Saud encouraged the

United States not to seek to renew the Dhahran lease, which was set to expire in 1962, and in a move especially risky for U.S. relationship, even seemed to court the Soviets.[10] Faisal's work behind the scenes, his reappointment as prime minister in 1962, and the near-complete marginalization of Saud at the same time, probably saved the Saudi-U.S. relationship from a catastrophic failure in the early 1960s. The 1962–1970 Yemeni civil war, and Saudi Arabia's prominent (if ultimately unsuccessful) role supporting its proxies against those of Nasser's Egypt, helped reinvigorate ties with the United States, strengthened further by Faisal's ascension to the throne in 1964.[11]

Under Faisal (1964–1975) the relationship with Washington was maintained, but it was sorely tested by the 1973–1974 oil crisis and embargo. The oil embargo was the result of the 1973 Yom Kippur/Ramadan War, in which Egypt and Syria, with wider Arab support, launched a surprise attack on Israel on October 6, during the Jewish holy day of Yom Kippur, seeking to recapture the territories lost to Israel in the 1967 Six Day War. As Israel struggled in the conflict, initially looking as if it could lose the war outright, the United States agreed to rearm and resupply Israel, which angered the Arab states. As a result, the Organization of Arab Petroleum Exporting Countries (OAPEC) and some OPEC members initiated an oil embargo on the United States and a reduction in supply to some other Western states supportive of Israel. Initially, several exporting states increased oil prices, but after the U.S. resupply of Israel began on October 12, a fuller OAPEC embargo commenced on October 17. The embargo was short lived, ending in March 1974, but it was severe in terms of its effects on U.S. fuel prices and availability, and reminded the United States of its vulnerability in ensuring its energy security.

Saudi Arabia had joined the embargo on October 20, and quite reluctantly. Faisal had previously suggested that the Saudi government would not use oil as a diplomatic weapon, but in the lead-up to 1973 this seemed to change.[12] The increase in prices just prior to and early on in the war suited the Saudis, but it was usually assumed in the West that Faisal would not join in any boycott. Certainly, Saudi Arabia was not keen on the embargo, joining it a couple of days later than several key exporters and taking its time with the initial production cuts.[13] The embargo was dropped after about five months, but as early as December 1973 the Saudis were arguing within OPEC for increased production. The United States also brought considerable pressure to bear on the Saudis, not surprisingly. The embargo arguably had a negative impact on popular U.S. perceptions of Saudi Arabia and other Gulf monarchies, but has not been used again since that time and is extremely unlikely to happen again now.

At the elite level, relations between the United States and Saudi Arabia recovered surely if gradually from the embargo. The United States was perhaps cognizant that the Saudi regime felt compelled to join the embargo and did so only reluctantly. The "confrontation"—if that term is even appropriate—with the

United States was "a short-lived experience."[14] The Nixon administration had given Saudi Arabia a crucial role in its *twin pillars* policy, and while Iran was the more important pillar until its 1978–1979 revolution,[15] the Saudis were important nonetheless to U.S. energy security and as a local alternative to the British once London withdrew from "east of Suez" by 1971.[16] The oil crisis sharpened international perceptions of Saudi Arabia's diplomatic and economic importance, which probably encouraged the United States to nurture the relationship despite the tensions caused by the embargo. Furthermore, the Kingdom's skyrocketing oil income after 1974 gave them the means to purchase more arms and invest heavily in the United States, both of which they did, deepening and extending the relationship with Washington.[17]

For the Saudis, a return to the twin pillars role was attractive. In the mid-1970s, defense spending began a sustained rise, and the United States was one of their main arms suppliers. The Saudi sense of regional threat, including their rivalry with the Shah and their concern over his expanding military capability, drove this higher spending, even if increased oil revenues were what made it possible. The Iranian revolution, and Saudi fears that Tehran would export its revolution,[18] added to Saudi security worries. Defense spending almost doubled from 1973–1974 to 1974–1975, rose a further 150 percent the following year,[19] and had increased another 150 percent by 1980–1981.[20] Three "military cities" were constructed in the latter-1970s and early-1980s along the Saudi borders with Iraq, Yemen, and Jordan.[21] Saudi Arabia also sought to maximize their military self-reliance and to offset the quantitative advantages of rivals such as Iran and Iraq with a qualitative superiority. Their arms acquisitions in this period were massive. For air capability, Saudi purchases in this period included 64 F-5 fighter aircraft; 62 various types of the very advanced F-15 Eagle aircraft; various C-130 and KC-130 transports; and in the early 1980s, the very controversial purchase of E3-A airborne early warning and control aircraft.[22] For the navy, a corvette, four French frigates, oilers, maritime surveillance aircraft, and patrol boats and missile patrol boats were all acquired.[23] The army also gained a substantial qualitative improvement from the acquisition of French and U.S. medium tanks, armored personnel carriers, anti-tank missiles, surface-to-air missiles, and self-propelled artillery.[24] Other institutions, including the National Guard and the intelligence services, gained budget increases—often dramatic ones—in the late 1970s.[25] These defense and security modernizations were a feature of Khalid's reign over 1975–1982, when oil prices were on a sustained high, and it suited U.S. strategy to support the conservative, anti-Communist Saudis. While Saudi-U.S. relations improved over this time, it was driven above all by oil security and military matters, keeping it still a relationship of convenience for both sides.

Around the time King Fahd came to power in 1982, international oil prices began to decline, ending a decade-long price boom. Oil prices peaked at US $36–$37 per barrel in 1980, fell back slightly to the high US$20s per barrel in

1983, and then dropped to about US$14 per barrel in 1986 (the Brent price of $14.43 equating to US$30.23 in 2012 dollars), a fall of around half.[26] This hit Saudi oil revenues, which fell from SR121,348 million in 1984, to SR88,425 million in 1985, and then to SR42,464 million in 1986.[27] In other words, oil income fell by almost two-thirds in two years, at a time when other income was falling as well. This created a dire economic crisis, worsened by the uncertain regional dynamics resulting from the 1980–1988 Iran-Iraq War and the 1975–1990 Lebanese civil wars. Relations with the United States in the late-1970s were in many ways solid, given the arms trade and both sides' security worries, but were not particularly warm. The Saudis had felt that they were given little voice by the Carter administration,[28] that the United States had abandoned the Shah too easily as the Iranian revolution unfolded, and that Washington had not responded firmly enough to the 1979 Soviet invasion of Afghanistan.

It was only under the Reagan administration and especially after the AWACs sale in 1982 that faith in the relationship seemed to return to both parties.[29] Fahd sought to deepen the relationship, albeit discreetly, using military, political, and economic links. The Saudi leadership wanted to reconfirm the U.S. security guarantee, given the regional events of the 1980s, yet still had to keep in mind the clerical and societal opposition to the relationship that remained. Thus, Fahd's tactic of a "balance of dangers," in which the U.S. relationship was kept inconspicuous but strengthened and deepened, as it was seen as less dangerous than letting domestic pressures shape strategic decisions.[30] Given the security threats posed by the Iran-Iraq War, Fahd also provided financial support to Iraq. This aimed to keep Saddam content that the Saudis were on his side, while being unobtrusive enough to maintain simple ties with Iran and certainly to avoid outright hostility or conflict with Tehran.[31]

As the 1980s passed, the Saudis continued to purchase new arms and pursue its military modernization goals, albeit at a much-reduced pace given the fall in oil income.[32] The Saudis played a critical role assisting the U.S. efforts against the Soviets in Afghanistan, during the USSR's decade-long conflict there over 1979–1989. The Saudi intelligence service was a key source of funding for anti-Soviet *mujahideen* militia, providing perhaps as much money as the United States did.[33] While the Afghanistan war would later prove a security issue for the Al Saud, given the number of Saudis who were radicalized by their time fighting there[34]—famous among them, Osama bin Laden—at the time the Saudi role in Afghanistan greatly aided their relations with the United States.

Yet, the Saudis were still cautious about the U.S. relationship being too deep or overt. Despite the shared interests and involvement in Afghanistan, through the latter 1980s the Saudis continued to deny U.S. requests for access to Saudi military bases, and at times there was tension when the Saudis felt that the United States was being too overt about the relationship.[35] However, this Saudi hesitation toward the United States would change, and their approach be tested, by the August 1990 Iraqi invasion of Kuwait and the 1990–1991 Gulf War, which profoundly changed Saudi security perceptions toward the United States, and had a lasting effect on Saudi security perspectives and debates toward the Gulf.

SAUDI-U.S. RELATIONS AND THE 1990–1991 GULF WAR

In the early hours of August 2, 1990, Iraqi tanks that had been massing on the border crossed over into Kuwait and began a rapid invasion of the small sheikhdom, beginning an occupation that was ended only by a U.S.-led coalition military action against Iraq in January–February 1991. It was the first war of the post Cold War era—Saddam probably miscalculated during the crisis as a result of his continuing to adopt a Cold War mode of thinking about how the superpowers would respond to his invasion of Kuwait—and it also markedly restructured the strategic environment in the Gulf.

Soon after the invasion, the United States came to the view that Saudi Arabia could also be in Saddam's sights. On August 3, senior U.S. officials briefed the Saudi ambassador in Washington, Prince Bandar bin Sultan, raising the perceived risk of Saddam's forces continuing south into the Kingdom and outlining a plan to send U.S. forces to Saudi Arabia to defend it against this possibility. Whether Saddam was eyeing Saudi Arabia remains unclear and very contested; given that the Saudis possessed around one-quarter of the world's proven oil reserves, perhaps the risk should have been taken seriously regardless, although there is scant evidence that any attack on Saudi Arabia was being prepared at that stage, and Saddam's rhetoric prior to August 2 targeted Kuwait and the UAE rather than Saudi Arabia.[36] The Saudi agreement to the U.S. positioning of forces came on August 6, after then secretary of defense Dick Cheney led a delegation to Saudi Arabia to convince King Fahd to agree. Cheney reportedly showed the Saudi monarch further satellite images suggesting a likely Iraqi attack. The king was also aware of how quickly the Iraqi military had seized Kuwait, and that the northeast of Saudi Arabia was similarly vulnerable given the sheer size of Iraq's armed forces. Fahd's agreement came with strict conditions, though, that were in line with past considerations: that the United States keep the deployment secret until it was underway; that any attack on Iraq from Saudi soil be approved in advance by Riyadh; and that the United States give a written undertaking that its forces would leave the Kingdom once the Iraqi threat was over.[37]

Several things are notable about this, especially Fahd's agreement to host U.S. forces. One is the speed with which such agreement came: regardless of how real a threat Saddam was to Saudi Arabia, Fahd obviously *thought* the threat was very acute; indeed, he later said that the decision to agree to the U.S. forces' positioning in the country was one of the fastest decisions he had ever made.[38] The Saudi contribution to the war included its own troops and air force, probably not just the result of feeling obliged to assist, but also reflecting a genuine concern that the Kingdom required defending. It also served to create an impression at home that Arab forces, including Saudi ones, were at the forefront of the war, and—despite the reality—that they were integral and equal partners in the liberation of Kuwait. Second, the Saudis also bankrolled a substantial proportion of the war. The war cost in total around US$170 billion in the dollars of the time—over double that in 2014 dollars—with direct costs for the actual U.S.-led war (Operation Desert Shield) being around US$70 billion. The Saudis contributed some US$16.8 billion to the United States and US$1 billion to the United Kingdom to offset some of the direct military costs, and provided aid and other assistance to the Arab world worth at least another US$6 billion.[39] The Saudis claimed after the war to have spent some US$45 billion on it, equal to about 57 percent of one year's GDP.[40] Finally, it is notable how clearly Fahd made the United States agree to the positioning being a temporary one, undertaking to remove the troops as soon as the Iraqi threat had passed. Critically, they did not leave, staying in Saudi Arabia through the 1990s—something that tested the relationship again much later.

The war itself was a military success, and it deepened the relationship between the United States and Saudi Arabia at the strategic, military, and even economic levels, but it also introduced new problems and challenges at home for the Al Saud. The presence of the U.S. troops on Saudi soil was an issue in Saudi domestic politics, and it added opposition in some quarters to the ruling family. For many, the simple question raised was one of legitimacy: why had the Al Saud spent so much on defense and security, and claimed in part that their right to rule was based on protecting the Saudi people and the holy cities of Islam, but then proven so unable to do so when threatened by Iraq? The U.S. presence, and the implication that the Saudis were a weak, junior partner to Washington, was a humiliation to many.[41] While the official, senior clerics all fell in line and supported the Saudi regime's invitation to U.S. forces, many figures, especially junior clerics, publicly criticized the regime, in many cases also painting the United States or the West, rather than Iraq, as the true threat and enemy.[42] This reflected a widespread fear that Saudi values and morals were threatened by the West rather than the Arab world, even though the crisis had begun because of actions by an Arab leader. These themes were often interwoven by critics, who would claim that the Saudi regime was weak, had thus invited foreign forces in to protect the Saudi people since the royal family could not do so, and that this in turn undermined both Saudi values and especially its Islamic values. The conclusion, by such argument, was that the Al Saud was at best incompetent, at worst illegitimate. The attempts by the royals to counter such opposition were not very successful. The senior *ulema* support for the U.S. deployment was seen simply as a reminder of how coopted those clerics had become, and claims that the decision was necessary for the preservation of the Kingdom or the Al Saud's role in protecting Islam led to Saudi princes coming under direct attack.[43] The Gulf War marked a genuine political crisis for the Saudi royal family and those, such as the senior clerics, who were closest to it.

Perhaps most famously and more important to later global events, the Saudi invitation to U.S. forces stoked Osama bin Laden's rage toward the Saudi royals. After the Iraqi invasion of Kuwait, bin Laden went to the Kingdom and met with senior figures, including the defense minister and intelligence chief, and laid out his own proposal for a self-defense of the country, and claiming that the defeat of the Soviets in Afghan showed the potential power of a popular mobilization to defend against Saddam.[44] Not surprisingly, his offer was dismissed, and the U.S. deployment approved shortly afterward. As much as bin Laden was opposed to the secular, Arabist politics of Saddam Hussein, that the Saudi royal family would let foreign, non-Muslim forces into the Kingdom became his weightiest grievance.[45] He continued to vocally challenge the Al Saud, until moving into exile in 1992.

The arguments, including those of bin Laden but even more of Saudi religious figures whose sermons and speeches were widely distributed in the Kingdom during and after the Gulf War, both reflected and increased the anger in many Saudi circles about the U.S. deployment. The Al Saud felt the popular concern, and at times anger, directed toward them, and could not have avoided noticing the new calls for reform that characterized the early 1990s. They responded to such pressure through a combination of reform and repression. Yet, during the crisis and war, there was little that the regime could do except to suppress the most vocal of opposition and continue working quietly with the Americans. They were careful to keep Saudi and other Arab forces as visible as possible during the build-up and then the war against Iraq.

THE 1990s

The 1990–1991 Gulf War was a military success, but it created new problems for the Saudi regime. The neutralization of Iraq as a regional power was a welcome outcome for the Saudis of the conflict, of course, but the war also led the United States to become far more actively and overtly involved in the Gulf. Its deployment in Saudi Arabia shifted into a smaller but long-term military commitment in the region. This was partly the result of the post-war situation in Iraq, especially the passage of UN Security Council Resolution (UNSCR) 688 in April 1991, after Saddam used air assets and his army to suppress uprisings that began in March among the southern Iraqi Shia and the Kurds in the north.[46] Following UNSCR 688, allied forces led by the United States introduced no-fly zones in Iraq to stop the Iraqi regime's aerial suppression of these populations. As a result, the United States needed to retain considerable military capability, especially air power, in the region. Saudi Arabia was an essential base and area of operations for the United States in enforcing the southern no-fly zone. Thus, while the bulk of U.S. forces left Saudi Arabia after the war, some 5,000 remained there, staying until the early 2000s. U.S. air basing in the Kingdom remained important, with Saudi Arabia hosting the main U.S. air coordination facility in the region, the U.S. Air Combat Operations Center, in the east of the country. Some of the U.S. strikes against Iraq in the 1990s were carried out by U.S. aircraft based in Saudi Arabia.[47]

Given that the original U.S. deployment was unpopular and supposedly only to be for the duration of a war with Iraq over Kuwait, the longevity of the U.S. military presence in the Kingdom exacerbated criticisms within the country of both Washington and of the Al Saud. It was also, as Niblock has noted, a reminder that the nature of the relationship and of U.S. power projection in the Gulf had changed as of 1990.[48] The Gulf War gave Washington a renewed focus on the region and a higher degree of direct strategic involvement there, but also coincided with the collapse of the Soviet Union in 1991 and a new unipolar global setting in which the United States was the sole global superpower. This was a reason why the United States could demand Saudi funding for the war itself, and perhaps why they gained agreement to retain some forces in the Kingdom too. The Saudis, arguably, benefited less from the post-1991 order, especially if the domestic and regional political costs of the Gulf War are taken into account. They did take advantage of access to new arms, signing contracts worth some US$17 billion just over 1991 to 1993 alone,[49] and the U.S. presence probably suited Riyadh by deterring greater Iranian assertiveness in the Gulf. But for the Saudi royals, the strategic rewards of the Gulf War and the U.S. relationship came at the expense of new and greater domestic opposition.

Starting almost immediately after the war, there were a series of petitions to the government seeking reform, and a rise in Islamist oppositional activity shortly after that. While not solely a response to the war and the U.S. deployment in the Kingdom, these were contributing factors, while the war also provoked new debates among Saudis about the need for reform in the Kingdom. The first petition was essentially secular in nature, published in early 1991 by 43 prominent and public figures, calling for political reform such as greater consultation with society, media liberalization, and a curbing of the *Mutawwa'*.[50] In May that year, a more religious petition was signed by 52 people, including prominent religious figures, and called for greater religiosity of politics and society and closer adherence to Islamic law. It was followed by a lengthier petition to Abd al-Aziz bin Baz in 1992, which made extensive calls for reform of religious power, Islamic-based human rights, and economic reforms to reduce inequalities in wealth and opportunity.[51] These petitions, while coming from different quarters of society, were unsettling for the Al Saud. They showed the cleavages that existed between state and society, and the similarities in many of the criticisms from both religious and secular strands of society. The royal family never gained proper support or popular endorsement for its position on the Gulf War, which itself, and along with other problems and grievances, brought matters to the point where many figures were willing to speak openly about the need for reform.

The regime's response to this dissatisfaction with the existing order was to initiate a set of reforms, while also suppressing more serious opposition figures. The reforms in 1992 included the promulgation of the Basic Law, the development of a Consultative Council, and other changes, as discussed in Chapter 2. At the same time, there was greater repression of more vocal or menacing opposition figures. Bin Laden's exile was in effect prompted by this regime crackdown. There were also a series of arrests, in particular of Islamist figures, and far more active surveillance of opposition rallies and of mosques with potentially troublesome or critical clerics.[52] The state-controlled media also became more critical of such opposition, increasingly speaking about the dangers of dissent and of the risks to Saudi values from those it termed (and who sometimes were) "extremists."[53]

Yet, the opposition had momentum behind it, and the regime found little success in such tactics. The Islamist opposition in particular found a stronger voice and was more activist in the first half of the 1990s than previously. One example was the Committee for the Defense of Legitimate Rights (CDLR), set up in May 1993 by some key intellectuals, religious scholars, and others to, they stated, promote human rights in the Kingdom according to Islamic principles and to push for the full implementation of Islamic law, or *shari'a*.[54] The group was almost immediately declared illegitimate by the senior *'ulema* and banned by the government, which probably further radicalized it, but unable to operate in Saudi Arabia it moved into exile in London. It was an influential group and a source of gossip about corruption and political machinations in the Kingdom until a schism in 1996 saw it succeeded by another group.

Even more important than such groups was the rise of al-Qa'eda and such like-minded Islamic extremists. When Osama bin Laden's rhetoric became increasingly hostile to the Saudi regime, his citizenship was withdrawn in 1994. Bin Laden and others also increasingly spoke in revolutionary or violent terms against both the Al Saud and the United States, and sometimes about the relationship between the two. This brought him to the attention of the United States by 1996, when he was expelled from Sudan (with Khartoum almost certainly influenced by pressure from both the United States and Saudi Arabia), and once he found haven in Afghanistan he started to actively recruit and train jihadists to fight both the Saudis and the West. By the time of the U.S. embassy bombings in Nairobi and Dar-es-Salaam on August 7, 1998, his intentions and the reality of the threat he posed to the United States were clear.

At that time, the Saudis were facing an internal terrorist threat as well, from both Sunni and Shia extremists. The first major attack was the November 13, 1995, car bombing outside a U.S. training facility in Riyadh that killed six people. On June 25, 1996, a major bombing took place at the Khobar Towers in eastern Saudi Arabia, killing 19 U.S. service personnel. The Riyadh car bombings were perpetrated by Sunnis. Responsibility for the Khobar attack remains unclear: the Saudis blamed al-Qa'eda for them, but the United States blamed Iran and named as the perpetrators *Hizballah al-Hijaz* ("the Party of God of Hijaz," a Shia extremist group). It remains more likely that al-Qa'eda members or closely like-minded Sunni extremists were behind it.[55] Other smaller incidents took place after that, followed by an extensive insurgency in the early-mid-2000s. While almost certainly not directly ordered by bin Laden, many of the attacks in the 1990s were probably incited by his rhetoric.[56] The insurgency in the 2000s, more profoundly, was dominated by al-Qa'eda and very similar types.

Coming on top of the attacks on the World Trade Center in New York City in 1993 and the 1998 East Africa bombings, the al-Qa'eda attacks in Saudi Arabia in the late 1990s demonstrated the links between Sunni extremism and the Saudi-U.S. relationship. The attacks both stemmed from, and impacted, that relationship. For the United States, this was the downside of a decade in which its power in the Gulf was ascending. The Clinton administration pursued a dual containment of both Iran and Iraq, which required the relationship with the Saudis, even as ties with other states such as Qatar and the United Arab Emirates (UAE) were developed. It was not lost on the Saudi leadership that the U.S. relationship was a dynamic with domestic linkages, but Riyadh wanted the relationship to continue for various reasons such as arms purchases, military capability development, and economic opportunity.

It was also a time of economic reform in the Kingdom, which also motivated Riyadh to maintain and develop the U.S. relationship. The economic liberalization of 1999 to 2005 and beyond was driven by the problems caused by low oil prices from the mid-1980s until the early 2000s. By the late 1990s, this was essentially a financial crisis. It stretched the royals' ability to meet their end of the rentier bargain, and with oil prices at such levels there was little capacity to generate new, meaningful economic activity.[57] Financial problems added to opposition toward the Saudi leadership and their legitimacy. This renewed the urgency they attached to economic diversification and employment generation, which meant broadening and strengthening the indigenous private sector and attracting foreign trade and investment. Beginning in the late-1990s, the Saudi government implemented a series of economic reforms and promised many others; some, such as initiatives to develop trade, investment, and grow the private sector, did occur, while more controversial policies such as privatization were instigated much more waveringly.[58] Such reform necessitated a close relationship with the United States—if still a cautious one at many levels—to encourage stability, attract foreign direct investment, improve finance and capital markets, reform the labor market, and above all to gain support for the Saudi bid to join the World Trade Organization (WTO). The process of seeking WTO membership began in 1999, and required considerable reform, which was a focus through until 2005 when they were successful in joining the Organization.

The 1990s also saw additional Saudi arms purchases, which remained central to its relationship with the United States. The 1980s had been a period of particularly high arms purchases because of high oil prices for much of the decade; over 1983–1989 Saudi Arabia imported a total of some US$48.1 billion worth of arms, a remarkable 14.1 percent of all arms purchases in the developing world.[59] Yet over 1990–1999 inclusive, when oil prices were sharply lower, Saudi Arabia still imported a total of almost US$99.5 billion in arms.[60] The purchases were driven by the experience of the Gulf War but also by Riyadh's strategic rivalry with Iran and its quest for greater regional influence. The problem, as with previous military modernizations, was that while the Saudi purchases delivered new platforms and systems, the Kingdom's military capability did not increase to its full potential. The necessary associated improvement in maintenance, support infrastructure, and interoperability was for the most part neglected.[61]

It is notable how central the United States was as an arms supplier to the Saudis as of the mid-1990s.[62] In earlier years, Saudi Arabia imported its arms from a range of suppliers, and the United States competed with the United Kingdom, France, Germany, and others. In the mid-1970s, the United States supplied only around half of the Saudis' arms. In the 1980s, the *Al-Yamama* deal meant that the United Kingdom became a larger source of Saudi arms, and over 1987–1991 the British sold the Saudis about three times as much arms, by value, than did the United States. Then, in the mid- and late-1990s the United States returned to supplying around half of Saudi arms imports, and the British the majority of the remainder. Most new Saudi orders then went to the United States as of the late-1990s.

Yet, there remained other, albeit minor, problems in the relationship. In the latter 1990s, the U.S. troop presence in Saudi increased, from less than 2,000 in 1997 to over 7,000 in 2000,[63] leading the Saudis to be more vocal about what they felt was a U.S. inability to deal with the on-going nuisance caused by Saddam Hussein. At the popular level, however, the U.S. military presence grated with many Saudis. Further, as Bronson notes, the Arab-Israeli peace process also tested the relationship: to the Saudis, the United States marginalized the Kingdom and only consulted it on Arab-Israeli matters superficially or when Washington needed something such as financial or diplomatic support.[64] Finally, as the United States and Saudi Arabia grew closer in the 1990s, domestic criticism of each other increased within both polities. The U.S. military presence affected how many Saudis viewed the United States and its foreign policy, and Saudi human rights issues gained attention from both nongovernmental organizations and from the U.S. State Departments reports on human rights around the world.[65] Although Osama bin Laden's status was greatest among radicalized

Saudi youth, and his ability to build widespread support in the Kingdom was limited, his criticisms of U.S. foreign policy and the U.S. military presence in the Kingdom were very popular.[66] At the same time, human rights and Saudi funding to international and Palestinian extremist groups started to gain greater attention in the United States and to influence public opinion there against the Saudis.[67]

9/11 AND THE SAUDI-U.S. RELATIONSHIP

At the start of the twenty-first century, Saudi Arabia and the United States had solid relations in several key areas, but there remained issues of tension and areas of deliberate neglect in what was still, ultimately, a relationship of convenience. In the early months of the George W. Bush administration, there was a marked shift in U.S. policy toward Israel. This was based in part on the failed peace talks at Camp David in mid-2000 and the Palestinian *al-Aqsa intifada* (or uprising) that followed after September 2000, but also stemmed from Bush's personal views and his intention to avoid spending too much energy or political capital on the peace process, as he felt Clinton had done.

Arab-Israeli matters thus received little attention after Bush took office in January 2001. Yet for the Saudis, and the Arab world, the issue was at the forefront of political debate. At the official level, the Saudi leadership had assumed that relations with the United States would be renewed and strengthened with a second member of the Bush dynasty now in power.[68] At the popular level, Israeli-Palestinian dynamics dominated the news, and there was enormous popular anger toward U.S. policy, which was seen as having always been supportive of Israel but of being especially pro-Israeli under the new Bush administration.[69] On August 27, 2001, Saudi concerns about U.S. policy reached the point where the Saudi ambassador in Washington, Prince Bandar bin Sultan, met Bush at the White House and delivered a letter from Crown Prince Abdullah.[70] The stern letter was highly critical of the U.S. failure to address Israeli-Palestinian dynamics and the violence that was becoming routine as the *al-Aqsa intifada* worsened. Bush promised to reexamine U.S. policy on Israel and the Palestinians, but nonetheless, Abdullah's letter reflected real tension in the relationship; it was probably the moment of greatest strain since the oil embargo.

The deepest event in the relationship was the terrorist attacks on the United States on September 11, 2001. The events themselves are well covered elsewhere, but it is crucial to reiterate a few key points about them. The first is that, since 15 of the 19 hijackers that day were Saudi nationals, the popular impression of the Kingdom in the United States was immediately impacted. Popular U.S. views on Saudi Arabia plummeted, and remained negative for many years.[71] This was probably a deliberate goal of bin Laden, who in choosing so many Saudis for the attacks, was almost certainly seeking to cleave or break the Saudi-U.S.

relationship that he so resented. The popular U.S. anger toward the Kingdom was partly because of the lack of public contrition and sympathy expressed by the Saudis.[72] When public gestures were made, they were often ineffective, such as when Prince Alwaleed bin Talal made a public donation to New York City after the attacks but then saw the money refused because of his linking of the Israeli-Palestinian issue to 9/11.[73] The Saudi response to 9/11 was not as adroit or sensitive as it should have been.

A more underlying problem, but perhaps the most critical one, was the fact that Saudi money had for years been supporting the promotion of Wahhabi ideology, and some such funds from individuals and charities had gone to extremist groups, including al-Qa'eda. A Council on Foreign Relations report on terrorism financing in 2002 put it bluntly: "[It] is worth stating clearly and unambiguously what official U.S. government spokespersons have not: For years, individuals and charities based in Saudi Arabia have been the most important source of funds for al-Qaeda; and for years, Saudi officials have turned a blind eye to this problem."[74] The same report showed that the Saudis had been lax in providing laws, regulation, and initiatives that would have diminished the capability of groups like al-Qa'eda to raise money or operate in Saudi Arabia.[75] A supplementary report by the 9/11 Commission on terrorism financing was similarly critical: "Saudi Arabia and the UAE, necessary partners in any realistic effort to stem the financing of terror, were ambivalent and selectively cooperative in assisting the United States."[76]

Such assessments influenced U.S. policymakers, as well as much of the public, to take a very critical view of the Saudis. The issue was more complex than often painted, however, since it was individuals, charities, and other nonstate actors that mostly had funded extremists, not the Saudi government. The Al Saud supported the clergy, of course, and some funds from more radical clerics probably flowed on to groups like al-Qa'eda, but the Saudi leadership would never have funded a group like al-Qa'eda that was as anti-Al Saud as it was anti-American. Furthermore, popular views at the time in both the United States and Saudi Arabia often ignored the fact that their own governments had built a pragmatic but in some ways thin relationship with each other. People in both countries often criticized their own government's apparent complicity with or support for the other, but this neglects the fact that both governments seem to have acted for a long time with the understanding that the two countries did not share a lot of values and had very different political cultures.

Other issues that stemmed from 9/11 also shaped the bilateral relationship. The U.S. decision to tighten visa rules and border security was seen as attacking Saudis as a group. Student visa applications subsequently declined sharply, as did Saudi tourist arrivals in the United States, when people who had previously been able to obtain a same-day visa now faced a long wait for one, and sometimes found themselves denied one at all.[77] At the leadership level, the relationship fared little better. The Saudi leadership continued to talk about the Israeli-Palestinian dynamic, when the United States most wanted to focus on activities against terrorism. When Bush and Abdullah met in April 2002, the meeting was tense. The United States and the Saudis made some concessions on Palestinian issues and support for extremism respectively, but otherwise the meeting dragged along and demonstrated just how deeply the 9/11 attacks had affected the relationship. Soon after that, the U.S.-led 2003 war against Iraq added further pressures and complexity to what had become a sorely tested relationship.

THE 2003 IRAQ WAR AND AFTER

The second signature event for the Middle East in the new century, after 9/11, was the 2003 Iraq War. A controversial war in the West but especially so in the Arab and Muslim worlds, the conflict was a military success in conventional terms, but quickly established a new strategic reality in the region characterized by instability in Iraq itself—still an issue today, if less so than in the 2000s—and a changed geopolitical environment in the Gulf that suited Iran, but few others. This all had implications for Saudi security and its will to be a regional power.

In mid- and late-2002, as the likelihood of a U.S.-led war against Saddam's regime increased, the Saudis wavered in deciding their stance on it. In October the Saudi foreign minister Saud al-Faisal suggested that the Kingdom would openly support the war and allow U.S. forces to operate from Saudi territory if the war had United Nations backing, but a month later, in November, then stated the reverse position.[78] This uncertainty probably stemmed in part from the tensions in the U.S. relationship after 9/11. More important, however, it reintroduced an old dilemma for the Saudi regime, that of wanting, on the one hand, to maintain its strategic and defense relationship with the United States, but on the other hand, being fearful of the unpopularity of that relationship and of the domestic opposition that would come from any war against Iraq. This dilemma, while an old one, seems to have been thorny enough that some of the royals were split on how they handle it.[79]

Ultimately, on March 18, 2003—the very eve of hostilities—the Saudis announced that they would not support the war or allow Saudi territory to be used by the United States to fight it. Very inconspicuously, they did allow the United States to undertake some noncombat activities from bases in the Kingdom.[80] In a strategic and military sense this made little difference for the United States, which operationally could execute the war from other Arab states, but nonetheless, for the message it sent, it further undermined Saudi-U.S. relations. In U.S. foreign policy circles, there was anger that the Saudis, seemingly having done little to stop the rise of al-Qa'eda and then acted only half-heartedly against it after 9/11, was then failing to support the United States in Iraq as well. This view was represented in actions such as that of U.S. Senator Arlen Specter, who in November 2003 tabled a *Saudi Arabia Accountability Act*, which among other things threatened to place restrictions on Saudi arms purchases and diplomats' movements if the Saudis were deemed to not be fully supporting U.S. anti-terrorism activities.[81] Congressional debate on the Act was vigorous, and was a chance for U.S. figures to again publicly criticize the Al Saud, although the bill was never enacted.

At a strategic level, while the 2003 Iraq War removed from power an Iraqi leader that was unfriendly toward the Saudi leadership and a strategic rival to them in the Gulf, there were significant downsides for the Saudi leaders from regime change in Baghdad. These included the risk of the conflict spreading into Saudi Arabia, and of course the concern that expanded Shia power in Iraq would lead to the Saudi Shia also making new or greater demands for reform on the Saudi leadership.[82] Later, as Iraq destabilized and descended into substantial levels of internal conflict, the Saudi government feared that extremists would shift their attention to Saudi Arabia and create a new wave of terrorism in the Kingdom. There was some justification for such concerns. Young Saudis went to fight as insurgents in Iraq in sizable numbers—a conservative estimate is that one thousand or more Saudis went to Iraq,[83] but the actual number may be higher[84]—and some of them then returned home radicalized by their Iraq experience. The Saudi crackdown on extremists in the early-mid-2000s was at least in part driven by this fear that Iraq had radicalized some Saudis.

The withdrawal of nearly all U.S. military personnel from Saudi Arabia in 2003 helped the Al Saud build or repair their support among the less violent opposition figures and forces, but it made little difference to more extremist elements that still denied the legitimacy of the Al Saud and sought to confront the regime violently.[85] This period of domestic terrorism lasted throughout 2004 and most of 2005.[86] Even once al-Qa'eda in Saudi Arabia had been largely suppressed by the regime, its remnants continued attacks after that time, albeit at a lower tempo, led by a younger generation of Saudis still very radical but lacking the same skills and coordination shown by extremists back in mid-decade.[87] While this insurgency was not a product of the Iraq War, the war certainly did not assist the regime.

The relationship throughout the remaining years of the George W. Bush administration continued to be dominated by impacts of the war on terrorism, the Iraq War, and the strife in post-Saddam Iraq. The relationship did gradually start to improve after Abdullah formally took the throne in 2005 and proved to be relative moderate and reformist. But the relationship continued to be hampered by the Arab-Israeli conflict. Between the negative impacts on the Kingdom of 9/11 and the Palestinian *intifada*, the Saudis in the early 2000s were prompted to become more involved in regional peace efforts. Thus, they proposed an Arab-Israeli peace plan, sometimes called the Abdullah Plan. This was a comprehensive peace proposal, adopted at the Arab League summit in Beirut in March 2002. It essentially promised that in exchange for a full Israeli withdrawal from all territories occupied after June 5, 1967, the creation of an independent Palestinian state with Jerusalem as its capital, and an acknowledgment of the Palestinian refugees' "right of return," the Arab states would establish a full peace with Israel, including complete normalization of relations across the diplomatic, economic, and cultural spheres.[88] While ambitious and potentially attractive in some quarters, the plan did not develop into the basis for peace negotiations.[89] Some Arab states were either lukewarm toward it or, like Libya, rejected it outright. The United States was outwardly supportive of the plan, but in practice was focused on terrorism and the forthcoming war with Iraq at the time, and so gave it little attention. Israel was skeptical about the plan, eventually raising numerous issues with it but not rejecting it outright.

The plan did not die at that stage, however, and was reapproved again at an Arab League meeting in March 2007. Again, and despite European Union backing, the plan did not lead to concrete peace developments, mostly because by mid-2007 Hamas had gained control of Gaza, meaning that the plan would not be able to be transformed into action. The peace plans have proven useful in image terms for the Saudis, enabling Abdullah to claim that he is willing to take some diplomatic initiative on the Arab-Israeli issue: "Saudi leaders managed to create the posture of regional coordinator; a status that has the ability to link Arab states and superpowers together in a coordinated attempt to bring stability to the Middle East."[90] Valuable as that may have been, the nature of the peace plan and the intractability of the Israeli-Palestinian dimension in particular, meant that the prospects for the plans was always poor.

In the same period, the Bush administration's diplomatic initiatives in the Middle East after 2003 did not sit particularly well with the Saudis. While Saudi economic reform through much of the 2000s was consistent with U.S. goals in the region, Riyadh was unsettled by the administration's democracy agenda. The *Greater Middle East Initiative* (GMEI) in particular was a problem. It was developed by the United States in the first half of 2004 and presented at the G8 meeting in June that year, promoting good governance, education, and economic growth as its pillars.[91] However, it was widely viewed in the region as an attempt to force democratization on the region, about which many leaderships, not least of all the Saudi one, were suspicious. The Saudi government was openly critical of the GMEI, and saw U.S. free trade agreements made with other Gulf states as undermining Riyadh's position in the region and as attempting to force political reform on the Al Saud.[92] While these free trade agreements were more prominently attached by the United States to attempts to create a U.S.-Middle East Free Trade Area (U.S.-MEFTA), to Riyadh all such steps appeared to both undermine and marginalize Saudi influence in the Gulf and assert U.S. power there.

That said, the United States and Saudi Arabia agreed on some things, especially on the strategic challenge from Iran after the Iraq War. Political change and conflict in Iraq meant that the Saudis became the only Middle Eastern regional power able to compete with Iran. This created, in effect, a Saudi-Iranian rivalry over Iraq, and a Saudi fear of greater Iranian influence and boldness there and in the wider Gulf.[93] For obvious reasons, the Saudis shared U.S. concerns about Iran's nuclear program and were keen for that program to be challenged and opposed, fearful of both the proliferation and regional strategic results of an Iranian bomb or even threshold capacity.[94] The 2003 Iraq War helped Iran by enhancing Shia power in Iraq and undermining the sense of security in the GCC states by changing the strategic dynamic. The perceived rise of Shia power in Iraq after about 2006 was deeply worrying to the Saudis, as was the rise in Hezbollah's regional support after the Israel attacks on Lebanon in the summer of that same year.[95] There was also a concern about a more ambitious or aggressive Iranian policy closer to home, above all as to whether Iran would seek to become more involved in Bahrain, where the Sunni Al Khalifa dynasty ruled over a population that was 70 percent Shia. Later events, especially the 2011 Arab Spring and the uprisings in Bahrain, as well as Iranian and Saudi rivalry in the Syrian civil war after 2011, further fed this concern in Riyadh.

What helped the Saudi regime through this period, both in terms of its regional influence and the security that the Al Saud felt at home, were the high oil prices over 2004 to 2008. Prices rose from an average of US$28.83 in 2003 (US$35.97 in 2011 dollars) to US$97.26 in 2008 (US$103.71 in 2011 dollars), before falling back in 2009 but rising again after that to US$111.67 in 2012.[96] This provided a massive windfall of funds to the Saudis: oil revenues went from US$105 billion in 2004 to US$298 billion in 2008 and were above US$300 billion in 2011 and 2012.[97] This helped to cushion some of the impacts of economic reforms over the period, and allowed the government, in the eighth five-year plan of 2005–2009, to be far more ambitious in public spending plans, diversification initiatives, the reduction of poverty, and even the promotion of women's roles in the economy.[98] High oil prices permitted these reforms, which otherwise would have been unaffordable or politically difficult. The regime's co-optive capacity, including its scope for discretionary spending, was far greater in the 2000s than it had been in the previous decade.

High oil prices also meant that the Saudis maintained a central role in the global energy sector, and as a U.S. ally in the region. Overall defense spending rose consistently through the 2000s; it almost doubled in nominal value over 2000 to 2009, while falling slightly as a percentage of GDP in that period but only because of the massive injection of oil rents into the state's coffers.[99] Arms imports did not rise as spectacularly as might be assumed, but mostly because previously placed or postponed orders came in at the time, and also because orders placed in the mid-2000s often were not delivered until some years later.[100]

Major initiatives at the time also included upgrades and enhancements to facilities, and some major new platforms later in the decade, and then an enormous and ambitious procurement agreement with the United States, as will be discussed shortly.

SAUDI-U.S. RELATIONS IN THE OBAMA ADMINISTRATION AND BEYOND

Various dynamics came together in the mid- and latter-2000s to improve Saudi-U.S. ties slightly after the shock of 9/11, including Abdullah's rise to power, the economic conditions in the Kingdom, the concerns about Iran's nuclear program, and after 2008, the decline in violence in Iraq. Still, relations had taken years to recover—and even then, only partially—from the damage caused by 9/11. In 2008, his final year in office, George W. Bush visited Saudi Arabia twice, and Abdullah had made three visits to the United States during Bush's tenure. In this sense, there was considerable communication between the United States and Saudi leadership, although a warming of the relationship was a different matter. Only under the Obama administration, after early 2009, did Saudi-U.S. relations even come close to returning what they were in the 1990s, and even then, this was in large measure because the regional dynamics of the Gulf had so shifted in the interim. Saudi Arabia had emerged as the key Sunni state, engaged in a tense regional sectarian rivalry with Shiite Iran, and then once the 2011 Arab uprisings began, Saudi Arabia was integral in countering Iranian influence in Syria and elsewhere. However, the relationship still faced challenges, and in 2013 began to deteriorate again as the Saudis became more openly critical of U.S. policy and more worried about the civil war in Syria.

Obama's first term approach to the Middle East was dominated by a focus on the drawdown of U.S. troops in Iraq, and dealing with the security situation in Afghanistan. The Saudis shared many U.S. concerns, especially about the long-term stability of Iraq and the need for consensus there to avoid future political turmoil or conflict, but the prime ministership of Nouri al-Maliki has been characterized by rising authoritarianism and favoritism toward the Shia. At the time, however, the Saudis increasingly came to treat Iraq as a security threat, as well as a field in which Iran could seek greater sway. Beyond Iraq and Afghanistan, however, Obama pushed for political reform in the Arab world, especially through his Cairo speech in early June 2009, in which he sought closer ties with the region but also reiterated a U.S. desire to see political reform, human rights, and economic transformation in the region.[101] His only mention of Saudi Arabia in the speech was a fairly positive one, on interfaith initiatives in the region, but much of what he said was interpreted negatively by the Saudi leaders. Obama's calls for democratization, greater religious freedom, and the advancement of women's rights, if pushed on the Al Saud dynasty, all had the potential to undermine the ruling bargain and the stability of the regime, as well as being matters with which the Wahhabi clerics and some other allies of the Saudi royals, would likely take issue.

Obama also took up the matter of U.S.-Iran relations early in his tenure, initially seeking to improve the relationship through a new year's message to the Iranian people in April 2009, but this made little progress. By 2010, with the relationship not improving and showing no signs that it might, the United States ramped up the pressure on Iran over its nuclear program. On July 1, 2010, Obama signed the Comprehensive Iran Sanctions, Accountability, and Divestment Act, which expanded sanctions on Iran, including placing restrictions on third countries trading with and investing in the Islamic Republic. Further international sanctions against Iran's oil sector in 2012 were especially damaging to its exports and its economic conditions. In these moves, the Saudis were supportive of the United States and shared its concerns about Iran. Were Iran to develop a nuclear weapon, this would completely change the strategic dynamics of the Gulf and give the Iranians hegemony in the subregion and, indeed, the Middle East more broadly. It would thus allow them a much more aggressive regional role, and dramatically increase the risk that they would seek to intervene into Saudi or GCC domestic politics, including sectarian dynamics in Saudi Arabia, Bahrain, and Kuwait.

This is perhaps a reason why the United States, also in 2010, agreed in principle to a massive future sale of arms to the Saudis. This was announced on October 20, 2010, when the State Department informed the U.S. Congress of its intention to allow the purchase of some US$60 billion worth of arms by Saudi Arabia over 15–20 years.[102] This included upgrades to 70 existing Saudi F-15 fighter/interceptors; the purchase of 84 additional new F-15s; extensive new helicopter capability (including 70 Apache attack helicopters, 36 AH-6M Little Bird light helicopters, and 72 Sikorsky Black Hawk transport helicopters); and munitions, parts, and other equipment. In late 2011, the Saudis exercised their prerogative under the program and signed contracts under this deal worth around US$30 billion.[103] The deal signified several things. One was that the Saudi-U.S. relationship was returning to a more functional and positive basis, if still not a close one. Second, the deal was a gesture of support from the United States for the Saudi regime, both at the time and longer term as the royal family faces a transition period of older leaders and generational change in its top ranks.[104] Finally, the deal highlighted the shared security concerns of both Washington and Riyadh. While the two sides did not state that the deal stemmed from an Iranian threat or rivalry, few analysts missed the chance to see it in such a light: "US military assistance to the Kingdom has been a significant part of Washington's strategic relationship with Riyadh and joint efforts to contain Iranian power in the Gulf region"[105] as one prominent analyst noted. Other agreements followed, including supplementary purchases from the United States and a renewed arms agreement with Britain, all of which enhanced the Saudis ability to project power and defend their air and ground space, even if inadequate training, infrastructure, and battle space management remain hindrances to their ability to maximize the capability of these platforms and systems.[106]

The arms trade also helps reduce the imbalance in a trade relationship that is very firmly in Saudi Arabia's favor. In 2012, Saudi Arabia exports to the United States were some US$55.67 billion, while their imports from the United States were worth US$17.97 billion.[107] These are substantial sums in themselves, but account for only a fraction of U.S. trade in goods and services, which totaled almost US$5 *trillion* that year (specifically, US$4,955 billion in total imports and exports). Likewise, important as the United States is economically to Saudi Arabia, and usually its largest or second-largest trading partner overall, it was projected to be only 14.3 percent of Saudi exports and 13.2 of Saudi imports in 2012.[108] Saudi investment in the United States may help offset this imbalance, but only slightly. Moreover, the trade is very skewed: nearly all U.S. imports from Saudi Arabia are oil and petrochemical products, while U.S. exports to Saudi Arabia are more diverse but still dominated by arms and related goods and services.

Beyond the arms trade, the other dynamic influencing relations in Obama's first term was the Arab uprisings from late 2010 onward. This so-called Arab Spring had a deep impact on the Saudi leadership. The protests led to a significant refocus of Riyadh's diplomatic energies once the risks of the regional protests for the Al Saud became obvious. The Saudi king and elite sought in particular to use its foreign policy to help "contain" the uprisings.[109] This is another reminder of how intertwined domestic and external security dynamics are in the minds of the Saudi leadership. For a time, especially in the initial months of 2011 as the uprisings unfolded, they strained Saudi-U.S. relations because the Saudis, especially the most senior royals, felt that the United States had not sufficiently supported U.S.-allied leaders in the region such as Egyptian president Hosni Mubarak, and that this lack of U.S. support contributed to his downfall.[110] The arms contracts of 2011 and 2012 perhaps helped improve that strained relationship, serving as an implied U.S. endorsement of the Saudi regime and a public commitment to the security of Saudi Arabia and its regime.

Ultimately, the United States and Saudi Arabia has enough shared interests that the Arab uprisings did not damage the relationship in the longer-term. The United States did not want to see the Saudi regime destabilized or overthrown, as much as many U.S. foreign policy makers perhaps would have liked to see greater social or economic reform in the Kingdom. Initial strains notwithstanding, the Saudi elite and the Obama administration quietly agreed on the need for the Bahraini regime neither to collapse nor for Bahrain to fall under Iranian influence. The two also shared similar goals in Syria, where the dynamics between the al-Asad regime and opposition forces deteriorated in 2011 and especially early 2012 into a civil war, which became a proxy conflict between Shia Iran, which backed al-Asad as Tehran's most important ally in the Arab world, and key Sunni states, including Saudi Arabia and Qatar most prominently. Even in Yemen, the United States and Saudi Arabia shared concerns about a collapse of the state or a civil conflict that might spill over into Saudi Arabia, as well as fears of Iranian intervention there too. Thus, in combination, the Arab uprisings on balance brought the United States and Saudi Arabia close together, but only to a limited and tactical extent.

The future of the Saudi-U.S. relationship—in light of regional rivalries, the Arab uprisings, the arms trade, the oil trade, and the broader Saudi-U.S. trade and investment relationship—is not under any serious threat. While a dramatic event such as the 9/11 attacks or the 2003 Iraq War has sorely tested the relationship in the past—and an event of similar gravity would test it again just as deeply—the benefits of the relationship and the elite consensus in both Washington and Riyadh about the need to maintain and develop ties ultimately dictate the marriage of convenience between the two states. For the Saudis, this means balancing the U.S. relationship against opposition to it among some domestic constituencies, but Saudi national security and the position of the regime are ultimately served by the links with the United States. For Washington, somewhat similarly, there are many ideological and practical reasons why the relationship is often seen and portrayed in the public realm in a negative light, but the U.S. elite seems to accept the benefits of the relationship and to be committed to its future preservation and development.

NOTES

1 For more detail on the meeting see Rachel Bronson, *Thicker than Oil: America's Uneasy Partnership with Saudi Arabia* (New York: Oxford University Press, 2006), 36–42.

2. David Long, *The Kingdom of Saudi Arabia* (Gainesville: University of Florida Press, 1997), 62, cited in Madawi Al-Rasheed, *A History of Saudi Arabia*, 2nd ed. (Cambridge: Cambridge University Press, 2010), 90.

3. Al-Rasheed, *A History of Saudi Arabia*, 90–91.

4. Al-Rasheed, *A History of Saudi Arabia*, 99.

5. Nadav Safran, *Saudi Arabia: The Ceaseless Quest for Security* (Ithaca: Cornell University Press, 1988), 65.

6. Ibid.

7. Ibid., 65–70.

8. Ibid., 103–104.

9. Ibid., 104–105.

10. Bronson, *Thicker Than Oil*, 78–79.

11. Ibid., 84–89.

12. Al-Rasheed, *A History of Saudi Arabia*, 131.

13. Ibid., 132.

14. Ibid., 135.

15. Gary Sick, "The United States and the Persian Gulf in the Twentieth Century," in Lawrence G. Potter (ed.), *The Persian Gulf in History* (New York: Palgrave Macmillan, 2009), 296–298.

16. Ibid., 296.

17. Al-Rasheed, *A History of Saudi Arabia*, 136–137.

18. The Iranian claim that it would "export" its "revolution" has been widely cited and discussed, but see for example F. Gregory Gause III, *The International Relations of the Persian Gulf* (Cambridge: Cambridge University Press, 2010), 46–51, 77, 86–87.

19. For the exact figures see Safran, *Saudi Arabia: The Ceaseless Quest for Security*, 182–183 (Table 3).

20. Ibid., 423 (Table 15).

21. Al-Rasheed, *A History of Saudi Arabia*, 136–137.

22. Safran, *Saudi Arabia: The Ceaseless Quest for Security*, 434–435 (Table 19); Al-Rasheed, *A History of Saudi Arabia*, 137. Importantly, some platforms such as the F-5 were delivered without the more advanced equipment and avionics necessary for attack/strike missions; see Al-Rasheed, *A History of Saudi Arabia*, 137, 285n3.

23. Safran, *Saudi Arabia: The Ceaseless Quest for Security*, 434–435 (Table 19).

24. Ibid., 434–435 (Table 19).

25. For details of the specific budget figures over various years, broken down by service/capability, see Ibid., 428 (Table 18).

26. Oil price figures and 2011 equivalent are from the "Historical Data Work Book" attached to the *BP Statistical Review of World Energy 2013* (London: BP, June 2013), http://www.bp.com/en/global/corporate/about-bp/statistical-review-of-world-energy-2013.html, accessed July 30, 2013.

27. Figures are from Tim Niblock with Monica Malik, *The Political Economy of Saudi Arabia* (London: Routledge, 2007), 56 (Table 3.2) and 101 (Table 4.2).

28. Al-Rasheed, *A History of Saudi Arabia*, 136.

29. Ibid., 154–155.

30. Ibid., 156.

31. Peter W. Wilson and Douglas F. Graham, *Saudi Arabia: The Coming Storm* (Armonk: M. E. Sharpe, 1994), 103–105; Bronson, *Thicker Than Oil*, 163–167.

32. Wilson and Graham, *Saudi Arabia: The Coming Storm*, 101–108, 151–160.

33. William Maley, *The Afghanistan Wars* (Basingstoke: Palgrave Macmillan, 2002), 81–82; a similar point is made in Tim Niblock, *Saudi Arabia: Power, Legitimacy and Survival* (London: Routledge, 2006), 147–151.

34. This is discussed in greater detail later in the book, and has been assessed in multiple sources. See for example Thomas Hegghammer, *Jihad in Saudi Arabia: Violence and Pan-Islamism since 1979* (Cambridge: Cambridge University Press, 2010), 38–48.

35. Wilson and Graham, *Saudi Arabia: The Coming Storm*, 106; Al-Rasheed, *A History of Saudi Arabia*, 156.

36. Dilip Hiro, *Desert Shield to Desert Storm: The Second Gulf War* (London: Paladin, 1992), 109–133.

37. Ibid., 116; Bronson, *Thicker Than Oil*, 191–196.

38. Bronson, *Thicker Than Oil*, 195.

39. Yahya M. Sadowski, *Scuds or Butter? The Political Economy of Arms Control in the Middle East* (Washington: The Brookings Institution, 1993), 19–21.

40. Hiro, *Desert Shield to Desert Storm*, 397.

41. Al-Rasheed, *A History of Saudi Arabia*, 159–160.

42. Ibid., 160.

43. Stéphane Lacroix, *Awakening Islam: The Politics of Religious Dissent in Contemporary Saudi Arabia* (Cambridge: Harvard University Press, 2011), 158–164.

44. Yossef Bodansky, *Bin Laden: The Man Who Declared War on America* (New York: Random House, 2001), 28–32.

45. Niblock, *Saudi Arabia: Power, Legitimacy and Survival*, 153.

46. Charles Tripp, *A History of Iraq*, 3rd Edn (Cambridge: Cambridge University Press, 2007), especially 246–249.

47. Niblock, *Saudi Arabia: Power, Legitimacy and Survival*, 151.

48. Ibid., 151–152.

49. Ibid., 151.

50. Al-Rasheed, *A History of Saudi Arabia*, 163.

51. Ibid., 163–166.

52. Ibid., 169–171.

53. Ibid., 170–171.

54. Several sources discuss the CDLR in some detail: see for example Daryl Champion, *The Paradoxical Kingdom: Saudi Arabia and the Momentum of Reform* (New York: Columbia University Press, 2003), 226–230, 248–252; Lacroix, *Awakening Islam*, 189–193; and Al-Rasheed, *A History of Saudi Arabia*, 171–180.

55. The Saudi government initially blamed al-Qa'eda-linked Sunni extremists for the bombing and suggested that it may have involved people linked to those behind the late-1995 Riyadh car bombing. The United States, however, after a lengthy investigation, claimed that Iranian-backed Shia were behind it. Iran denied this. Some of the evidence garnered by the *National Commission on Terrorist Attacks Upon the United States* (the 9/11 Commission), and statements by senior officials such as former-U.S. Secretary of Defense William Perry and former-Saudi Interior Minister Prince Nayef, cast doubt on the FBI's claim that Iran was behind the attack. The question of responsibility remains unresolved.

56. Niblock, *Saudi Arabia: Power, Legitimacy and Survival*, 155.

57. Niblock with Malik, *The Political Economy of Saudi Arabia*, 173–175

58. For more detail on the Saudi economic reforms of 1999–2005, see Ibid., 180–199.

59. Anthony H. Cordesman, *Saudi Arabia Enters the Twenty-First Century: The Military and International Security Dimensions* (Westport: Greenwood Publishing, 2003), 90

60. Ibid., 92 (Table 3.14).

61. Ibid., 93–94.

62. Ibid., 94–102, 98 (Chart 3.18).

63. Bronson, *Thicker Than Oil*, 219.

64. Ibid., 229–230.

65. Niblock, *Saudi Arabia: Power, Legitimacy and Survival*, 160.

66. Ibid., 162.

67. Ibid., 163.

68. Bronson, *Thicker Than Oil*, 234.

69. Ibid.

70. Ibid., 232–233.

71. Ibid., 235.

72. Ibid.

73. Ibid.

74. Maurice R. Greenberg, William F. Wechsler, and Lee S. Wolosky, *Terrorist Financing: Report of an Independent Task Force Sponsored by the Council on Foreign Relations* (New York: Council on Foreign relations, 2002), 8.

75. Ibid., 18–20, 30–31.

76. National Commission on Terrorist Attacks Upon the United States (the 9/11 Commission), *Monograph on Terrorist Financing: Staff Report to the Commission* (Washington: National Commission on Terrorist Attacks Upon the United States, 2004), 6, http://govinfo .library.unt.edu/911/staff_statements/911_TerrFin_Monograph.pdf, accessed August 6, 2013.

77. Bronson, *Thicker Than Oil*, 239–240.

78. Madawi Al-Rasheed, "Saudi Arabia: The Challenge of the U.S. Invasion of Iraq," in Rick Fawn and Raymond Hinnesbusch (eds.), *The Iraq War: Causes and Consequences* (Boulder: Lynne Rienner, 2006), 155–156.

79. Ibid., 156.

80. Ibid.

81. Niblock, *Saudi Arabia: Power, Legitimacy and Survival*, 168.

82. Al-Rasheed, "Saudi Arabia: The Challenge of the U.S. Invasion of Iraq," 159–160.

83. Hegghammer, *Jihad in Saudi Arabia*, 223.

84. For example, see the discussion about numbers captured, intelligence gathered, and likely insurgent movements in Christopher M. Blanchard et al., *Iraq: Regional Perspectives and U.S. Policy* (Washington: Congressional Research Service Report to Congress, October 6, 2009), 19–20.

85. Niblock, *Saudi Arabia: Power, Legitimacy and Survival*, 168–169.

86. The phases of this 2003–05 wave of terrorism are laid out in Hegghammer, *Jihad in Saudi Arabia*, 202–213.

87. Ibid., 217–226.

88. Gawdat Bahgat, "Saudi Arabia and the Arab-Israeli Peace Process," *Middle East Policy*, 14:3 (Fall 2007), 53.

89. Ibid., 53–54.

90. Joseph Kostiner, "Saudi Arabia and the Arab–Israeli Peace Process: The Fluctuation of Regional Coordination," *British Journal of Middle Eastern Studies*, 36:3 (December 2009), 429.

91. "They grumble, but they move," *The Economist*, March 4, 2004, http:// www.economist.com/node/2482203, accessed August 9, 2013.

92. Niblock, *Saudi Arabia: Power, Legitimacy and Survival*, 166.

93. See Toby C. Jones, "Saudi-Iraq Relations: Devolving Chaos or Acrimonious Stability?," in Henri Barkey, Scott B. Lasensky, and Phebe Marr (eds.), *Iraq, Its Neighbors, and the United States: Competition, Crisis, and the Reordering of Power* (Washington: United States Institute of Peace, 2011), especially 102–108.

94. Bronson, *Thicker Than Oil*, 253–254. "Threshold capacity" refers to a point where a state has the capability to assemble a working nuclear weapon quickly, but does not keep an assembled stockpile of nuclear weapons and does not declare itself a nuclear weapons' armed state.

95. Joshua Teitelbaum, *Saudi Arabia and the New Strategic Landscape* (Stanford: Hoover Institution Press, 2010), 31–33.

96. These figures are from the "Historical Data Work Book" attached to the *BP Statistical Review of World Energy 2013* (London: BP, June 2013), http://www.bp.com/en/global/corporate/about-bp/statistical-review-of-world-energy-2013.html, accessed July 30, 2013.

97. These are nominal figures, but even adjusted for inflation, the rise in overall income was dramatic. The figures are from the U.S. Energy Information administration page on "OPEC Revenues Fact Sheet" and the Excel spreadsheet covering 2004–2012 data attached to it, http://www.eia.gov/countries/regions-topics.cfm?fips=OPEC, accessed August 9, 2013.

98. Niblock with Malik, *The Political Economy of Saudi Arabia*, 183–185.

99. On this see *SPIRI Fact Sheet: Military Spending and Arms Procurement in the Gulf States* (Stockholm: Stockholm International Peace Research Institute, October 2010), 2–3, http://books.sipri.org/files/FS/SIPRIFS1010.pdf, accessed August 9, 2013.

100. Anthony H. Cordesman, *Saudi Arabia: National Security in a Troubled Region* (Santa Barbara: ABC-CLIO/Center for Strategic and International Studies, 2009), 140–141.

101. For a full text of the speech see "Text: Obama's Speech in Cairo," *The New York Times*, June 4, 2009, http://www.nytimes.com/2009/06/04/us/politics/04obama.text.html, accessed August 16, 2013.

102. "U.S. announces $60 billion arms sale for Saudi Arabia," *Reuters*, October 20, 2010, http://www.reuters.com/article/2010/10/20/us-usa-saudi-arms-idUSTRE69J4ML20101020, access August 16, 2013.

103. Mark Landler and Steven Lee Myers, "With $30 Billion Arms Deal, U.S. Bolsters Saudi Ties," *The New York Times*, December 29, 2011, http://www.nytimes.com/2011/12/30/world/middleeast/with-30-billion-arms-deal-united-states-bolsters-ties-to-saudi-arabia.html, accessed August 16, 2013.

104. Christopher M. Blanchard, *Saudi Arabia: Background and U.S. Relations* (Washington: Congressional Research Service Report for Congress, November 27, 2012), 5–6.

105. Anthony H. Cordesman and Robert M. Shelala II, *The Gulf Military Balance Volume III: The Gulf and the Arabian Peninsula* (Washington: Center for Strategic and International Studies, June 6, 2013), 89, http://csis.org/files/publication/130530_Iran_Gulf_Mil_Bal_III.pdf, accessed August 16, 2013. This document also provides detailed context on Saudi-Iranian rivalry and the U.S. role in the region, see pages 34–41 and 75–91 in particular.

106. Ibid., 90.

107. "Trade in Goods with Saudi Arabia," *United States Census Bureau, U.S. Department of Commerce* Web site, http://www.census.gov/foreign-trade/balance/c5170.html, accessed August 16, 2013.

108. Central Intelligence Agency, *CIA World Factbook* (Washington: Central Intelligence Agency, 2013), https://www.cia.gov/library/publications/the-world-factbook/geos/sa.html, accessed August 16, 2013, n.p.

109. Crystal A. Ennis and Bessma Momani, "Shaping the Middle East in the Midst of the Arab Uprisings: Turkish and Saudi Foreign Policy Strategies," *Third World Quarterly*, 34, 6 (2013), 1130–1134

110. This was widely reported at the time; see as examples Christopher Boucek, "U.S.-Saudi Relations in the Shadow of the Arab Spring," *Carnegie Endowment for International Peace* Web site, June 21, 2011, http://carnegieendowment.org/2011/06/21/u.s.-saudi-relations-in-shadow-of-arab-spring/1il#decline, accessed August 15, 2013; and Nawaf Obaid, "Amid the Arab Spring, a U.S. Saudi split," *The Washington Post*, May 15, 2011, http://articles.washingtonpost.com/2011-05-15/opinions/35263284_1_saudi-arabia-saudi-government-saudi-leaders, accessed August 16, 2013.

CHAPTER 4

Saudi Arabia and the Region

Saudi Arabia is both a regional military power in the Middle East and a significant economic power in the region and beyond it. It also faces strategic rivalry from its neighbors; all states do, to some extent, but in the Gulf this is accentuated by strong historical animosities and a lack of strategic architecture. Regional dynamics therefore impact Saudi Arabia, strongly shaping its strategic and security perceptions, and at times influencing its strategic culture. As stressed in the previous chapter, domestic factors and imperatives and foreign dynamics bear upon each other strongly, influencing Saudi views of its main strategic rivals, their views of the Saudis, the need for Riyadh's relationship with Washington, and the regional responses to the U.S. role in the Middle East.

FACTORS SHAPING SAUDI APPROACHES TO THE REGION

Saudi Arabia's strategic position and posture, and its security perspectives, are the product of both external and internal factors. Among the former, the regional power balance, rivalries between regional actors, and external intervention are important. Internally, dynamics within the Kingdom such as its strategic culture, elite relationships, and the leadership's ambitions and calculations are all notable. While their relative importance may fluctuate, all these dynamics have been both context and explanation for the role that Saudi Arabia has been able to take, and has chosen, over recent decades.

The broad changes in the international relations environment of the Middle East since the early 1990s have been important in allowing Saudi Arabia the incentive, scope, and opportunity to become more active regionally and even globally. As Kamrava has noted, there has been a gradual power shift from Arab republics such as Egypt and Syria to the Gulf in recent decades,[1] as a result of the end of the Cold War, the declining importance of traditional military power in the region, the globalization of the region, and the increased importance of economic power. The old powers of the Arab world are increasingly politically stagnant—the Gulf increasingly dynamic and energetic.[2] Moreover, it could also be argued that the demise of Arab nationalism freed the Saudi regime from many of the regional pressures it previously had faced, especially the need to be seen to be acting in accordance with overarching Arab interests. Legrenzi's idea that a specific *khaliji* (loosely translated as "Gulfy") identity has emerged in the Gulf, in the wake of Arab nationalism and with the economic rise of some Gulf states, is a convincing one.[3] A distinct subregional (i.e., Gulf) identity helps account for security arrangements such as the Gulf Cooperation Council (GCC), he argues, but it also helps explain the Gulf's rising economic power—and intra-GCC economic rivalry—and their willingness since the 1990s to act on their own, specific foreign policy incentives. For Saudi Arabia, this means there is now a strong incentive to lead and quietly dominate the Arab Gulf subregional security hierarchy, engage with the world diplomatically and strategically in support of economic goals, and even to become more activist when faced with rivalries in the wider Middle Eastern arena.

All of this makes for a very different international relations context to what the younger Saudi state faced from the 1950s through to the 1970s and even into the 1980s. The Kingdom has always engaged rivals for regional influence, most famously Egypt during the "Arab cold war" of about 1952 to 1970.[4] This included a proxy conflict with Egypt in the Yemeni civil war of 1962–1970, as well as the Saudis trying more generally to limit and undermine the influence of Arab nationalism in the region. The demise of Egyptian regional power after the death of Nasser in 1970, and again after Sadat's 1979 peace treaty with Israel, dramatically reduced the risks to the Saudi regime from Egypt. Later, and closer to the Kingdom's borders, older subregional rivalries and competition changed as well, reformatting and reorienting Saudi regional policies and security strategies. Iran, which under the Shah had been the main rival to Saudi Arabia for hegemony in the Gulf, was greatly diminished by the 1978–1979 revolution and then by the tortuous 1980–1988 Iran-Iraq War. This did not remove Iran as a rival, but stopped it from becoming a hegemon in the Gulf and allowed Saudi Arabia far greater reach and influence than it would otherwise have had. Then, in 1990, after Iraq foolishly invaded Kuwait and set in motion events that would lead to the 1991 Gulf War, Iraq too was neutralized as a strategic rival to Saudi Arabia. It remained a militarily capable neighbor and a source of some security threats, but after 1991, with the impact of sanctions and Saddam Hussein focused on his political survival, Iraq was no longer a major Gulf military power. The increased U.S. role in the Gulf after the 1991 war, while a problem for the Saudi regime in some ways, was useful for them, too, in increasing the perceived importance of the Kingdom to Washington and in the eyes of some Gulf actors.

Since that time, economic change and the impacts of globalization have increased Saudi influence and capability. Although the Kingdom lacks the population to dominate the Middle East, it wields enormous economic power because of its oil income, which also buys it other types of influence. The oil boom of 2004–2008 further helped Saudi Arabia, improving its budgetary position and letting it accumulate massive surpluses, which have been invested more cleverly and sustainably than in past oil booms.[5] The 2000s oil boom also paid for new qualitative military capability, and especially with the modernization of its forces in the 1990s and 2000s, it now possesses enough strategic reach and qualitative capacity to credibly offset Iran's and Iraq's quantitative military advantages. Within the GCC, the rise in Gulf economic power is a double-edged sword: it has given Saudi Arabia greater power relative to less wealthy but more populous large states, but it has also allowed small rentier states such as the United Arab Emirates (UAE) and Qatar to challenge Riyadh in the economic and "soft power" spheres, weak as they may be militarily. This had added additional complexity to intra-GCC relations.

This is not to deny that Saudi Arabia and its regime face real security threats. While Iran and Iraq have lost some power and strategic capacity relative to Riyadh since 1990, Iran is still a determined rival to Riyadh. The security environment has also become more complicated as new, often-unconventional threats have emerged, such as terrorism, weapons of mass destruction, food security, and water insecurity.[6] The regime is justifiably concerned about internal instability and the risk of it being stoked by external actors, given that it rules over a diverse set of social groups, and a society with multiple local and sectarian loyalties. At the same time, it faces all the traditional security concerns of a sovereign state: concerns over border security; a desire for regional stability, in the interests of economic development and regime security; and the need for secure transport and shipping lanes to and from its territory. The Saudi leadership, therefore, acts not only to enhance its strategic position and reach and to influence regional dynamics but also to defend its interests and ensure the stability and maintenance of its rule.

This suggests some merit in Gause's argument that the Gulf ought to be treated as a regional security complex; that is, as a subregion or collection of states that share a mutuality of fear or threat about each other and whose primary strategic and security concerns are each other rather than states further afield.[7] This approach helps explain why the Gulf lacks complete or proper security architecture, and is especially useful in explaining the posture of the major actors—Iran, Iraq, and Saudi Arabia—over the longer term toward each other, where a major actor can only feel secure if it possesses enough military capability to become perceived by the others as a threat. It also explains the desire of smaller states to seek some security and economic ties at a regional level with Saudi Arabia, while also ensuring a security guarantee from the United States. As Gause notes, this approach does not exclude consideration of other nearby states either, nor does it exclude the region from being part of a larger Middle East region.[8] It should not, moreover, preclude single-country studies such as this one from illuminating aspects of Gulf international relations, even if a single country study cannot explain Gulf regional security dynamics exhaustively.

Just as the U.S. relationship has been strongly influenced by domestic dynamics, such as the royal-*'ulema* dynamic and wider state-society issues, so too do such dynamics shape Saudi policy in the Gulf and Middle East. Saudi Arabia is the dominant conservative Sunni power in the Arab world; arguably, it is the dominant Sunni power overall at present, given Egypt's political malaise in the 2000s and then the turmoil during and after the uprisings against Mubarak. This, given the Al Saud alliance with the Wahhabi clergy, means that religion is tightly linked with Saudi foreign policy. The Kingdom promotes conservative social values and interests in its regional engagement, and the senior clerics are themselves foreign policy actors, providing support for religious initiatives and institutions abroad. As previously discussed, Saudi religious conservatism has at times influenced other aspects of foreign policy, including Saudi-U.S. relations.

Internal factors also inform state strategies and tactics in the international arena. In this regard, economic goals have been especially important in the past couple of decades. Oil prices and the politics of oil are an example. There is a correlation between oil prices and the Saudi regime's ability to balance its budget, buy arms, and pursue development initiatives that contribute to the regime's legitimacy and support. It is not coincidental that Riyadh's moves toward joining the World Trade Organization (WTO) began in the late 1990s, in a period of sustained, remarkably low oil prices. Such were the political pressures from budgetary strains, and the risks of them to the regime, that the elite undertook substantial economic liberalization and other reforms with the aim of obtaining WTO membership.[9] Saudi Arabia uses other international mechanisms and processes too, such as the Group of 20 (G20) and the GCC, to promote its economic interests—which in turn assist the legitimacy of the region—through international engagement. Even the U.S. relationship, as already noted, has strong economic drivers.

Perhaps the regime's greatest fears about internal instability and opposition come from its concerns about instability among the Saudi Shia. This, too, shapes its regional foreign policy. Indeed, it is a key reason why the regime interfered directly in Bahrain in March 2011 during the uprisings there. The Al Saud were deeply worried that the fall of the Sunni Al Khalifa regime in Bahrain—which, briefly, appeared possible at that time—would provide a colossal strategic boost to Iran and its influence on the Arab side of the Gulf, encouraging Tehran to support the Saudi Shia and to try to destabilize the Saudi regime. Ultimately, a Sunni-Shia rivalry is a key source of Saudi-Iranian rivalry, although there is a large measure of secular strategic and economic competition behind it, too. Still, sectarian concerns, especially about Iranian influence over the Saudi Shia, is a fundamental source of Riyadh's determination to be the dominant military force on the Arab side of the Gulf, and to compete with—and ideally, out-compete—Iran.

Finally, the post-2010 Arab uprisings created a new strategic imperative for Saudi Arabia and drove it to become more activist in the region, including in Bahrain and, later, in Syria. The Al Saud took the Arab uprisings as a sign to seek out more self-sufficiency and engagement in ensuring their regional security: "President Hosni Mubarak was pushed from power in what many influential Saudis saw as U.S. abandonment of a traditional ally. Ever since, the Saudis and other Gulf states have been arguing, publicly and privately, that U.S. power is waning and that they must take more responsibility for their own security."[10] This argument is convincing, given the bolder Saudi involvement in the region as of early 2011, especially the Saudi leadership's security emphasis in responding to the Arab uprisings. There is much at stake for Riyadh. Although the Saudis have made strategic gains out of the shift in economic and strategic power in the Middle East since the early 1990s, more recent events such as the Arab uprisings threaten many of these gains, and add to the already-complex environment in which foreign policy is conducted sand security sought.

SAUDI ARABIA AND THE GCC

The Cooperation Council for the Arab States of the Gulf—more commonly known as the Gulf Cooperation Council—is at one level very important for Saudi Arabia. It represents one of the more successful experiments—at least compared to others in the Middle East—in creating a subregional international arrangement, and has been quite effective in developing closer economic ties among its six member-states of Saudi Arabia, Bahrain, Kuwait, Oman, Qatar, and the UAE. That said, it remains far more modest than an economic bloc such as the European Union, where member-states surrender considerable economic sovereignty to a supranational organization.[11] The GCC has also showed some capacity to operate, albeit to a limited extent, as a security body. It has been partially successful as a shared institutional front for Arab Gulf states to pursue their security concerns; however, its inability to counter real military threats such as the August 1990 Iraqi invasion of Kuwait and the 1992 Iranian seizure of full control over Abu Musa island, emphatically demonstrate its very limited strategic authority in situations of real conflict. These examples are a reminder, moreover, that the GCC does not include two major Gulf actors, Iraq and Iran.[12]

In fact, the exclusion of Iran and Iraq from the GCC reflects both the timing of its creation and the underlying political goal for it as a conservative Arab monarchical grouping rather than a comprehensive subregional security body. The timing of its formation was the result of the outbreak of the 1980–1988 Iran-Iraq War, and Gulf monarchies' fears that the conflict could expand to include the wider region. There had long been a caution toward Iraq among many Gulf states, and the 1978–1979 Iranian revolution and then the commencement of Iranian-Iraqi hostilities added fears about revolutionary Iran to the conservative states' list of security concerns. Later, the 1990 Iraqi invasion of Kuwait would appear to support the fears of small states in the Gulf toward major powers in the subregion such as Iraq, while for the Saudis, a more united front among the conservative states would suit its goals for both greater security and, if possible, further strategic reach in the region.

Yet, for its members, the benefits of being in the GCC vary, and while its member-states devote varying amounts of attention and resources to the GCC, they all engage with it to a certain degree and in some key initiatives. The smaller member-states of Bahrain, Kuwait, Oman, Qatar, and the UAE engage with the GCC to the extent that it suits them, especially in economic and social initiatives and, to a more limited extent, by providing contributions to the GCC's rapid deployment force, Peninsula Shield. Ultimately, however, these states realize that even the combined military power of the GCC states is probably insufficient to repel a direct, major military attack from Iran or Iraq. The GCC's capability is an important deterrent to such belligerency, but not a guarantee of survival against a threat that serious. This has prompted all the GCC states into close military, security, and economic ties with the United States, a far more important security guarantee against external military threats for Gulf rulers than the GCC.

For Saudi Arabia, there is somewhat greater motivation in enhancing the capacity of the GCC, given the Saudi dominance of the Gulf: in 2009 Saudi Arabia accounted for some 46 percent of GCC GDP; a majority of the GCC's total population, around 67 percent; and some 83 percent of the GCC's total territorial area.[13] For the Saudis, therefore, the GCC is attractive as a body of like-minded conservative Sunni leaderships; as a mechanism for greater economic development and collaboration between member-states; and to a more limited extent for certain military benefits such as the coordination of air defenses and improved interoperability between GCC militaries. At the formation of the GCC, a key driver for the Saudis was the opportunity to fuse and strengthen its leadership on the Arabian Peninsula and over the smaller monarchies in the Gulf; previously, the Saudis had sometimes found their influence in these smaller states checked or offset by the links that the small states' leaders established with Iran or with major external powers such as the United Kingdom or later the United States.[14] The Iranian revolution and then the Iran-Iraq War both made the small Gulf states willing, as of the early 1980s, to accept a much stronger Saudi role in both the economic and security spheres. However, it also placed a natural limit on the degree to which such states would engage with the GCC, and at times they have tried to challenge Saudi dominance of it.

Between the structural problem of Iran's and Iraq's exclusion, and the propensity of states to engage with the GCC only as far as it suits their ambitions, the development of the GCC has always been very slow. Member-states have given it only a limited capacity to institutionalize security problems, and little true power, much less sovereignty, has been ceded by member-states' regimes. The 1980s and 1990s bear out some of these problems, and even more recently, the GCC has been more of a forum for states such as Saudi Arabia, rather than a genuine supranational body.[15] The GCC may transition in the future to a body with such supranational authority and more activist agendas, but it lacks them for the time being and remains instead a much more modest diplomatic forum.[16] Even the Saudis, keen to use the GCC as a means of greater influence over their smaller neighbors, have not tried to cede real sovereignty to the Council.

However, Saudi Arabia has still benefited from the GCC. They were able to use it as a vehicle for communication with Iran during the early years of the Iran-Iraq War, when Riyadh was supporting Iraq in that conflict, and at other times, it has been an outlet for the Saudis to be openly critical of Iran using a multinational body rather risking doing so directly.[17] The Saudis have also used the GCC to push for other diplomatic processes in the region, and almost certainly view the body as a forward defense against the spread of conflicts into the Arab Gulf monarchies.[18] In such respects, the GCC need not be an unbridled success or a body of deep international collaboration for it to serve the purposes of member-states, and this has especially been the case for Saudi Arabia.

Later, after the 1990–1991 Gulf War and again after September 11, 2001, and the 2003 Iraq War, Saudi influence over the smaller Gulf states was again somewhat offset by the closer relations that several of these states developed with the United States. These states realized that they could enhance their security not only via the relatively limited collective security arrangements within the GCC but also by incorporating into the U.S. defense posture in the region. For Kuwait and Qatar, as examples, hosting U.S. bases has proven as an attractive way to gain an implicit security underwriting from Washington. These two states were central to the U.S. war effort against Iraq in 2003 and to U.S. operations in the region in the years afterward. Critical too was the Saudi leadership's refusal to the United States fighting the 2003 Iraq War to any substantial degree from Saudi soil. Some states have remained close to—even clients of—Riyadh, most notably Bahrain. There, the Al Khalifa dynasty has relied on the Saudis to bolster their economy and guarantee the regime's survival. Even then, however, the United States and Bahrain have an established strategic relationship dating back to 1949, and with Bahrain hosting the U.S. Fifth Fleet, the Al Khalifa regime have a strong degree of implied U.S.-backed security as well. The other small states, Oman and the UAE, have also developed more sophisticated or detailed sets of ties with the United States since 1990, and moreover, all the small states have been able to enhance relations with the United States without it having a substantial impact on the level of popular domestic support enjoyed by the leadership. This is in contrast to Saudi Arabia, where the relationship with the United States has been controversial and at times a cause of popular resentment.

For Riyadh, the 1990s and especially the 2000s were marked by a mixture of goals in which the GCC needed to play a role. When rivals to Saudi Arabia emerged—Iraq in 1990, Yemen in the 1990s to a lesser extent, and above all Iran after its revolution but especially since 2003—the Saudis have typically sought to engage with them afield and keep them at bay on the Kingdom's doorstep. Thus, the Saudis tried to use the GCC in the 1990s and 2000s to develop hegemony among the small Gulf monarchies, build economic and commercial ties with these small allies, and engage more widely but selectively in the region using the GCC as a multilateral front. The Saudi balance of threat approach, and its ability to exert strong influence but not achieve hegemony in the broader Middle East, is why Riyadh has shifted position and changed policy toward some actors at various points in time. It is why it supported Iraq over Iran during the 1980–1988 war between the two, but then linked with Egypt, Syria, Turkey, and others to back the U.S.-led Gulf War against Iraq in 1990–1991. It is why, later, Riyadh both competed and collaborated with Mubarak's Egypt at various stages, depending on what was at stake, while at times being a rival with Mubarak for the position of chief Sunni Arab power. It is why the Saudis have been extremely critical of Israel at certain times, while in the 2000s going further than most Arab states ever had by proposing the formal, comprehensive 2002 peace plan.

The intra-GCC dynamics of the 1990s and 2000s also shifted because of the declining role of military capability and the rise in economic and "soft" cultural power, above all in the Gulf. Dubai, and through it the UAE, became a major economic actor in the Middle East and even globally as of the 1990s. Its rise as a stable regional headquarters for international investors and as a perceived case study in economic diversification and transformation gave it first a commercial, and later a popular, reputation in the West that the Saudis continued to lack. The development of Dubai was the most marked example of an active globalization and economic transformation, but was followed after the late 1990s by somewhat similar strategies by Qatar and, less successfully, Kuwait. For these small states, there was less incentive to collaborate deeply with Saudi Arabia when their economic importance was rising and since Saudi Arabia did not have the same degree of trade diversity or cultural openness that were becoming increasingly important as a measure of a state's power and influence. For most small Gulf states, the U.S. relationship underwrites their fundamental security from external threats, but also has let them expand their economic and soft power without needing the same endorsement from Riyadh than otherwise would probably be the case.

The GCC did continue to develop and deepen its economic, social, and other roles in the 1990s and 2000s, notwithstanding the changes to the security environment and economic dynamics of the Gulf. The Saudis pushed or supported initiatives in the GCC on specific economic, social, and technological ones, and security and defense arrangements grew too, if only to the extent that GCC dynamics permitted. Therefore, the GCC has had some achievements, especially in the economic and commercial areas. Its goal of creating in effect a single "economic citizenship," per Article 4 of its Charter, has largely occurred, with an almost complete freedom of movement and employment, and very liberal rules on economic interaction, for GCC member-states' nationals.[19] The GCC has also been important in trade and investment promotion, initiatives to encourage technology transfer and innovation in members' economies, and in areas such as patents and intellectual property. A customs union was announced in 2003, but in practice its implementation was plagued by difficulties, although it ultimately made some progress.[20] A common market, launched at the start of 2008, has been more significant, placing all GCC firms and nationals on the same footing across the GCC bloc and allowing them extensive freedom in trade and investment activities within the GCC economies.[21]

The security realm has seen a few modest successes, but overall has seen fewer achievements than in the economic realm. The Peninsula Shield rapid deployment force, which was created in 1982, is perhaps the key strategic achievement of the GCC. However, it is a small force, set at brigade strength for its initial 14 years and only expanded slightly, to around two brigades (some 7,000 troops in total) in 2006. This is despite occasional calls for it to be dramatically enlarged and its capabilities enhanced and for the necessity of such an expansion if the GCC is to become an important strategic body.

Other smaller security initiatives have included the development of a communications network, the coordination of military communications, and the development of a coordinated air defense capability and improved interoperability among GCC militaries. Closer intelligence coordination and exchange since 2004 has been important, especially for counterterrorism. Beyond such security initiatives, however, the GCC has achieved far less in the defense and security realm than might be expected of it. This is largely because of the strategic and policy variations between member-states. The six GCC leaderships have, at various times, disagreed over central matters such as the threat from terrorism; the 2003 Iraq War; policy toward Iran; whether to open membership to states such as Yemen and seek closer engagement with other regional actors; and whether individual states' bilateral free trade agreements with external powers are a positive or a negative for other GCC states.[22]

What the GCC has ignored, or failed to accomplish, is also telling. Not only did the common market fail to develop in its first decade or more, but through the 2000s the GCC had an ambitious plan to implement a single currency by 2010. This became shaky when Oman announced in 2006 that it would not participate for the foreseeable future, and by late in the decade the currency union plan had been shelved. It is unlikely to be revived in the foreseeable future, if ever. The failure to expand the rapid deployment force into a major capability is a reminder of the limited strategic outcomes from the GCC, even though member-states operate with substantial regional insecurity and agree on many aspects of security. An optimist might argue that the regular meetings that take place under the GCC banner, from annual leadership summits to quarterly ministerial-level meetings, are important opportunities for dialogue across security, economic, and other realms. This has some merit. Yet, for a body that is over three decades old, and whose member-states share so many similarities and perspective, the GCC's successes have been surprisingly modest.

The GCC took many observers by surprise when it announced in 2011 that it was offering membership to Jordan and Morocco. At a basic level, the offer to these potential new members—Jordan seems likely to join; Morocco may do so in the longer term but seems less keen—is simply a demonstration that the primary aim behind the GCC is to ensure coordination and collaboration among like-minded conservative Sunni Arab monarchies. In this light, the offers to Jordan and Morocco were simply designed to consolidate the region's monarchies, turning the GCC into a grouping based on regime type rather than geography. Coming only months after the post-2011 Arab uprisings began, the expansion of membership was also probably a counterrevolutionary move, using the GCC as the institutional mechanism for enhancing solidarity among the conservative Arab regimes. However, there is more to the new membership offers than just these reactive explanations. In the case of Jordan in particular, the offer has as its basis a security-economic exchange. It brings Jordan into the GCC partly for economic reasons but above all for its military capability and its geographic reach beyond the Gulf and across to the Levant, in particular adding Jordan's sizeable, quality armed forces to the GCC's existing defense capabilities. In exchange, Jordan is offered the chance to enhance its trade with the GCC, attract new investment, and act as a trade and investment bridge between the GCC and the Mediterranean. This suits the regime in Amman, which once had a thriving transit trade from Iraq, which ended with the Iraqi invasion of Kuwait. The offer of membership to Jordan may be one of convenience, but it is likely to proceed because it is so attractive to both sides. It also shows that, even if the successes of the GCC have been modest overall, and the goals for the GCC change over time, it still has utility for its members in some important respects.

For the Al Saud in particular, the GCC therefore serves an important purpose but is only one of several mechanisms it has available to pursue security and economic goals. A recent and controversial example of where the GCC is useful to Riyadh, in this case providing it with a veneer and validation for its actions, was the March 2011 intervention in Bahrain to suppress the uprisings there against the Al Khalifa dynasty. The Saudi and Emirati forces that were sent to Bahrain came from the GCC rapid deployment force, arriving under the banner of a GCC initiative to support the Bahraini leadership, and legitimized by reference to the mutual defense agreement that forms part of the GCC Charter.[23] This was a far more attractive option for the Saudi regime than a bilateral intervention. It also allowed Saudi Arabia (and to varying extents the other GCC leaderships) to mask their strategic concerns about Iran and its influence on the Arab side of the Gulf by declaring that the intervention, and follow-up financial and political support for the Bahraini regime, was based on supporting an ally and reestablishing regional stability.

Beyond the GCC dynamic, the 2011 Bahrain intervention was a reminder of just how deep Saudi Arabia's security concerns ran through neighboring states, and Bahrain above others. While Bahrain is only a small set of islands close to the Saudi northeast coast, it is of deep strategic value to the Saudi regime and its security. The primary concern in Riyadh is that the Al Khalifa remains in power as a key conservative Sunni ally of the Saudis and as a bulwark against the spread of Iranian influence across to the western side of the Gulf. Post-revolutionary Iran was thought to be behind an attempted coup against the Al Khalifa in 1981, and there have been suspicions since then that Tehran is seeking greater influence into Bahrain. More radically but still important, Iran has at times claimed sovereignty over Bahrain, based on the indirect control and at one time Persian possession of the islands from the sixteenth to the eighteenth centuries. Bahrain also matters for Gulf sectarian politics. The Al Khalifa are a Sunni minority, ruling a population that is some 70 percent Shia and which resents the ruling dynasty's treatment of the Shia majority. The Saudi regime is concerned about their own Shia population and its grievances,[24] and the proximity of Bahrain to Saudi Arabia's own Shia population links to this worry. Finally, Bahrain is of economic and strategic value to the Saudis. There are strong economic links between the two Kingdoms, including oil export pipelines running between them. The main Saudi super-field, *Ghawar*, has a pipeline running to Bahrain. Bahrain is also an economic force in itself as a commercial and financial hub with links on to other states such as Saudi Arabia, and of course the Saudis retain considerable investments in Bahrain in tourism, infrastructure, and some industrial plants.[25]

Bahrain is a classic example of the breadth and interrelatedness of Saudi security concerns in the Gulf, and of how traditional defense and security dynamics are increasingly interacting with other considerations. Similar arguments could be made, if to a lesser extent, about Saudi views toward other GCC states. The increased economic integration among the GCC states, for example, means that the trade and investment linkages between them have broadened and deepened in the past decade or so. Despite the rivalry that sometimes takes place in the economic sphere or over attempts to host major sporting or cultural events, the GCC states have sufficient ties between them to mean that an economic problem or security threat to one, is likely to have ramifications into the political economies of others. For the Saudis, the other GCC states are important because of the value of Saudi investments in many of them, the Saudi use of their financial and business services, and the transfers and exchange of technology, labor, and capital among them. At a strategic level, even if the GCC has been of limited success as a security body, the Saudis have interests in the security and stability of the smaller Gulf states, which they pursue through the GCC as well as bilaterally and using other channels. The U.S. role is important subregionally for security, too. Beyond the U.S.-Saudi relationship, Riyadh also sees its role as supporting the U.S. relationships with the smaller Gulf states, perhaps partly out of wanting to keep an eye on these relationships but also because they assume it will in turn support or reinforce their own relationship with Washington. Certainly, many aspects of these relationships, such as arms sales, interoperability, and shared defense capability improvements, rely on collaboration between several or all the GCC states and the United States.[26]

That noted, the specific bilateral relations between Saudi Arabia and the smaller monarchies beyond Bahrain have varied over time, and in a few cases have been tense or hobbled by a particular disagreement. There was notable tension in 2002 and 2003 over the then-imminent U.S.-led war against Iraq, which Kuwait, Qatar, and Bahrain openly supported, but which the Saudis viewed adversely. This flowed through into GCC tensions; in particular, the Saudi position was publicly stronger than the GCC's position, and more important, the GCC member-states disagreed fundamentally about the strategic case for the war.

In other cases, such as Qatar, specific matters have previously impaired relations with Riyadh. The Qatar-Saudi border was long disputed, and in the past there were several incidents on the border, including a clash in 1992 that killed two Qatari border guards.[27] The border issue is now resolved, after a 1999 agreement and then a final deal demarcating the border in 2001. However, Saudi-Qatari relations have been strained at other times, especially given the independent and activist foreign policy pursued by Qatari Emir Hamad (r. 1995–2013) and since then Tamim (r. 2013–). Prior to Hamad's rule, Qatar was very compliant in its dealings with Saudi Arabia, but no longer, while some Qatari initiatives such as the development of its bold, critical media channel Al-Jazeera has affected Saudi-Qatari relations when the Saudis have taken offense At Al-Jazeera's reporting on the Kingdom.[28] In short, it has been frustrating for Riyadh to discover that, despite its size and economic power, some smaller Gulf states can and will still pursue their own separate foreign policy and development goals, and seem to be doing so increasingly often and confidently.

Similar dynamics have impacted Saudi-UAE relations. First, a border dispute between the two has also lurked in their relationship and at times been a thorn. Although the boundary between the two was meant to have been resolved by a 1974 agreement, the UAE has not ratified this agreement, and in 2006 the UAE reignited the issue by complaining about the legality and some territorial losses in the 1974 agreement. While the border issue never caused a serious breach in relations, it is a persisting problem.[29] It has soured relations at times, as in August 2009 when travel between the two states was affected by a dispute over the map on UAE identity cards (which showed the UAE-claimed border rather than the border according to the 1974 agreement),[30] and then in March 2010 when there was a naval clash at sea over the Saudi-UAE maritime boundary.[31] Second, as with Qatar, the UAE has sought to pursue its own development and foreign policy goals, often at variance with Riyadh's preferences. For the UAE, the overriding driver in their external relations has been economic considerations, and they have, like Qatar and others, sought to construct their own close relationship with the United States. Again, these dynamics are a reminder of the limitations and hurdles that the Saudis face in trying to gain hegemony in the Arabian Peninsula. Even Oman has followed a unique foreign policy, being much more open to trade and other relations with Iran and seeking to balance the interests and influence of various actors in its foreign policy.[32]

Riyadh does not always get its way. In the case of Bahrain, it is much more likely to be able to exert influence, given how strongly the Al Khalifa rely on Riyadh for their political survival and seeks such influence given the rivalry with Iran that is played out over Bahrain.[33] Yet, even then, at times the priorities of the two have been at variance: Bahrain's pursuit of a free trade agreement with the United States in 2005 created considerable tensions with Saudi Arabia, because it was seen by Riyadh as undermining the economic initiatives and priorities of the GCC.[34] However, after the post-2011 Arab uprisings, and the threat that Bahraini protestors posed to the Al Khalifa, the Saudis arguably have again gained greater influence over Bahrain than in the years prior.

In contrast, Saudi Arabia and Kuwait have quite solid and well-founded relations.[35] The two have a shared concern about Iraqi power and the risk of Baghdad again threatening neighbors as it did with the invasion of Kuwait in 1990, as well as close societal and cultural ties, backed by strong economic links. The relationship is also an historical one between the two ruling families: it was the Kuwaiti Al Sabah family that provided Ibn Saud with safe exile during his youth and it was from there that he launched his successful campaign to retake Riyadh in 1902 and establish the third Saudi state. Even then, minor issues remain. There is a small underlying border dispute between the two over two islands,

Qaruh and Umm al Maradim, and as mentioned earlier, the two were at variance over the U.S.-led 2003 Iraq War. Nonetheless, the general characteristic within the GCC has been that Saudi Arabia has had stronger ties, and been able to exert greater influence, over the more northern states of Kuwait and Bahrain, while the central and southern Gulf states, being closer to Iran and having strong trade and economic links with it, have sought more of a balance in their relationships. While Qatar, the UAE, and Oman have remained close to Saudi Arabia, they have also sought to maintain economic links and cordial diplomatic relations with Iran, and above all tried to avoid anything that might destabilize the Gulf. This has meant that Saudi Arabia, while the main economic power on the Arabian Peninsula and far and away the most militarily powerful member of the GCC, has not been able to simply dictate GCC policy or the policies of its member-states. Riyadh has had to negotiate and bargain with other GCC states on varying terms, and has not always gotten its way.

SAUDI-IRAN RELATIONS

As already noted, Saudi Arabia has long been a rival for influence in the Gulf and beyond that in the wider Middle East. But, the Saudi will to power has been checked by the quantitatively larger military capacity of Iraq prior to 1990, and above all remains contained by the enormous numerical military strength of Iran. Strategic rivalry is only one aspect of the dynamic between these two subregional powers, however, and the tensions and animosity between them are multiple, long established, and dictated by various dynamics. A combination of conflicting strategic cultures, history, regional-level rivalry, and the security dynamics of the Gulf all account for the complications, contentions, and at times the enmity, that have plagued Saudi-Iranian relations.

At the highest levels of strategic culture and security perceptions, there is a propensity for Saudi Arabia and Iran to see the other as a threat or rival.[36] Both claim a particular importance in history and to the region. Saudi Arabia feels unique in being home to Mecca and Medina, the two holiest cities in Islam, and given that Islam originally emerged in what is today Saudi Arabia. Iran, meanwhile, claims a three-millennium civilizational history and is the global center of Shiism and the largest Shia state in the modern world. There is something bordering on chauvinism in how the two see themselves. To the Saudis, the modern state is simply a new rational-legal construct overlaid on a society that is ancient and which has had cultural, trade, and other links with the rest of the world for several millennia. Modern Saudi Arabia also sits at the geographical heartland of the Arab world. In contrast, Iran sees the Arab side of the Gulf as an area that has historically been underdeveloped, and uses this as a benchmark against which to claim that its own culture is highly refined and developed through three thousand years or more of great empires and societies.

Many of these issues lead to friction when one side considers that the other does not appreciate its own historical perspective or sense of accomplishment, or where historical dynamics such as past conflicts or conquests are presumed to still drive diplomatic strategy today. Other historical bequests, especially the sectarian difference, are especially important in driving concerns about each other. The perceived rise of Iranian influence and power in the Middle East since the 2003 Iraq War, and the Saudi fear that there is a Shia resurgence occurring in Iraq that threatens to spread elsewhere in the Arab world, has added further to the strength of this dynamic in shaping Saudi security perceptions.

Particular later events have been more concrete in their impact. While Saudi Arabia and Iran were the "twin pillars" of U.S. doctrine toward the region during the Nixon administration, since the 1978–1979 Iranian revolution the tension, and at times animosity, between the two subregional powers has been substantial. While Iraq was omitted from the GCC at the latter's creation primarily because it was a strategic rival with Saudi Arabia, Iran was excluded for far more substantive reasons. It was seen as a destabilizing force in the region, and as posing a genuine threat to Bahrain and, via its reasserted Shia identity, to stability in other states with large Shia populations such as Kuwait and Saudi Arabia itself. Iran's claims that it sought to "export" its revolution fueled such fears. For these reasons, the Arab Gulf states backed Iraq in the Iran-Iraq War, albeit to varying degrees, but Kuwait, the UAE, and Saudi Arabia were especially firm in so doing.[37] This caused genuine tensions with Iran in the 1980s, including cases of direct and public Iranian threats against Riyadh.[38]

Later issues into the 1990s and 2000s have proven even more substantial, and many remain hurdles in the relationship to the present day. The strategic and security setting after 1988 changed somewhat, with Iran needing time to reconstruct its economy after the war with Iraq, and then with changes in policy and approach after the death of Iranian supreme leader Ayatollah Khomeini in 1989. Still, there remained an underlying rivalry and military competition between Iran and Saudi Arabia. This was, and remains, driven in large part by the nature of the two states. Iran is a geographically and economically diverse state with a population of some 76 million, as of 2012, but its wealth per capita is modest compared to Saudi Arabia—Iran has around 25–30 percent of Saudi Arabia's nominal GDP per capita—and its economy has been eroded by war, mismanagement, and sanctions over several decades. In contrast, Saudi Arabia has considerable wealth per capita and access to U.S. military platforms and weapons, but with a population of only around 27 million—less than 21 million of them Saudi nationals—the Kingdom does not have the same geographic or population base as Iran. As a result, the two have competed in strategic and military terms in markedly different ways. Saudi Arabia has sought a qualitative advantage in platforms and equipment, and by having an important security relationship with the United States. In contrast, Iran has competed through the size of its armed forces, through its asymmetrical combat capabilities, and by encouraging a strong nationalist zeal in its military and across society. Such differential competition, however, is a risk because it means that both qualitative and quantitative changes by one side can be construed as a threat, and certainly an enhanced capability, by the other. Such rivalry also leads smaller states to feel less secure and thus to pursue closer ties with Riyadh and Washington, while inhibiting the development of the very security architecture that might otherwise have emerged and subdued such rivalry.

Adding to this is a genuine variation in how the two states perceive themselves. Iran truly believes that it is a nonaggressive force for stability in the Gulf, while the Saudis view it as a serious threat given the past calls for the export of revolution, the perception of Iranian involvement in Bahrain, and the Iranian seizure from the UAE of the Abu Musa and Greater and Lesser Tunb islands in the lower Gulf. Meanwhile, the Saudis see themselves as vulnerable, because of their oil wealth but much smaller population than Iran or Iraq, while Iran sees them as exporting ultraconservative Sunni Islam and seeking a strategic reach far beyond what they should be demanding.

The Saudi relationship with the United States is itself a dynamic in Saudi-Iranian relations, given the hostility between Tehran and the United States since the Iranian revolution. Iran perceives Saudi Arabia as being, in effect, a U.S. proxy in the region, and as a result acting against most local interests and as a force for instability in the Gulf. As an element of this, Iran also sees Saudi Arabia as seeking to check Iranian influence on behalf of the United States, given past U.S. basing in the Kingdom, the level of U.S.-Saudi trade and especially of arms sales. At times specific issues have arisen, as in October 2011 when the United States claimed that Iran had been planning to assassinate the Saudi ambassador in Washington, Adel al-Jubeir—something that led to venomous rhetoric by both the Saudis and Iranians, and increased tensions coming so soon after (or perhaps because of) the March 2011 Saudi intervention in Bahrain.[39]

Iranian attitudes have been hardened by what they see as an unfair international response to their development of a nuclear capability. They are also angered by U.S. sanctions on Iran; both those introduced because of the nuclear issue, and others that date back as far as the Iranian revolution. These two issues have accentuated the other Saudi-Iranian problems already mentioned, and contributed to an Iranian perception that the Saudis are opportunistically trying to undermine Iran economically and diplomatically through the nuclear issue and sanctions. For the Saudis, however, this all looks very different. To them, the nuclear issue is a profound strategic issue. Riyadh fears that Iran might be seeking a nuclear weapons capability or a threshold capability, which in either case would completely restructure the strategic setting of the Gulf. Above all, it would give Iran something close to unchallengeable hegemony in the region, and even if Saudi Arabia could gain security under a U.S. nuclear umbrella, Riyadh's relative power and sense of security would be devastated by an Iranian nuclear bomb or even by realistic ambiguity about Tehran's capability. This is probably why the Saudis have previously appeared supportive of a U.S. strike on Iran. Among the U.S. cables leaked by Wikileaks, some of the most significant are those that demonstrate just how seriously Riyadh considered Iran's nuclear program to be, with the Saudi king supporting a U.S. strike on Iran, if necessary, during meetings with U.S. officials in the mid-2000s.[40] More recently, although Hassan Rouhani's election as president of Iran in 2013 seems to have brought to power someone interested in improving Iran's foreign relations, and allowed for an interim nuclear deal with the international community, whether this will positively impact relations with Saudi Arabia is far from certain. The two remain intense rivals in Syria's civil war and are competing with or suspicious of each other in various other arenas. It will take a marked shift by the leaders and foreign policy elite of both states to significantly improve the relationship and reduce the tensions in it.

All of these dynamics have created the underlying mistrust and tension that has steered particular events in the relationship. It has meant, for example, that the two have engaged in indirect confrontation and proxy conflict, where either it has suited their purposes or where they have feared giving some strategic opportunity or gain to the other if they do not act. This mistrust and tension has surfaced when particular incidents have occurred. Clashes at the annual Hajj pilgrimage in Mecca, most notably in 1987, and the uprisings in Saudi Arabia at several times, have stoked Saudi suspicions of Iran and heightened tensions that were often already significant. Finally, strategic culture has meant that oil and a shared interest in stable energy trade has not usually brought the two sides together. Only to a very limited extent have the two states' views converged, such as in the mid-late-1980s when oil prices were especially low and they both felt financially squeezed as a result. At other times, in contrast, their rivalry and fears have extended into the energy sector. Saudi Arabia sees oil income as giving Iran a greater military capability than it would otherwise have, and a stronger capacity to intervene in other states. Iran sees Saudi Arabia as a powerful swing producer able to attract more trade and investment than Iran, and interprets this as a risk.

SAUDI ARABIA IN THE WIDER MIDDLE EAST REGION

The Saudi-Iranian rivalry has regularly positioned the two states on opposing sides of regional conflicts and enmities. One of the most prominent and enduring examples is the Israeli-Palestinian arena, in which the two sides seek to gain leverage with Palestinian client groups and an international role for themselves as external actors. Another is in Lebanon, where both sectarianism and the symbolic and commercial opportunities available there have motivated Saudi Arabia and Iran to seek political influence.[41] The Saudi role in these two dynamics, and the Saudi patron-client networks in both, are often explained primarily as deriving from symbolic goals: of rivalry in the Gulf spreading to other parts of the region; of Saudi hopes to embarrass Iran or to cow it by ensuring it suffers some tactical defeats around the region; and by reinforcing Saudi claims to be a dominant diplomatic actor and key strategic player in the region. This is part of what motivates Riyadh. However, also important are the more practical and tangible goals of engaging Iran indirectly in these arenas. For one thing, there are broader rivalries at play. Not only is Saudi Arabia seeking to curtail Iranian influence in Lebanon and among the Palestinians but also Syrian influence (Syria is the closest Arab ally of Iran, but is a rival of Saudi Arabia, too) and even Egyptian and Jordanian, especially the former given the competition between Cairo and Riyadh over leadership of the Sunni Arab world. Furthermore, Lebanon and the Palestinian issue link back to Al Saud domestic legitimacy, and the latter in particular demands some involvement by the Saudi regime as a result. The Arab-Israeli issue is widely watched and of broad, deep concern in the Arab world, including among Saudis. By supporting the Palestinians and their aspirations—and being seen to be doing so at home—the Saudi leadership is also seeking to solidify its support and legitimacy in the domestic context.

Other regional conflicts and issues have engaged Saudi Arabia and Iran in indirect competition or proxy conflict too, often for similar reasons of prestige, leadership aspirations, sectarianism, and economic ambitions. One has been the Houthi conflict in Yemen, where the Sunni Yemeni regime of Ali Abdullah Saleh, and the subsequent elite after Saleh's removal from power in 2012, have fought against an uprising led by the Houthi (sometimes "Huthi") family and drawing support from people in the mostly Shia areas of northern Yemen.[42] The conflict began in mid-2004, and despite the diversion of a popular uprising against Saleh in 2011 and his removal in early 2012, the uprising in northern Yemen continues at the time of this writing (early 2014). Over much of the conflict, the Yemeni and Saudi regimes both assumed Iranian involvement in support of the Houthis, and often publicly alleged it. There were regular claims in the late-2000s that Iranian revolutionary guards, and fighters from the Iranian-backed Lebanese Hezbollah militia, had provided advice and training to Houthi combatants. Iranian naval deployments in the northern Indian Ocean after 2009, ostensibly to help counter piracy in the area, have often been construed by the Yemenis and Saudis as in fact aimed at influencing the Yemeni government in the Houthi conflict. The Saudis even became directly involved in the conflict in 2009, undertaking airstrikes against Houthi forces after they had crossed the border into Saudi Arabia and killed two Saudi border guards in the process.[43] This in itself angered Tehran, but to the Iranians the nature of the conflict is seen very differently. Yemeni Shia are seen by Iran as an oppressed group, with that oppression blessed and aided by the Saudis. It is also a chance, more opportunistically, for Iran to pull the Saudis into a conflict close to their border. To both sides, ultimately, there are political justifications, both ideological and practical, for engaging with the Yemeni conflict.

There are several key relationships and roles played by Saudi Arabia in the greater Middle East region, and indeed beyond it, which are not derived from the rivalry with Iran and instead serve and further Riyadh's security interests and needs in other ways. The Saudi-Iraqi relationship is worth exploring, as it is the other great subregional power rivalry—at least in the past and especially from the start of the republican period in Iraq in 1958 through to the 1990–1991 Gulf War or even the 2003 war—that has occupied much of the Saudi elite's attention. For much of the early republican period relations were tense.[44] The Saudis suspected that Iraq was trying to destabilize the Kingdom by sponsoring or supporting radical political movements; this, recall, was the period when pan-Arabism was still a genuine domestic threat to the Saudi regime. As Iraqi foreign policy became more moderate in the latter-1970s, relations with Saudi Arabia began to improve,[45] and albeit opportunistically, were further improved by the 1978–1979 Iranian revolution and the threat that both Iraq and Saudi Arabia perceived from post-revolutionary Iran. Obviously, the 1980–1988 Iran-Iraq War profoundly shaped Iraq's perspective on regional security and power dynamics, although Saudi support and funding for Iraq's war effort was driven by pragmatism and a fear of revolutionary Iran, not by warmth toward Baghdad, which the Saudis continued to view with great suspicion and presumed to be a longer-term rival or threat.[46]

Saudi suspicions of Iraq were seemingly confirmed by the August 1990 Iraqi invasion of Kuwait, although Saddam's grievances against Kuwait were quite specific and few could have been applied to Saudi Arabia as well. Even the March 1989 Saudi-Iraqi nonaggression pact meant little to the Saudis when the decisive moment arrived where Iraqi forces were in control of Kuwait and reached the Kuwaiti-Saudi border. To the Saudis there was a genuine risk that Saddam would push on into northeastern Saudi Arabia, and Riyadh was poorly equipped to repel such an attack. While the Saudis hoped for a diplomatic resolution to the crisis in the lead-up to the January–February 1991 war, the reality is that "Once they accepted the U.S. military presence [in Saudi Arabia], the Saudis were in effect committed to the U.S. strategy of confrontation with Saddam."[47]

The subsequent U.S.-led 1990–1991 Gulf War came to affect Saudi-Iraqi relations in several ways. Perhaps most important, the wide scale destruction of Iraqi military and economic power removed Iraq as a genuine existential threat to Saudi Arabia; no longer did Baghdad possess the ability to overrun Saudi Arabia and defeat its military comprehensively, and the United States had established a precedent against such aggression by coming to the aid of Kuwait and reversing the Iraqi occupation. At the same time, the U.S.-Saudi relationship expanded and deepened greatly as a result of the war.[48] Second, contentious among Saudis at the time, the fact that the United States kept some of its forces in the Kingdom for years after the war probably provided an even stronger security guarantee, which made the chance of any serious Iraqi attack on Saudi Arabia negligible. Third, the conflict motivated the Saudis to push the GCC toward a greater security role. While, as already discussed, this has been of only limited success, the fact that Saudi Arabia and several other GCC states sought, after 1991, to achieve greater defense self-reliance and improved qualitative capability is important. The 1990s and 2000s witnessed, as discussed in a previous chapter, a substantial modernization of the Saudi armed forces and security services, which can be explained in large measure by the shock that the Saudi political leadership felt as a result of the 1990–1991 Gulf War.

The following decade at the start of the 2000s came to be especially catastrophic for Iraq, and while the 2003 Iraq War and the removal of Saddam's regime further weakened Iraq and its capacity to threaten the region, the post-2003 dynamics in Iraq were complex and extremely challenging for Saudi Arabia to maneuver in. The removal of Saddam Hussein was, at one level, welcomed by the Saudis and others (especially Kuwait). Diplomatic relations were reestablished in 2004,[49] and the beginnings of new aid, trade, and cultural links between the two became evident by the mid-2000s[50] and especially as of 2010 or so.[51] Yet, this has been neutralized to a great extent by the rise of Shia power in Iraq and the greater potential for Iran to develop ties with the post-Saddam Iraqi government and other political actors. There has been considerable Saudi mistrust, even enmity, toward the post-Saddam Iraqi government, and especially toward Iraqi prime minister Nouri al-Maliki personally and toward his administration. The Saudi hostility toward al-Maliki, who they viewed as being too sympathetic toward Iran, dates to around early 2007, and in the years after that there were multiple snubs by the Saudis[52] and disagreements between the leaders of the two states. The Saudis have some reason to be anxious about al-Maliki if only because the strategic opportunity that regime change in Iraq gave Iran was substantial; it "raised the possibility for unprecedented Iranian influence in Iraq," and Iran did play a much greater role in Iraq, including in security and political roles, after 2004.[53] While the Iranians probably viewed post-Saddam Iraq as an opportunity to consolidate some of their interests there and reduce the chances of future Iraqi aggression against Iran, to the Saudis, there was a much deeper fear at work, in which Iran would transform Iraq into a Shia-dominated client state,[54] and in turn that this would create a new and grave threat to Saudi security along the Kingdom's northern flank. Again, it is a reminder of the depth of strategic concern in Saudi Arabia toward Iraq, but even more than that, it is a sign of the degree to which Saudi-Iranian rivalry and tension impacts Saudi relations with other states in the region.

It is also another reminder of the Saudi leadership's fears about sectarian threats. The empowerment of Iraqi Shia after the removal of Saddam has concerned, even panicked, the Saudi elite, and at least some of the animosity toward al-Maliki is also the result of Saudi sectarian worries and the view that the Iraqi prime minister embodies, or even promotes, sectarian disunity.[55] For the Saudis, there was and remains a genuine anger at the state of Iraq's Sunni population, including their reduced power after 2003 and, during the worst of Iraq's civil conflict over 2004–2008 or so, an anger that the Sunni were such routine victims of sectarian violence and crime. While the Saudis had not supported the 2003 war, once it took place they then were vocal in calling for the United States to remain in Iraq and to stabilize it before attempting any withdrawal. They argued that any premature U.S. departure would lead to a massacre of Iraq's Sunnis by the newly empowered Shia majority.[56] This shows some of the deeper fears that the Saudi leadership held about Iraq's future at the time, although it obviously ignores the enormous financial and moral support, which came from Saudi Arabia to the Iraqi Sunni population during this period of civil conflict in the mid-2000s.[57]

Still more important for Riyadh was the domestic aspect of what was happening in Iraq, and the risk that political stability inside the Kingdom was threatened by an invigorated Iraqi Shia political force. The Saudi concerns were that their own Shia population would be agitated by Iraq's Shia or by Iran, or that the Saudi Shia would use regime change in Iraq as a reason to demand greater freedoms or power within the Saudi political system.[58] This was not only a sectarian concern, however, and the Saudis were concerned about various types of "spill-over" from Iraq, including terrorism, radicalization of their Sunni population, threats from large-scale refugee movements, and even from worsening international relations within the region if Iraq collapsed.[59] This is yet another reminder of the emphasis that domestic political risks and imperatives are often given in Saudi foreign policy making, and especially of the interactions between sectarianism, regime maintenance, and regional strategic rivalry in several Gulf states, including Saudi Arabia.

The Saudi response to the post-2011 Arab uprisings brought to the surface several of the Saudi leadership's key fears for the region and for its own survival. Bahrain has been perhaps the most urgent example of the Al Saud need to support allied Arab regimes, as discussed. The same issues—sectarianism, strategic rivalry with Iran, and the Saudi goal of ensuring stability among the conservative Arab monarchies—drive the Saudi response to the Arab uprisings beyond the Gulf and in the wider region. By its very nature, the Saudi regime has always sought to counter revolutionary impetuses in the region, and this is true too of any unrest, which might unsettle not only the existing power structures of allied or like-minded states, but even those that threaten more distant, even barely tolerable states. If the Al Saud cannot dominate the Middle East, then the next best path is to ensure political stability and strategic balance instead.

It is notable how irate the Saudi royal leadership was by the perception that the United States had failed to properly and more fully support Egyptian president

Hosni Mubarak as protests there unfolded in early 2011. To the Saudi regime, Mubarak's loyalty to the United States and support for its aims in the region demanded in return a far stronger level of U.S. support, and more public support, than what was provided. Even if the uprising in Egypt had the potential to weaken a key Sunni Arab rival of Saudi Arabia, countering this was the Saudi fear of a "reborn" Egypt, poor but energized by revolution.[60] Mubarak's eventual removal from power in February 2011 created a genuine sense of duplicity and infidelity among the Saudi elite, and with the U.S. concern about the Saudi intervention in Bahrain as well there was significant new tension in the relationship as of spring 2011.[61]

More generally, the Saudis became deeply worried about the range of other changes and upheavals in the region in 2011, including dynamics in North Africa, the risk of state collapse in Yemen, and protests elsewhere, all of which had, in Riyadh's eyes, the potential to stoke instability, sectarianism, and political Islamism.[62] Later, when Egyptian president Muhammad Morsi was removed from power by the Egyptian military in early July 2013, it was no surprise that the Saudis prominently backed Egypt's military: to the Al Saud, a populist, democratically oriented Muslim Brotherhood was a deep threat to regional stability but above all to Al Saud legitimacy at home.[63]

Perhaps the greatest concern for the Al Saud from the Arab uprisings has been the Syrian civil war. The Saudis became increasingly interested and involved in the conflict, especially as the level of violence increased from spring 2012 onward and as Syria increasingly became a battleground for Sunni-Shia—mostly Saudi-Iranian—rivalry and strategic competition. For the Saudi leadership, Syria is a pressing matter. If Iran were to prop up the al-Asad regime in Damascus or manage to replace it with another elite sympathetic to Tehran, this would be a threat to Saudi strategic interests but also at the sectarian level. Saudi policy on Syria also comes from a fear of the Syrian conflict spreading into neighboring states such as Jordan and Lebanon. The upsides of the Syrian conflict for the Saudi regime are lesser, but include, if al-Asad is removed and replaced with a Sunni leadership, the chance to check Iran's influence in the Arab world, perhaps even to diminish it significantly, by ending or greatly weakening Tehran's only strategic alliance in the Arab world. As a result, the Saudis have engaged in proxy conflict with Iran in Syria, supplying arms to Syrian rebels, appointing their intelligence chief Prince Bandar bin Sultan to the project to topple al-Asad, and pressuring the United States to respond resolutely to al-Asad's alleged use of chemical weapons in the conflict several times in 2013.[64]

The complexity of the Syrian conflict and of the proxy actors and sponsors engaged in it is highlighted by some of the points of disagreement between the Saudis and other anti-Asad actors. Among the GCC members, there has been considerable tension between Saudi Arabia and Qatar over which opposition groups should be supported, especially with arms transfers. This accounts for the Saudis sending arms through Jordan to specific, more moderate groups, compared to Qatar backing more Islamist opposition forces and sending arms to them through Turkey and into northern Syria.[65] Saudi Arabia's strong advocacy of international action against Asad for his alleged use of chemical weapons was also a point of difference with many allies. The Saudis were implicitly critical of the September 2013 U.S.-Russian deal over Syria's chemical weapons, claiming through media and indirect statements that a diplomatic outcome could strengthen al-Asad or encourage his regime to intensify the civil war.[66] Despite concerns that the situation in Syria was aggravated in 2012 and beyond by the proxy actions of regional and international actors, there was little chance that the Saudis would not become involved in the conflict. With Iran on the opposing side, fighting for the very survival of its only Arab ally, too much was at stake strategically in Syria for the Saudis to ignore the conflict or leave intervention in it to others. Coming as it did out of the Arab uprisings, and given the Saudi sense of insecurity in the region once the uprisings commenced, Syria by 2013 was perhaps the key strategic battleground for the Saudi regime, and one which, once resolved, the Al Saud assumed would dictate the security environment in the Middle East for years afterward.

The above issues constitute only some of the Saudi regime's foreign policy priorities and areas of strategic and diplomatic participation. Beyond the region, the Saudis have links with major external actors, not only with the United States, of course, but with other powers. Increasingly they are engaging with emerging economic and strategic Asian powers such as China, India, and others, something that is taken up again in Chapter 6. Furthermore, and beyond economics and simple security concerns, Saudi foreign policy also links to religion, including to the unique royal-cleric bargain that underpins domestic politics in the Kingdom. The Saudis consider their international role to include the propagation of Wahhabi Islam, and the promotion of Islamic values in general, through the Muslim world. The state acts in support of this strategy in some situations, but the clerics also have considerable scope to engage internationally toward such ends. This is discussed in the chapters that follow as well, as the discussion now turns to the question of Islam and security in Saudi Arabia, including the Saudi role in the rise of political Islamism in recent decades and above all after September 11, 2001.

NOTES

1. Mehran Kamrava, *Qatar: Small State, Big Politics* (Ithaca: Cornell University Press, 2013), see especially 16–40.

2. Ibid., 17–19.

3. Matteo Legrenzi, *The GCC and the International Relations of the Gulf: Diplomacy, Security and Economic Coordination in a Changing Middle East* (London: I. B. Taurus, 2011), 50–51.

4. Malcolm H. Kerr was the creator of the term "Arab Cold War" to describe the rivalries between Nasser's pan-Arabist, republican Egypt and the more conservative monarchies, especially Saudi Arabia. See for example Malcolm H. Kerr, *The Arab Cold War: Gamal 'Abd al-Nasir and His Rivals, 1958-1970*, 3rd ed. (London: Oxford University Press, 1971).

5. Bessma Momani and Matteo Legrenzi, "Introduction: The Geo-Economic Power of the Gulf," in Matteo Legrenzi and Bessma Momani (eds.), *Shifting Geo-Economic Power of the Gulf: Oil, Finance and Institutions* (Farnham: Ashgate, 2011), 1.

6. Nora Bensahel and Daniel L. Byman, "Introduction," in Nora Bensahel and Daniel L. Byman (eds.), *The Future Security Environment in the Middle East: Conflict, Stability, and Political Change* (Santa Monica: RAND Corporation, 2004), 1–2.

7. F. Gregory Gause III, *The International Relations of the Persian Gulf* (Cambridge: Cambridge University Press, 2010), 3–4.

8. Ibid.

9. On Saudi accession to the WTO, see as one of many sources William Clatanoff, C. Christopher Parlin, Robert Jordan, Charles Kestenbaum, and Jean-Francois Seznec, "Symposium: Saudi Arabia's Accession to the WTO: Is a 'Revolution' Brewing?," *Middle East Policy*, 13, 1 (Spring 2006), 1–23.

10. David Ignatius, "Saudi Arabia Stirs the Middle East Pot," *The Washington Post*, August 23, 2013, http://www.washingtonpost.com/opinions/david-ignatius-saudi-arabia-stirs-the-middle-east-pot/2013/08/21/51dce448-09c5-11e3-8974-f97ab3b3c677_story.html, accessed August 26, 2013.

11. A full background on the structure and governance of the GCC is beyond the scope of this book, but for more information on this see Legrenzi, *The GCC and the International Relations of the Gulf*, especially Ch. 2 (27–39).

12. Joseph Kostiner, "GCC Perceptions of Collective Security in the Post-Saddam Era," in Mehran Kamrava (ed.), *International Politics of the Persian Gulf* (New York: Syracuse University Press, 2011), 94.

13. These figures are presented in Alexis Antoniades, "The Gulf Cooperation Council Monetary Union," in Mehran Kamrava (ed.), *The Political Economy of the Persian Gulf* (London: Hurst & Company, 2012), 180.

14. Gause, *The International Relations of the Persian Gulf*, 72.

15. Matteo Legrenzi, "Gulf Cooperation Council Diplomatic Coordination: The Limited Role of Institutionalization," in Jean-François Seznec and Mimi Kirk (eds.), *Industrialization in the Gulf: A Socioeconomic Revolution* (Abingdon: Routledge, 2011), 103.

16. Ibid., 103–104.

17. This point is made several times in Ibid., especially over 104–111.

18. Kostiner, "GCC Perceptions of Collective Security in the Post-Saddam Era," 108.

19. Legrenzi, *The GCC and the International Relations of the Gulf*, 58–60.

20. "Profile: Gulf Co-operation Council," *BBC News*, February 15, 2012, http://news.bbc.co.uk/2/hi/middle_east/country_profiles/4155001.stm, accessed September 25, 2013.

21. For a brief summary of some of these, and other, initiatives of the GCC see Ibid.

22. Noted in "Profile: Gulf Co-operation Council," n.p. and explored in more detail in Legrenzi, *The GCC and the International Relations of the Gulf*, passim. See also Reyadh Alasfoor, *The Gulf Cooperation Council: Its Nature and Achievements. A Political Analysis of Regional Integration of the GCC States, 1979–2004* (Lund: Lund University, 2007).

23. Ethan Bronner and Michael Slackman, "Saudi Troops Enter Bahrain to Help Put Down Unrest," *The New York Times*, March 14, 2011, http://www.nytimes.com/2011/03/15/world/middleeast/15bahrain.html, accessed September 25, 2013. For a scholarly analysis see Mohammed Nuruzzaman, "Politics, Economics and Saudi Military Intervention in Bahrain," *Journal of Contemporary Asia*, 43, 2 (2013), 363–378.

24. Nuruzzaman, "Politics, Economics and Saudi Military Intervention in Bahrain," 371. On the Shia uprising in the Eastern Province see Frederic Wehrey, *The Forgotten Uprising in Eastern Saudi Arabia* (Washington: Carnegie Endowment for International Peace, 2013), http://carnegieendowment.org/files/eastern_saudi_uprising.pdf, accessed September 25, 2013.

25. Nuruzzaman, "Politics, Economics and Saudi Military Intervention in Bahrain," 368. Nuruzzaman argues, in fact, that economic reasons were paramount in motivating the Saudi regime to undertake the 2011 intervention.

26. Some context on U.S.-GCC relations is in Rebecca Puckett, Joshua Abel, and Sara Keefe, *Exploring the U.S.-GCC Relationship: A Discussion of Trade, Investment, and Commercial Opportunities* (Washington: Elliott School of International Affairs, The George Washington University, April 2008), 14–16, http://elliott.gwu.edu/assets/docs/acad/itip/us_gcc_itip_capstone.pdf, accessed September 24, 2013.

27. Saudi-Qatari relations are briefly discussed in Matthew Gray, *Qatar: Politics and the Challenges of Development* (Boulder: Lynne Rienner, 2013), 186–191.

28. Ibid., 168–169, 186–188.

29. Christopher M. Davidson, *Dubai: The Vulnerability of Success* (London: Hurst & Company, 2008), 276–277.

30. "Saudi and UAE Border in Dispute over ID Cards," *Reuters*, August 23, 2009, http://in.reuters.com/article/2009/08/23/idINIndia-41923020090823, accessed September 26, 2013.

31. Richard Spencer, "Naval Battle between UAE and Saudi Arabia Raises Fears for Gulf Security," *The Telegraph* (London), March 26, 2010, http://www.telegraph.co.uk/news/world news/middleeast/unitedarabemirates/7521219/Naval-battle-between-UAE-and-Saudi-Arabia-raises-fears-for-Gulf-security.html, accessed September 26, 2013.

32. Kamrava, *Qatar*, 70–71; Marc J. O'Reilly, "Omanibalancing. Oman Confronts an Uncertain Future," *The Middle East Journal*, 52, 1 (Winter 1998), 70–84; and Frederic Wehrey et al., *Saudi-Iranian Relations since the Fall of Saddam: Rivalry, Cooperation, and Implications for U.S. Policy* (Santa Monica: RAND Corporation, 2009), 51–53.

33. Wehrey et al., *Saudi-Iranian Relations since the Fall of Saddam*, 53–55.

34. Michelle Wallin, "U.S.-Bahrain Accord Stirs Persian Gulf Trade Partners," *The New York Times*, December 24, 2004, http://www.nytimes.com/2004/12/24/business/world business/24gulf.html, accessed September 26, 2013.

35. Wehrey et al., *Saudi-Iranian Relations since the Fall of Saddam*, 55–57.

36. A detailed outline of the various ideological, sectarian, and other dynamics in the Saudi-Iranian relationship can be found in Ibid., especially Ch. 2 (11–43).

37. On this see Stephen C. Pelletierre, *The Iran-Iraq War: Chaos in a Vacuum* (New York: Praeger, 1992), 60–63.

38. On Saudi-Iranian tensions and threats in the latter years of the war see Dilip Hiro, *The Longest War: The Iran-Iraq Military Conflict* (London: Paladin, 1990), 213–215.

39. Craig Whitlock and Liz Sly, "For Iran and Saudi Arabia, Simmering Feud Is Rooted in History," *The Washington Post*, October 11, 2011, http://articles.washingtonpost.com/2011

-10-11/world/35276886_1_saudi-iranian-relations-saudi-arabia-saudi-ambassador, accessed September 26, 2013.

40. For a summary on this see "Saudi King Urged U.S. to Attack Iran: WikiLeaks," *Reuters*, November 29, 2010, http://www.reuters.com/article/2010/11/29/us-wikileaks-usa-idUSTRE6AP06Z20101129, accessed September 26, 2013.

41. Wehrey et al., *Saudi-Iranian Relations since the Fall of Saddam*, 78–89.

42. For some background on the Houthi conflict, see Barak A. Salmoni, Bryce Loidolt, and Madeleine Wells, *Regime and Periphery in Northern Yemen: The Houthi Conflict* (Santa Monica: RAND Corporation, 2010), especially the Introduction (1–16).

43. "Iran military denounces Saudi 'killing' in Yemen," *Reuters*, November 17, 2009, http://www.reuters.com/article/2009/11/17/idUSDAH749814, accessed September 26, 2013.

44. Joseph McMillan, "Saudi Arabia and Iraq: Oil, Religion, and the Enduring Rivalry," *United States Institute of Peace Special Report 157* (Washington: United States Institute of Peace, January 2006), 5.

45. Ibid., 5.

46. Toby C. Jones, "Saudi-Iraq Relations: Devolving Chaos or Acrimonious Stability?," in Henri Barkey, Scott B. Lasensky and Phoebe Marr (eds.), *Iraq, Its Neighbors, and the United States: Competition, Crisis, and the Reordering of Power* (Washington: United States Institute of Peace, 2011), 100–101.

47. F. Gregory Gause III, "Saudi Arabia: Desert Storm and After," in Robert O. Freedman (ed.), *The Middle East after Iraq's Invasion of Kuwait* (Gainesville: University Press of Florida, 1993), 210.

48. Ibid., 211.

49. Jones, "Saudi-Iraq Relations," 100.

50. See McMillan, "Saudi Arabia and Iraq," 11–12.

51. "Analysis: Saudi Wants Bigger Role in Iraq to Counter Iran," *Reuters*, August 2, 2010, http://www.reuters.com/article/2010/08/02/us-saudi-iraq-idUSTRE6712K620100802, accessed September 26, 2013.

52. Jones, "Saudi-Iraq Relations," 100.

53. Ibid., 105.

54. Ibid., 106; also McMillan, "Saudi Arabia and Iraq," 9–10.

55. Jones, "Saudi-Iraq Relations," 109–110.

56. Ibid., 110.

57. Ibid., 112–114.

58. Ibid., 109–110.

59. These points, although primarily discussed from a U.S. point of view, are made in Daniel L. Byman, "Regional Consequences of Internal Turmoil in Iraq," in Mehran Kamrava (ed.), *International Politics of the Persian Gulf* (New York: Syracuse University Press, 2011), 145–163.

60. Bob Dreyfuss, "Saudi Arabia's Fear of Egypt," *The Nation* (New York), February 13, 2011, http://www.thenation.com/blog/158523/saudi-arabias-fear-egypt#accessed September 27, 2013.

61. Helene Cooper and Mark Landler, "Interests of Saudi Arabia and Iran Collide, With the U.S. in the Middle," *The New York Times*, March 17, 2011, http://www.nytimes.com/2011/03/18/world/18diplomacy.html, accessed September 27, 2013.

62. Robert F. Worth, "Unrest Encircles Saudis, Stoking Sense of Unease," *The New York Times*, February 19, 2011, http://www.nytimes.com/2011/02/20/world/middleeast/20 saudi.html, accessed September 27, 2013.

63. Rod Nordland, "Saudi Arabia Promises to Aid Egypt's Regime," *The New York Times*, August 19, 2013, http://www.nytimes.com/2013/08/20/world/middleeast/saudi-arabia-vows-to-back-egypts-rulers.html, accessed September 27, 2013.

64. On the proxy conflict see: Fahad Nazer, "Saudi Arabia's Proxy Wars," *The New York Times*, September 20, 2013, http://www.nytimes.com/2013/09/21/opinion/global/saudi -arabias-proxy-wars.html, accessed September 27, 2013; and on the role of Prince Bandar: Adam Entous, Nour Malas, and Margaret Coker, "A Veteran Saudi Power Player Works To Build Support to Topple Assad," *The Wall Street Journal*, August 25, 2013, http://online .wsj.com/article/SB10001424127887323423804579024452583045962.html, accessed September 27, 2013.

65. See David B. Ottaway, "The Saudi-Qatari Clash over Syria," *The National Interest*, July 2, 2013, http://nationalinterest.org/commentary/the-saudi-qatari-clash-over-syria-8685, accessed September 27, 2013; Mariam Karouny, "Saudi edges Qatar to control Syrian rebel support," *Reuters*, May 31, 2013, http://www.reuters.com/article/2013/05/31/us-syria-crisis-saudi-insight-idUSBRE94U0ZV20130531, accessed September 27, 2013.

66. "Mixed response from media to Syria chemical weapons deal," *BBC News*, September 16, 2013, http://www.bbc.co.uk/news/world-middle-east-24111098, accessed September 28, 2013.

CHAPTER 5

Saudi Arabia, Islamism, and Sunni Extremism

At a popular level in the Western world, common knowledge about Saudi Arabia is often limited to a basic picture of Saudi Arabia an as ultra-conservative Muslim country sympathetic to extremist groups. The September 11, 2001, terrorist attacks on the United States reinforced this image. Damaging Saudi Arabia's image in the United States, and relations with Washington, was probably one of Osama bin Laden's goals, given that of the 20 hijackers chosen for the attacks and the 19 who were involved on the day, 15 were Saudi nationals.[1] This damaged Saudi-U.S. relations, as discussed, as well as the popular American impression of Saudi Arabia; by one poll, the Saudis went from having 56 percent of Americans viewing them favorably in early 2001 to only 24 percent still doing so by December of that year.[2] The image of Saudi Arabia as home to strict Islamism and to supporters of extremist groups like al-Qa'eda is built on some important realities. The Saudi government is highly conservative, and needs to be so given its ties with the Wahhabi clerics. The freedom given to the clerics to promote Wahhabism, including abroad, has meant that more radical Saudis have supported groups with anti-Western agendas, sometimes including violent groups such as al-Qa'eda.

However, the Saudi relationship with Islamism and Sunni extremism is more complex than this. As this chapter will show, while the Saudi regime has sometimes been a force for Islamism and Islamization, at home and abroad, it has complex relationships with both conservative elements and more extremist ones within the country. The regime's security, and Saudi security in general, has been sought through a balancing of dynamics, as at an international level the Saudi rulers have also sought to balance their bonds with and reliance upon the United

States against the forces that oppose this relationship. At times, and from certain groups, the Saudi regime has been a victim of terrorism and extremism; at other points, it has done too little, if anything, to erode the support base or legitimacy of Islamist groups and ideologies.

THE WAHHABI TRADITION AND CONTEMPORARY SAUDI ARABIA

One of the most common impressions of Saudi Arabia and Saudi Arabians in the West is that they are religiously ultraconservative. Specific policies such as the complete ban on alcohol and the prohibition on women driving cars are assumed to reflect Saudi support for an officially sanctioned, puritanical Sunnism. Certainly, to the extent that it is possible to generalize, there is a strong conservative religious current among the Saudis. Wahhabism, previously discussed, is often equated with extremism because it is, in essence, a type of *salafi* Islam. *Salafi* Islam or *salafism* is puritanical and fundamentalist in the literal sense of demanding a return to the fundamental principles and "foundational texts and to the practices of the *salaf al-salih* (the 'pious forefathers')"[3] of the early few generations of Islam. However, *salafism* does not necessarily construct or dictate extremism: it seeks a renaissance of what it sees as the true practices and beliefs of Islam, unadulterated by change or modernity but still adaptable to change within the parameters of its principles. Thus, as Niblock notes, there is scope for reform within Wahhabi ideology, although a more rigid religious structure has, in practice, been dominant.[4] It has had a powerful impact on society and on societal perspectives, often condemning or discouraging change, while at the elite level the Al Saud need for clerical endorsement has seen the family grant the Wahhabi clerics more reach into society than clerics elsewhere normally enjoy.

The strong religious current in the Kingdom is in many ways not surprising. Its geographic position at the very center of the region where Islam was born, encompassing the area from which the Prophet Muhammad received the Qur'an and from where the Islamic religion spread, gives Islam profound importance to many Saudis. In its modern form, the Saudi state is warden for the two holiest cities in Islam, Mecca and Medina. King Fahd and now Abdullah have adopted the title of "Custodian of the Two Holy Mosques," arguably above all for political legitimization, but also reflecting a genuine view in Saudi Arabia that the country has a unique role and obligation toward Islam by hosting its two holiest cities. At a political level, religious piety is enforced in the public realm and encouraged in most aspects of daily life for these reasons, but furthermore because of the power of the clerics. It is also a reason why the *Mutawwa'een* (the "religious police") have, in the past but still today, been permitted considerable power in and over society and social dynamics. Very puritanical policies such as a ban on women driving cars are absent in other parts of the region, but exist in the Kingdom because of its history, identity with Islam, and more practically, because of the role given to the clergy. Some observers have claimed that there is a Saudi sense of *khususiyya* ("exceptionalism").[5] This captures the popular sense of Saudi uniqueness, informed by history and its links to Islam. However, Saudi Arabia is not the only contemporary society to consider itself unique or exceptional; *khususiyya* is not fundamentally different to the ideas of American exceptionalism and virtue that underpins *manifest destiny*, or Japanese *nihonjinron* (roughly, "theories of the Japanese [uniqueness]"), or other forms of national exceptionalism and chauvinism.

Therefore, important as religious tradition and popular identification with Islam has been, and continues to be, a generalization about the religiosity of Saudi society cannot proceed much further than this. The Saudi political system is deeply permeated by Islamic values and practices, but it is difficult to genuinely accept that the Saudi clerics are seeking to recreate some sort of Medinan *utopia*; and if they are, such an endeavor is almost certainly doomed to failure given the imperatives of the modern world and the modernity that has crept into Saudi government, statecraft, and society over the past century.[6] Any generalizations about the piety of the Saudis needs to incorporate an acknowledgement of the multiple and competing layers of political and social identity and loyalty, meaning that important as Islam is to many or even most Saudis, other units of allegiance such as family, tribe, ethnicity, and nationalism cannot be ignored.

The most objective measure available on the views of Saudis is probably opinion polling, and the result of opinion polls conducted with Saudi respondents reflects this diversity of allegiances and loyalties. It has never provided simplistic results where the overwhelming majority decides their opinions on the basis of religious tenets or instruction. An insightful case of surveying is that done by Shibley Telhami from the University of Maryland and the Brookings Institution. His 2010 survey included a regional sample of 3,976 over six states, of which 750 were Saudis in Riyadh, Jeddah, and Dammam.[7] There are other survey results available, and while the quality of some surveys can vary and it can be difficult for pollsters to design and conduct accurate surveys,[8] generally the better ones provide statistical results along the lines of Telhami's, including some surprising answers for those who see Saudi Arabian political culture and social values as driven purely by religious considerations. A couple of pertinent survey questions, and the responses, are presented in Tables 5.1 and 5.2.

Several features are immediately obvious. The first, in Table 5.1, is that the role of Islam in people's minds is important, but not uniquely or overwhelmingly so. In terms of identity, interestingly it is in Morocco, not Saudi Arabia, where the most people attributed to religion the highest priority in framing their identity. The percentage of Saudis who did so was only a minority, if close to half. A substantial share—around one-third—of Saudi respondents placed their Arab identity above their Muslim one. Similarly, from Table 5.2, Saudis do not stand out in their views on the Israeli-Palestinian conflict. One might expect their

Table 5.1 Saudi Opinion Poll Results, 2010—The Question of Identity Question: "Which of the following is your most important identity?"

	Muslim	National Identity	Arab	Cosmopolitan
Overall	39%	32%	25%	4%
Saudi Arabia	47%	19%	34%	0%
Egypt	31%	37%	30%	2%
Jordan	16%	58%	19%	6%
Lebanon	8%	55%	32%	4%
Morocco	61%	25%	4%	10%
UAE	23%	34%	31%	11%

Source: From figures provided in Shibley Telhami, *2010 Annual Arab Public Opinion Survey*, University of Maryland with Zogby International, slide 72, http://www.brookings.edu/~/media/research/files/reports/2010/8/05%20arab%20opinion%20poll%20telhami/0805_arabic_opinion_poll_telhami.pdf, accessed November 25, 2013. Used here with permission.

responses to be especially strong on this issue given the Muslim sympathy often assumed to exist with the Palestinians and the significance of Arab sovereignty over Jerusalem because of that city's importance in Islam. However, the Saudi responses were not especially at variance with the averages. Similar in its findings to the Telhami poll, an earlier poll in 2002 by the Arab American Institute found that the Saudi respondents did not vary greatly from other Arab respondents in the weight they placed on Islam or Arab-ness as a key source of their identity.[9] As elsewhere, very secular issues such as corruption and economic conditions often rate highest of all in people's minds when they are polled.[10]

Such results confirm that Saudi society or politics cannot be explained simply by religious dynamics. Islam is important, certainly, and perhaps slightly more

Table 5.2 Saudi Opinion Poll Results, 2010—the Arab-Israeli Issue Question: "When you look at the Israeli-Palestinian conflict, which of the following issues is the most central to you, assuming that they may all be important?"

	Establishment of a fully independent contiguous Palestinian state in WBG	Arab sovereignty over East Jerusalem	The right of Palestinian refugees to return to their homes
Overall	46%	31%	21%
Saudi Arabia	51%	23%	26%
Egypt	52%	30%	14%
Jordan	23%	38%	39%
Lebanon	27%	39%	34%
Morocco	33%	37%	30%
UAE	52%	32%	11%

Source: From figures provided in Shibley Telhami, *2010 Annual Arab Public Opinion Survey*, University of Maryland with Zogby International, slide 30, http://www.brookings.edu/~/media/research/files/reports/2010/8/05%20arab%20opinion%20poll%20telhami/0805_arabic_opinion_poll_telhami.pdf, accessed November 25, 2013. Used here with permission.

politically substantive than in some other Arab states, but other sources of social identity and political culture are crucial as well.

In the Saudi case, regionalism and regional identity is important. As discussed earlier, the modern Saudi state is the result of Ibn Saud's conquests. It is a conglomeration of regional areas, with distinct identities and historical trajectories. One scholar identified at least six distinct regions in the Kingdom, listing Najd, Hijaz, Asir, the Eastern Province, the northeast, and Najran in the south-central part of the country as distinct areas.[11] Across and even within these regions, there are then variations in history, the power of the clergy, the past reach of the Al Saud, the degree of tribalism, and trading history.[12] The traditional desert-dwelling *bedouin* ("nomads") are only one set of Saudis, standing in contrast to the openness, even cosmopolitanism, of a long-established port city such as Jidda.[13] Religion has varied in its regional role, too, and the power of Wahhabi clerics in the Saudi state is a product of the original Saudi alliance with abd al-Wahhab rather than something inherently and always "Saudi Arabian" in nature.

The speed and impact of social change in the Kingdom in recent decades has also informed social values and political culture. While it has prompted opposition from some Wahhabi clerics and very pious Saudis, it also reflects the large middle class that has emerged in the Kingdom and the members of which are secular, at least comparatively, in their views. The middle class has been strengthened by modern education, technological change, and contact with the outside world. A significant proportion of the pressure for political and social reform in the early 1990s came from these societal forces. It was secular women who protested very visibly in 1990 for the right to drive, and who periodically breach the ban in an ongoing current of opposition to it.[14] The middle class has driven the petitions and protests about the driving ban, which have increased since 2007 or thereabouts.[15] They have put other pressures on Abdullah for reform, petitioning for social and (limited) political change from 2003 onward,[16] and have been active in challenging Islamists and other counterreformists online.[17] This said, while the numbers of secular and reformist Saudis is extensive, they are not a majority and the most vocal calls for reform have come from an elite circle within the middle classes.[18] Some members of the middle class are a force for traditionalism and conservatism instead.

The middle classes' rise, and their relative openness to modernization and change, is often explained by the expansion of educational opportunity in the Kingdom in the oil era. Certainly, oil has paid for a lot of Saudis to receive a quality technical education, often at the tertiary level and overseas in the West, which may give them an appreciation for modernization and technology.[19] There remains a significant group of Saudis educated in the West each year; however, since 1979 or so, the domestic primary and secondary systems have put greater emphasis on transmitting religious values to students.[20] Beyond education, the number and share of Saudis who spend substantial time overseas is large.

Many Saudis spend summers abroad or otherwise travel abroad regularly. Often Saudis, especially Saudi men, behave in a far more secular manner abroad than they would ever dare to at home: not only is this a common complaint by their wives, but it reflects the fact that there is a strong underlying affinity for a more secular lifestyle, which can be explored abroad on vacation but not at home. Such time abroad, along with the emergence of online sources of information and the expansion of satellite television, means that Saudis can gauge much more easily than in the past what life is like around the world and how their own country compares.

The point here is not that religion or secularism is politically ascendant, but simply that the Saudi regime is faced with a highly diverse society, meaning that it needs to recognize and balance various views, even if its relationship with the Wahhabi clergy is especially important for its survival. At the level of policy the clerical role is important, but at the societal level, the degree to which religion and a conformist devotion to tradition dictates Saudis' political or social views cannot be indiscriminately labelled or categorized. Even within some larger families or tribes, people vary in the weight they give to religion. Even the Saudi royal family itself has relatively moderate and conservative branches within it,[21] and as Al-Rasheed had noted, "royal reputations are constructed, and are subject to change over time."[22] An understanding of Islam is essential to explaining Saudi politics and society and, in turn, to assessing its security setting, but is not a singular explanation for these dynamics.

THE REVIVAL OF ISLAM, 1979 TO 9/11

Notwithstanding the various streams of relative religiosity and traditionalism within Saudi society and the complexity of forces in it, Saudi society overall has become more religiously conservative in recent decades, especially since the late 1970s. The year 1979 was pivotal because the royals were forced to concede significant new influence to the clergy that year, as the price of obtaining *'ulema* endorsement for the state to violently end the siege of the Grand Mosque at Mecca. The siege coincided with the 1978–1979 Iranian revolution and the Soviet invasion of Afghanistan, at a time also when the clash between economic modernization and socio-political conservatism, whetted during the reign of former-King Faisal, was becoming increasingly strong. This rise in piety was visible in stronger public displays of religiosity, more radical preaching, more Islamist political argument, and a greater emphasis on Islam in the education curriculum as well as in the promotion of Wahhabi ideology abroad. The rise of rejectionist and violent Islam in the Kingdom, dating back some time but most prominent after the early-2000s, is a further example. While there have been substantial political or other reforms since 1979, the rise in religious conservatism since 1979, both in a nonviolent, socially conservative form and as a "militant" and extremist one, is undeniable.[23]

Adding to this Islamization, the state addressed the challenges of 1979–1980 by both promoting further economic modernization and through other rentier-based spending and development, while simultaneously reasserting its own Islamic credentials and supporting religious initiatives with even greater fervor.[24] Arguably, this introduced new security dynamics at home, as new Islamist groups started to emerge, and abroad, in the reputation that Saudi Arabia gained as a center of Islamism, even Islamic extremism.

The Grand Mosque siege was one of the first signs of violent Islamist undercurrent in the Kingdom, and of the inherent threats to Saudi stability and the regime itself from such groups and from confrontations couched in religious terms.[25] The message of Juhayman was not a complex theological one, and the siege reflected historical factors and a broader radicalization of Sunni Islam in the region, and was not just the product of a religious confrontation per se. The siege did, however, usher in a further and in many ways more violent Islamism in which Saudis were prominent. The Saudi role in the Soviet war in Afghanistan is a case in point.

The war in Afghanistan over much of the 1980s was the signal event that determined the nature and intensity of the Islamist challenge to the Saudi state that emerged in the following decade and especially in the 2000s. Many people who were later figures in al-Qa'eda, especially Al-Qa'eda in the Arabian Peninsula (AQAP),[26] cut their teeth in Afghanistan or were radicalized by the rhetoric that the war provoked. The war began with the Soviet invasion of Afghanistan on Christmas Day 1979, but with the Cold War dynamics in play at the time, the Soviet presence was stretched out to nearly a decade-long commitment to what became a counter-insurgency operation against Afghan *mujahideen*. The U.S., Saudi, and Pakistani governments collaborated to recruit and support volunteer resistance fighters who would fight alongside or assist the *mujahideen*. One early volunteer was Abdullah Azzam, a Palestinian who went to Afghanistan in 1980 and who "is widely acknowledged as the ideologue behind al Qaeda and [Osama] bin Laden's mentor."[27] His views were not as extreme as al-Qa'eda's would later be, but nonetheless he provided a consistent ideological message demanding of Muslims that they join the defense of Afghanistan.[28] When he was assassinated in 1989, the leadership of his *Maktab al-Khidamat* ("Office of Services") group passed to Osama bin Laden, whose 1998 *fatwa* declared a *jihad*, or religious war, against the United States on the basis of its political and cultural domination and the negative impacts for the Muslim world that he argued came from its hegemony.

Only a limited responsibility for the rise of al-Qa'eda in this period can be placed at the feet of the Saudi regime, but their strong and vocal support for the Afghans and the funding of the insurgency were still factors. Starting in the mid-1980s and becoming more extensive and formal around 1986, when efforts were more organized and the bulk of the travel costs for volunteers was paid, through intermediaries, by the Saudi government.[29] Some Wahhabi figures were even more important. Azzam claimed to have the support of a range of clerical figures, including key Saudi Wahhabi ones, and later, clerics encouraged and assisted the recruitment of Saudis volunteers for Afghanistan.[30] This is something the Saudi elite would have stopped if it had not approved of it, placing on the regime a certain amount of responsibility for the radicalization of some young Saudis at the time.

The main targets for recruitment to such groups were the young members of *al-Sahwa al-Islamiyya* ("the Islamic Awakening"), the dominant Islamist oppositional force in the Kingdom, and its more radical outgrowths. A network of like-minded religious scholars more than a formal group, *al-Sahwa* first emerged in the 1960s and gained greater prominence after the events of 1979; it was the main Islamist network or movement in the Kingdom from the 1960s to the 1990s. *Al-Sahwa* was strong on university campuses, among the middle classes, and with foreign workers in the country, especially those from Egypt and elsewhere who had been exposed to Muslim Brotherhood ideas at home before moving to the Kingdom. The *al-Sahwa* ideology was a blend of Wahhabi *social* ideas and perspectives with Muslim Brotherhood type *political* ideas, to form an informal, largely uncoordinated network that called for policy reform but which did not normally question the state's or royal family's overall legitimacy.[31] The al-Sahwa figures were different from the Saudi Wahhabi *'ulema* in this sense, but also because they debated current theological issues rather than more abstract or theoretical ones and because they were more open to modern technology than many traditional Saudi clerics.[32]

The Grand Mosque siege in 1979 reflected the split that had become wider between the mainstream, reformist *al-Sahwa* and the isolationist, "rejectionist or neo-Salafi"[33] offshoots of it, which drew inspiration from some of the more radical scholars who were prominent in Medina in particular in the 1960s and after. The most famous of these scholars, and the most important for the rise of more violent groups as of the late 1970s, was probably Muhammad Nasir al-Din al-Albani, who more than anyone else revivified the *ahl al-hadith* ("People of the Hadith") concept and led a faction of that name as a more radical and stricter offshoot of *al-Sahwa*.[34] The *ahl al-hadith* movement was a literalist one.[35] For example, where the Qur'an provided no or insufficient instruction on a matter, the movement, like the original eighth century *ahl al-hadith* adherents, opposed the use of reasoning to make a religious ruling on the matter, instead insisted on using the *Sunna* (the normative set of prescribed rules and behaviors based on the teachings and practices of the Prophet Muhammad). Scholars like al-Albani criticized the main Wahhabi clerics on several bases, including for using reasoning rather than exclusively relying on the Qur'an and the Sunna. He also differed from the clergy on some more minor theological points. His views were influential because they provided an ideological basis for

Salafist groups such as *al-Jama'a al-Salafiyya al-Muhtasiba* (loosely, "the Salafi group for ensuring righteousness," hereafter JSM), and it was from this lower-class, highly unyielding group that the leader of the Grand Mosque siege, Juhayman al-'Utaibi, came. The JSM claimed that mainstream Islam, including the official Saudi Wahhabism, had been corrupted and had to be purified of its misinterpretations and contaminations.[36]

Such views were not unpopular at the time; some of the most prominent religious scholars in the Kingdom held similar views, and JSM leaders drew inspiration from, and had extensive contact with, top figures such as Abd al-Aziz bin Baz and Abu Bakr al-Jazairi.[37] However, it evolved into a more extreme ideological force, and came into increasing conflict with the Wahhabi clerical class, but Juhayman was the first figure in the movement to challenge so violently the legitimacy of the Saudi state. JSM members were repressed after the Grand Mosque siege, or fled the Kingdom where possible, but their influence returned later, when a new wave of extremism appeared in the late-1990s and early-2000s.

The 1970s had also laid the groundwork for the radicalization that occurred during the Soviet war in Afghanistan. While the older leaders of *al-Sahwa* were relatively cautious and orthodox, many younger Sahwists were attracted to the opportunity to fight what they saw as a very literal *jihad* in defense of Muslim lands. The Muslim Brotherhood members in *al-Sahwa* were most of this mind, as Lacroix notes, probably because of their less stern attitudes toward other schools and ideas in Islam and given the prominence of Brothers in the Afghan jihad.[38] By the time that Osama bin Laden established al-Qa'eda in 1988, it was able to help support quite an extensive number of Arab volunteers and provide a link between these volunteers on the basis of their ethnicity and culture. It was acting consistent with the official view back in Saudi Arabia that the volunteers were serving a positive religious and national cause: the Saudi ones, upon their return, were treated as heroes in the late 1980s. It was only later, as of the early 1990s that Saudi veterans of Afghanistan started to be repressed, once the Saudi regime became concerned that they were too radicalized. The exact number of Saudis who went to fight in Afghanistan remains very vague and contested, with estimates ranging from a few thousand to 20,000 in total.[39] Most of these went only briefly and most never saw significant combat. Estimates of the number of Saudis killed in Afghanistan are in the range of 50 to 300, suggesting there were probably only a few thousand dedicated Saudi fighters, perhaps fewer than 1,000 at most times late in the war. Still, as Hegghammer notes, it was still "a remarkable figure, given the near-absence of a militant Islamist community in Saudi Arabia in the early 1980s. An entire movement had been created in the space of five years."[40] It was integral to the radicalization of some Saudis who were prominent extremists later.

The 1990s were very different to the 1980s in terms of the nature of Saudi Islamism. Briefly, the regime seemed to gain greater control over potential sources of opposition, but in fact they instead laid the groundwork for the violent opposition of the early-mid-2000s. Several factors accounted for the changing profile of Saudi Islamism at the time, including the 1990–1991 Gulf War, the changing international context, and above all to splits among the Islamists into both more liberal and more extremist variants. As a result, the primacy of *al-Sahwa* as the Islamist opposition was challenged, and the network was pushed into the background as its competitors gained a firmer foothold and a stronger political distinction from it.

The 1990–1991 Gulf War has already been discussed, but it is worth reiterating a few key aspects of it as they relate to Islamism. Most importantly, the crisis and war was an existential challenge to the Al Saud, or seen by them as such, meaning that they allowed the U.S. military deployment to the Kingdom despite knowing it would be unpopular. The fact that U.S. forces stayed afterward, however, riled the religious establishment, not to mention more radical Islamists, but there was little scope to mount opposition to it, since the establishment clergy were integrated into the political system[41] and more radical Islamists who spoke out were repressed. While many key *al-Sahwa* figures challenged the U.S. deployment and the mainstream clergy's endorsement of it, arguing that it would bring about creeping secularization,[42] their influence declined into the 1990s as several key figures were arrested or repressed by the Saudi regime. The famous and charismatic mid-ranking figures Salman al-Awda and Safar al-Hawali were arrested in 1994, when the regime feared they were inciting real unrest,[43] and their imprisonment eroded the dynamism of *al-Sahwa*.

Over the latter-1990s *al-Sahwa* was diluted as a political force and served as a warning to some other scholars and figures about the risk of speaking out. Then, after they were released from prison in 1999, al-Awda and al-Hawali pursued slightly varying but much more cautious, tepid roles. Al-Awda became far more orthodox in his pronouncements, responding favorably to regime demands to condemn terrorism after the 9/11 attacks, and openly opposing the violent insurgency against the Saudi state in the early 2000s.[44] Safar al-Hawali did not transform into a moderate, but still played a more mainstream role, positioning himself as a link between the Saudi state and the new opposition figures that were then emerging, and avoiding directly criticizing and challenging the state.[45] Al-Awda and al-Hawali did not become "mainstream," as some Islamist critics often painted them. They remained highly critical of the United States, and by implication of the U.S.-Saudi relationship.[46] Both were among 26 key Saudi clerics who, in November 2004, issued a religious statement endorsing *jihad* in Iraq.[47] Perhaps they were savvy enough to leave it to listeners to discern what they would from their statements, or maybe they were deterred from openly challenging the state but had not changed their underlying views.

The weakening of *al-Sahwa* over the late 1990s perhaps lulled the Saudi regime into a false sense that they were succeeding at neutralizing the Islamist opposition. However, the 1990s were also a period of further radicalization of some Saudis—this was a time when some of them ventured off to Bosnia, Chechnya, and elsewhere[48]—and in these years al-Qa'eda's influence began growing. The primary motivator for most Saudi *jihadis* seems to have been the chance at religious purification and what Hegghammer has called the "classical jihadism" ideology of Azzam and others.[49] He also notes that while few seem to have been motivated by opposition to the Saudi regime, this was about to change.

It perhaps should have been clearer than it was in the mid- and late-1990s that the Saudi regime could face a far greater Islamist threat, especially since the first acts of violence occurred at that time. The first dramatic one was the 1995 Riyadh bombing, where a 100kg car bomb was exploded in downtown Riyadh on November 13, 1995, outside a building used by a U.S. security contractor, killing five U.S. and two Indian nationals and wounding some 60 other people.[50] While responsibility for the incident remains debated, it was probably inspired by Osama bin Laden rather than specifically being an al-Qa'eda operation.[51] Most significant about it was its political messages: it was a statement against the U.S. military presence in the country, a message to the Saudi state against the repression of Islamist forces such as *al-Sahwa*, and a sign that militants were willing to engage in violence if they were ignored.[52] The following year, another attack shocked the Saudis. This time, on June 25, 1996, an explosives-packed vehicle exploded outside U.S. Air Force barracks in Khobar, in the east of the country. The massive explosion killed 19 U.S. personnel and injured some 400 people. It was initially assumed to be the work of al-Qa'eda, but the United States later claimed it was the work of the Shia extremist group Saudi Hezbollah.[53] The evidence later seemed to return to cast doubt on this, and suggest al Qa'eda after all, following some statements by key U.S. and Saudi figures. Ultimately, the question of responsibility remains uncertain and contested.

As a result of the bombings, the Saudi regime began further repressing Islamist figures, former foreign jihadists, and others. Over several years after 1996, more than 3,000 people were arrested.[54] This radicalized a large number of new people, including many who seem to have shifted from the "classical" pan-Islamist jihadis into highly critical, even violent, opponents of the Saudi regime. There were many further, if smaller, bombings inside the Kingdom in 1999, 2000, and 2001. By 2001, al-Qa'eda represented not only the views of a small number of absolute extremists, but was engaged in an anti-U.S., anti-Saudi campaign that had wider, albeit not majority or enormous, support among Saudis. Violent Islamism had become a central security threat to the Saudi state and the Al Saud regime.

ISLAMIC EXTREMISTS AND THE SAUDI REGIME IN THE 2000s

The 9/11 attacks had such dramatic impacts in the United States, and for Afghanistan, Iraq, and other countries, that its effects on Saudi Arabia, and the conflict that was fought in the 2000s between the regime and its violent Islamist opponents, is often overlooked or understated. In fact, 9/11 helped create some of the context in which the Saudi militant insurgency took place, given how extensively the so-called *war on terrorism* altered the international environment and motivated Islamists to mobilize against the Saudi state and even the United States.

9/11 began by forcing on the Saudi regime a new reality in its relationship with the United States. No longer did or could the United States treat the Saudis as any other regional ally, given the Saudi origins of bin Laden and 15 of the 19 9/11 hijackers. Moreover, as Niblock notes, there emerged the inescapable conclusion in the United States after the attacks that Wahhabi Islam could never harmonize with U.S. political and security interests in the Middle East.[55] The changed U.S.-Saudi relationship after September 2001, as discussed in the previous chapter, was almost inevitable given the nature of the attacks and the prominent role played by Saudis in them. Not only did the United States change the way it saw Saudi Arabia, not least of all in security terms, but the Saudis, likewise, sharply changed their approach to the United States as a result of the attacks and especially the "war on terrorism." The two sides' relationship shifted to much colder terms for many years.

However, the Saudi state and regime became, after 9/11, an even higher-profile target for violent Sunni extremists. What in the late 1990s had started to look like a small-scale terrorism threat in the Kingdom was, by 2001 and 2002, a more sweeping and dramatic conflict. It was possible until the 1995 Riyadh bombing to treat Saudi Islamic radicals as essentially a social movement; in the years following the Riyadh bombing this was more difficult, although those who would violently confront the state were considered a miniscule minority. But by the early 2000s this had changed. Unexpectedly, the 9/11 attacks created little sympathy for the United States among Saudis, partly because of the problems it produced in the bilateral relationship, partly because most Islamists treated it as suspect or declared it a conspiracy, and finally, because it ultimately spawned additional negative images once the 2003 Iraq War and the subsequent insurgency in Iraq were putting images on the evening news that many Islamists considered to represent U.S. aggression, not victimhood.

Indeed, Saudi feelings of hostility toward the United States began even with the U.S. operations, as of October 7, 2001, to remove the Taliban government in Afghanistan. Most polls around this time showed a large majority of Saudis angry at the U.S. invasion of Afghanistan, with many also declaring sympathy toward al-Qa'eda's ideology, especially its anti-American ideas; remarkably, one poll of educated Saudis in mid-October 2001 reported 95 percent of respondents as having such sympathies.[56] While this is a most dramatic poll result, most other surveys found a clear majority of Saudis opposed to the U.S. role in the region, including the United States, and a great many, typically a majority, holding anti-American views. Very soon after this, the images of prisoners captured by the United States being sent to Guantanamo Bay, Cuba, had a similarly sharply negative impact on Saudi opinion, especially since so many Saudis were among those now being held by the United States as "enemy combatants." Between Afghanistan, Guantanamo Bay, and U.S. policy on issues such as the Israeli-Palestinian conflict, the U.S.-led conflict that began with the 9/11 terrorist attacks on U.S. civilians had, in less than a year, come to be widely seen in Saudi Arabia (and elsewhere) as a war on Islam and Muslims.[57] Talk in the United States, starting as of the summer of 2002, about a possible war against Iraq only added to this widely held perception among so many Saudis.

This was at the popular level. Among key, more radical Saudi scholars, the anti-U.S. sentiment and rhetoric was stronger still. One of the more radical networks of scholars, called the "al-Shu'aybi school" after their highly conservative central Wahhabi figurehead Hamud al-Uqla al-Shu'aybi, had arisen in the mid-1990s as *al-Sahwa* became suppressed as a reformist voice and as some of the old establishment clerics such as Abd al-Aziz bin Baz died.[58] Key al-Shu'aybi figures became more radicalized in the late-1990s. So too did al-Shu'aybi himself, after he was dismissed from his job at Imam University in Burayda in 1994, in large part because of his role in *al-Sahwa*. His age made him a useful figurehead for radical Islamists, although he was not the operational leader or driving force of the network that bore his name. Still, he lent his name and reputation to *fatawa* ("religious edicts") that motivated some violent Saudi jihadists, including several of the Saudi 9/11 hijackers, plus at least one of the hijackers was recruited by an al-Shu'aybi school figure. Moreover, some *al-Sahwa* scholars became coaxed or cornered into taking more radical positions on the U.S.-led "war on terrorism," especially the U.S. invasions of Afghanistan and Iraq. On top of the popular mood at the time, therefore, there were few voices calling for moderation or opposing language that argued for a violent response to the United States and its allies.

At the same time, where moderate calls were made, they often had counter-productive effects. Some of the old *al-Sahwa* figures such as Salman al-Awda condemned the 9/11 attacks, but this simply allowed more extreme Islamists to paint former agitators like al-Awda as now having become submissive regime puppets. Quite paradoxically in a security sense, the Saudi crackdown on Islamists in the late 1990s had the counterproductive effect of pushing them underground, including the most extremist and violent ones, making it all the more difficult to track them and monitor their radicalization efforts. As a result, in 2001 and 2002, as young Saudis were being radicalized and mobilized for conflict with the Saudi state, little was done by the Al Saud, or could be done, to counter it. Moreover, when the Saudi leadership did eventually try to address this radicalization, in the lead up to the 2003 Iraq War, it initially did so in the same manner as it had in the 1990s.[59] In February 2003, the Saudi authorities arrested key al-Shu'aybi figures and drove others underground, but this achieved nothing like what was intended. It further angered these figures. It gave greater prominence to the Saudi state as an enemy of such interpretations of Islam, never shifting the focus away from the United States, but increasingly justifying terrorism and political violence, especially against Western targets, at home in the Kingdom. For those figures who were now fleeing from the authorities, there was little to lose in speaking in even more fanatical terms. They did exactly that. As the war approached, several major sheikhs who were in hiding from the regime openly reasserted their judgment that anyone assisting the United States in the war on Iraq was an apostate.[60]

Thus, the Saudi extremist struggle transformed from one that was initially, in the 1990s, focused almost exclusively on external enemies and that was dominated by intellectuals, to one by early 2003 that was more local in focus, increasingly critical of the Saudi regime and state, and for the first time willing to violently attack both Saudi targets and U.S., and other Western ones inside the Kingdom. Around the same time, the United States had fragmented bin Laden's main al-Qa'eda forces in Afghanistan and Pakistan after their late-2001 invasion and removal of the Taliban, so that what had previously been a single al-Qa'eda movement was by 2002 and 2003 a fragmented collection of al-Qa'eda and like-minded groups, operating in their own more specific areas.[61] This fragmentation, and some specific dynamics of the Saudi state's response to Islamism in earlier years, meant that it was the Saudi branch of al-Qa'eda that dominated the Saudi state's conflict with extremists from 2003 to approximately 2008.

The al-Qa'eda War on the Saudi State

As Hegghammer explains, in one of the most informative books on Saudi radicalism and Islamist violence, the conflict between the Saudi state and what became AQAP was the most substantial and protracted campaign of political violence that Saudi Arabia has experienced within its modern borders.[62] It killed at least 300 people, and injured several thousand others. It changed the nature of extremist Islamism from something that previously had only been violent abroad to something that now was a direct security threat to the Saudi leadership and state on the home front. It was a continuation of a political struggle that dated back to before 1990,[63] but the nature of this struggle was very new.

AQAP formed in late 2003, in the broadest terms, out of the original al-Qa'eda ideology and rhetoric of the 1990s, even if it later became a more localized and focused organization. Integral to its rise, however, was the recruitment, organization, training, and indoctrination of Saudis sympathetic to al-Qa'eda. More than any other figure, it was Yusuf al-Uyayri who was responsible for this.[64] He was a long-established jihadist. He went to Afghanistan as a teenager in the mid-late-1980s, becoming an instructor in one of the al-Qa'eda training camps there. He subsequently became one of bin Laden's bodyguards, then in the early 1990s fought in Somalia, before returning to Saudi Arabia to recruit and train Saudis to travel to the Bosnian conflict. He was arrested after the Khobar bombing and spent two years in prison, after which time he began writing jihadist texts. In the year 2000, he visited Afghanistan and seems to have reconnected with al-Qa'eda there. From then on, until his death in 2003, he was perhaps bin Laden's most important contact in the Kingdom, especially in terms of the radicalization of young Saudis and their preparation for armed conflict.

At the same time, al-Uyayri's role is a reminder of a fundamental debate among observers about AQAP: that of whether its goal was simply to evict the United States and the Western presence from Saudi Arabia, or whether in fact it wanted to overthrow and replace the Saudi government, as Hegghammer has noted.[65] The evidence is varied. Much of the material produced by AQAP figures was about evicting Westerners from the Kingdom, and until 2004, by which time the state-AQAP conflict was in full swing, there was little rhetoric against the Saudi royal family, state, or security services. At the same time, however, the rhetoric from bin Laden and other senior al-Qa'eda leaders suggests they wanted to overthrow the Al Saud. As the conflict with the Saudi state unfolded, and AQAP's rhetoric became increasingly revolutionary, it is likely that deposing the Al Saud and taking over the Saudi state became a more important, if still second-stage, goal of the organization.[66] Moreover, as Meijer and others have also noted, once AQAP branded leading Saudi figures as *kuffar* ("nonbelievers") and the conflict was an openly violent one, it is difficult to see the struggle as anything other than an existential one for the two sides.[67] In the case of al-Uyayri himself, his views in the 1990s seem to have been external in focus but included criticism of the Saudi government, and in facilitating violent extremism in the first few years of the 2000s, he was focused mostly on Afghanistan. But around 2001, he started putting aside some of the money from al-Qa'eda fundraising in preparation for a future fight against the Saudi state.[68] This purchased arms, funded training, and allowed for greater coordination and longer-term thinking; in short, it provided the capacity for the Islamists' war against the Saudi state that began in 2003.

That war started, by most assessments, with the Riyadh compound attacks on May 12, 2003, in which extremists from al-Uyyari's network used a mix of gun attacks and truck bombings against Western compounds in Riyadh, killing 36 and wounding over 160 people. The attack was by its nature a ruthless one. In attacking a compound, foreigners were key among the targets, and seven U.S. nationals were killed in the attacks, but the breadth of the attacks meant that they had multiple impacts, including also on the Saudi security services, the economy, and U.S. relations. But the attack sought not only to push foreigners out of the Kingdom: the large number of extremists killed, and the rhetoric and imagery of the attacks used in subsequent propaganda videos and the like, all also suggest that the attacks were meant to signify a "typical" al-Qa'eda type of "cosmic struggle" against evil.[69]

The attacks caused a massive police crackdown on Saudi Islamists. There were a range of arrests, including of scholars, ideological proponents of al-Uyayri's views, and militants. Yusuf al-Uyayri himself was killed in a shootout in late May 2003. The group, while dented by the crackdown, responded to it aggressively and proactively.[70] The network deliberately tried to become more adaptable and dynamic, changing and improving their structure and operations both for greater security from the state and to give the impression that the network was larger than it was. They established a media unit, and became cleverer and more coherent in appearance than previously, appearing to be a more cohesive and larger group than they actually were. Such tactics were quite effective at offsetting some of the damage done to the network by the regime's strong crackdown. Important too, and part of this new focus on their image, was the network's use of the organizational name "al-Qa'eda on the Arabian Peninsula" as of November 2003.[71] The group at this time was strongest in Riyadh and is thought to have consisted of three main clusters, two of them in or around Riyadh.[72]

On November 8, 2003, AQAP had sufficiently regrouped and reinvigorated to launch another large-scale attack, this time a truck bombing of the Muhayya compound in Riyadh. This greatly damaged AQAP's support, since most of the 17 killed and 120-plus wounded were Arabs and Muslims, including children. It lay low for some months, apart from the occasional small-scale gunfight with police, but in December its first attack on the Saudi security forces took place,[73] marking a shift in focus from targeting Westerners to taking on the security forces. Once the group had spent some time in the shadows, their attacks again increased in tempo and ferocity. They launched several car bomb attacks in the spring of 2004, had a number of shootouts with police, and began assassinating Westerners. They also launched some notable suicide attacks, such as the April 21 one on the traffic police headquarters, another on a firm in the western oil area of Yanbu, and the May 29 shooting spree at the Khobar compound.[74]

This period was the height of the AQAP violence, but the new tactics were notable, especially the assassination of Westerners. Over just a few weeks in May–June 2004, five Westerners were killed. On June 12, an AQAP cell took U.S. national Paul Johnson hostage, and six days later posted a video of his beheading online.[75] This caused considerable fear among expatriates in Saudi Arabia, and many quickly left the Kingdom. It ultimately turned out to be the peak of AQAP activity, however, and over the following year it was extensively incapacitated. Most of its key leaders and figures were killed by Saudi forces. As the Saudi intelligence capability grew, in part with U.S. assistance, AQAP was sharply weakened by arrests and the seizure of documents and weapons. There were still some gun battles and smaller attacks, with some cells clearly remaining effective, but overall the state's tactics and capabilities improved, and AQAP crumbled. A three-day shootout at a farm in al-Rass was a fatal blow to the old leadership of the group, most of whom were holed up at the farm and fought to the death. After this, "practically all of the militants who had been part of Yusuf al-Uyayri's original network were dead or captured."[76]

What followed this 2003–2005 phase of the "original network" was a slower-paced conflict led by a new set of leaders and cells. This "new generation"[77] did not possess the same momentum and urgency of the original group. While AQAP remained an active group, and some older tactics such as gun battles with police continued to occur, it had less success with major operations. It tried unsuccessfully to launch a truck bomb attack on an oil facility at Ubqaiq in February 2006, and killed some French tourists outside Medina in February 2007. Its relevance was sustained, however, only by its merger in 2009 with the Yemeni branch of al-Qa'eda, which gave it a markedly different profile. Perhaps because Yemen provides such an easier training and operational environment, the main activities of the group shifted there after the merger, and Yemenis dominate in the new merged group. The only case of a bold attack in the Kingdom around this time was the August 2009 attempted assassination of Prince Mohammed bin Nayef by a suicide bomber. He was a tempting target, as the head of the Saudi antiterrorism program and son of the then interior minister. The assassination failed, however, and otherwise its operations have predominantly been in Yemen or involved international activities coming out of Yemen. These are not insubstantial. The group claimed responsibility for the 2010 cargo plane bomb plot against the United States, and a range of attacks against the Yemeni government in the years after 2010.[78] While some Saudis who fled to Yemen to avoid crackdowns at home are members of the group, it is now much more strongly Yemeni in character and focus than it is Saudi.

AQAP in Saudi Arabia lost its war for a range of reasons, as Hegghammer has noted.[79] The Saudi state grew very effective at countering it, and this role was important at both the strategic and operational levels. The Saudis obtained significant assistance from the United States, the United Kingdom, and other states with intelligence, special forces training, and analysis. At the same time, the Saudi government dedicated enormous financial resources to fighting the group, which was used not only to expand its capabilities but to things such as higher wages to security services and police personnel. The morale of security personnel and police increased quite markedly in this period, as wages rose and the importance of their work were recognized. At the same time, the Saudi regime did not just bluntly kill and repress extremists. It also used many more "soft"[80] forms of counterterrorism, including targeting their funding, offering militants amnesty and other face-saving ways out of groups like AQAP, and running publicity campaigns to alienate the group from society and reduce its popular support.

The Iraqi Insurgency and Saudi Arabia

There was one other reason why AQAP struggled in its war with the Saudi state, and that is that the conflict coincided with the post-2003 Islamist fight in Iraq as well.[81] Iraq captured the attention of so many potential militants, and perhaps even outweighed many militants' focus on Saudi Arabia, because it was a chance to fight the U.S. military in a conflict begun by Washington's invasion of Iraq; fighting in Iraq could easily be justified to militants as a case of "defensive jihad," that is, of protecting Muslim territory from an infidel invader. The views of Saudi scholars varied somewhat on Iraq; while nearly all agreed that Iraq had been the victim of U.S. aggression, the more mainstream and establishment clerics were most likely to argue that it was a jihad with a collective obligation. This meant that it was a duty for Iraqis to engage in jihad against the United States, but Saudis had a choice in so doing. The more jihadist or radical scholars, in contrast, typically declared Iraq a jihad with individual obligation, meaning that all Muslims were obliged to wage jihad there. At the same time, however, offsetting such calls for jihad in Iraq was the more practical matter that Saudi jihadists such as AQAP leaders needed potential militants focused on Saudi Arabia, too. Many therefore argued that, important as Iraq might be, it was only one battleground in the conflict with infidel aggressors, and that a jihad could and should be just as urgently fought against the Western presence in Saudi Arabia. This debate quickly turned into a sharp ideological split among Saudi jihadists.

As with the 1980s foreign Islamist insurgency in Afghanistan—to which the 2000s insurgency in Iraq has sometimes been compared[82]—it is difficult to gauge the number of Saudis who traveled to the country and fought there. Hegghammer puts it at "over a thousand"[83] Saudis out of several thousand foreign fighters; another source from 2005[84] puts the number, even then, at as many as 2,500; while other sources sometimes put the figure much lower than either of these.[85] Over the main period that foreign fighters were traveling to Iraq, around 2004 to 2007 inclusive, the final number of Saudis probably did total over one thousand. They were certainly a substantial percentage of the foreign fighters: a number of plausible estimates put them at 40–60 percent of all foreign fighters. Even at 25 percent, since there were likely to have been around 3,000 foreign fighters in Iraq at any particular time in that period, over the four years the total would have exceeded 1,000.

More important than the number of Saudis alone is the overall number and the outsized role played by foreign fighters in Iraq at that time. Foreigners were especially radicalized, were seeking to expand and worsen the fighting with U.S. forces, and were disproportionately involved in suicide and mass casualty attacks. Therefore, even the conservative estimate of 3,000 foreign fighters in Iraq in 2005, a few hundred of them Saudis, was an alarming number and a significant issue for Saudi security. It is certainly plausible, indeed likely, that the Al Saud feared that such extremists would turn their attention to Saudi

Arabia if they were not so focused on Iraq: the fact that key Saudi jihadists were having an ideological debate around 2004 about whether Iraq or Saudi Arabia ought to be their priority suggests that the problems for the Saudis would have been greater still without some extremists being lured off to fight in Iraq. Turning a blind eye to Saudis traveling to Iraq as fighters would send a message that the Al Saud were quietly supporting them, or at least assenting to the jihadists, and in the middle of a crackdown on AQAP, the regime's boundaries would be clear: it is acceptable to fight in Iraq but not against the Saudi state back home.[86]

Around the same time, there were rumors that the Saudi royals were paying off or funding AQAP and other al-Qa'eda types as a way of avoiding being targeted by them, and certainly AQAP targeted police, security services, and sensitive foreign targets in the Kingdom, but somewhat strangely, until 2009 not the Saudi royal family. Whether valid or not, such ideas have been commonly recited by observers. They are backed at least by circumstantial evidence, and it would make sense that the Saudi regime would try to avert greater conflict on its own soil, especially while it faced a violent confrontation with some extremists anyway. Yet, there is probably also sufficient sympathy for extreme Islamist views in some quarters of the Saudi state apparatus, and even with some royals, that Saudi fighters would have found quite extensive support even if official policy had been to stop them traveling to Iraq.

For the Saudi state, therefore, there may have been little alternative to the tactic of simply ignoring the Saudis who were venturing off to Iraq. At any rate, the conflict in Iraq ultimately had an outcome that suited the Al Saud and the state, insofar as it very sharply divided the Saudi jihadists and many of their ideological leaders. AQAP was a key loser from the insurgency in Iraq, and it struggled to gain the financial support and recruits that it wanted.[87] The financial aspect of Iraq, in fact, was critical, since raising money within the Kingdom for a jihad was far easier when that jihad was to be waged in Iraq rather than on the streets at home.[88] This is probably why the Saudi state made some efforts to counter the flow of fighters—for example, by claiming to have cracked down on their recruitment, and by trying to seal the Saudi-Iraq border against infiltrators[89]— but did so inadequately and unenthusiastically. Finally, the Saudi-Iranian dynamic may have figured, with the Saudis keen to disrupt Iranian influence in Iraq even if it risked harming U.S. interests there as well.

Additionally, it was not only Iraq that had a radicalizing impact at the time. The insurgency in Afghanistan from the early 2000s into the 2010s also attracted a small number of Saudis as jihadi fighters. There were even reports of a handful of Saudis going to fight with the Palestinians against Israel in 2006 and with Sunni extremist groups in Lebanon in 2007.[90] For all of these reasons, therefore, the Saudi regime ended up pursuing an uncertain, lukewarm policy that achieved little. In not being as active in supporting the United States in the region as Washington wanted, it added to tensions to that relationship, while if it was trying to appear discreetly sympathetic toward jihadists or radical Islamists, it would not have impressed them.

Saudi Counterterrorism Efforts and Results

The hesitant, even contradictory, approach of the Saudi government toward the Iraqi insurgency is a reminder that the Saudi effort at counterterrorism and fighting extremism has been mixed, determined by an array of sometimes conflicting considerations. There are two major levels to the issue of extremism in Saudi Arabia, the ideological and the practical. This refers to the nature of Wahhabism on the one hand, and the practical concerns of Saudi politics on the other. As a strict, puritanical ideology in Sunni Islam, Wahhabism that is easily misinterpreted or exaggerated for the sake of extremist or fundamentalist causes, yet at the same time its senior clerics allied with Ibn Saud and subsequently have helped maintain the Al Saud in power. As Meijer has argued, this means that over the longer term:

> Saudi rulers tried to contain, regulate, and mobilize the powerful forces it unleashed to gain political power, it was difficult for the zealots to understand that in the end, pragmatic and self-serving objectives prevailed over [the Wahhabi doctrines that they believed the ruler ought to respect] ... Caught in the middle, the *'ulama'* might be able to sympathize with the wayward radicals who were willing to sacrifice themselves for higher goals; however, ultimately they knuckled down to the powers that be, aware of their own interests.[91]

Thus, there is always a propensity on the part of the royals to seek to control the Wahhabi forces on which they are so reliant, yet a certain amount of power and influence has to be ceded to the clergy and left with them for the Al Saud to survive. In this way, if the major concerns about Saudi support for extremism are a combination of "the official state ideology and the issue of terror financing,"[92] then considerably more could be done, even quite easily, about the latter, whereas the former touches on the very prospects of Al Saud survival. This will always make the Saudi counterterrorism and counterextremism efforts complex and, to many, controversial. When under direct threat, the regime's counterterrorism efforts have been strong and deliberate, as in the fight with AQAP over 2003–2005. This was, as noted, essentially an existential conflict. However, the Saudi regime has had less motivation to suppress other extremist actions, especially the targets of them are abroad. As a result, it has been responded to vocal and radical Islamism in varying ways. Thus, its antiterrorism and counterextremism approach since the early 2000s has had several aspects. First, of course, has been the "hard" counterterrorism tactics pursued against AQAP, especially after 2003. Second has been the Prevention, Rehabilitation, and Aftercare (PRAC) program, which sought to counter the ideological and intellectual bases of extremism. Third, the Saudis have made some efforts against the financing of extremist groups. Finally, the Saudis worked far more closely with external actors, especially Western states such as the United States, United Kingdom, and some European states, on specific initiatives and to improve their capability.

Two of these—the hard counterterrorism tactics and international cooperation—have already been mentioned. They are also somewhat interlinked, given that the Saudis most needed international assistance in areas that would support hard counterterrorism efforts, such as special forces training, counterterrorism intelligence gathering (especially electronic surveillance), tracking international financial flows and people movements, and other such areas.[93] This is important both for the practical reason that the conflict with AQAP had become violent, making a military and state security capability essential in at least some circumstances, but it was also a useful demonstration that the state was taking the threat of terrorism seriously—carrots work best when combined with sticks, it is typically argued. Yet, as noted, hard counterterrorism tactics were in fact used thriftily and judiciously by the Saudi state. The lessons from other Arab states were perhaps instructive: the Egyptian state, for example, fought an extensive conflict with Islamic extremists in the 1990s, and of course the 1992–2004 Algerian civil war was an especially tragic reminder of how pitiless and costly such conflicts could be. Although the Saudis were criticized for this softer approach, it has worked better than many critics expected, and was a sounder choice than a purely repressive strategy that might have created new sources of opposition to the state. Thus, while it was brutal when the circumstances demanded it, including in engaging with AQAP militants in armed fighting, the Saudi regime also tried to use a carrot alongside the stick, appealing to militants to give up their struggle, and providing them with opportunities to do so.

The Saudi moves against terrorism financing were quite significant, remembering however that this was an area in which the government received enormous criticism for not having done enough prior to 9/11. While the *9/11 Commission Report* in 2004 found no explicit evidence of Saudi government funding for al-Qa'eda, donations from the Saudi government sponsored al-Haramain Islamic Foundation may have reached al-Qa'eda, according to the *Report*, and certainly the evidence that Saudi individuals provided financial support to al-Qa'eda cells is very clear.[94] Reinforcing the argument that the Saudi government addresses financing when its own position is at stake, the state cut off bin Laden's assets and holdings in the Kingdom when he lost his Saudi citizenship in 1994, and they also tried very actively, and quite successfully, to block his direct fundraising in the country in the late 1990s.[95] Other financing was more difficult to block, however, given how effectively and discreetly extremist scholars and sympathizers were able to raise and funnel money to groups, and even to particular cells. Moreover, the lines between funding for social purposes versus more militant or violent ones was blurred, as were the lines between funding that went to al-Qa'eda, whether to bin Laden or AQAP, versus funding for overseas causes such as Chechnya.[96]

The Saudi efforts against fundraising, especially by bin Laden, al-Qa'eda, and affiliated and sympathetic groups and individuals, obviously increased massively after the 9/11 attacks, and became an important part of the Saudi efforts at counterterrorism and anti-radicalism. In the initial years, the government shut down the al-Haramain Islamic Foundation, tightened laws on international financial transfers out of the Kingdom, placed charities under much greater scrutiny, and publicly encouraged people to provide funding to groups and causes at home.[97] They also created greater state capacity against extremist fundraising, as with the formation of the Saudi Anti-Financial Crime Unit, designed both to investigate terrorist financing and to share intelligence on it, and by amending or updating laws on banking, cash collection, unofficial money exchange, and greater control over the informal money and remittance transfer system *Hawala*.[98] Such measures do appear to have helped stem the flow of funding to groups such as al-Qa'eda.

Where the Saudi government also focused its efforts after 2001 was in the PRAC program. The PRAC was implemented as of 2003, and therefore not so much because of the 9/11 attacks but in response to the AQAP threat and the concern among key members of the leadership about the more general rise in political Islamism and extremism in the Kingdom in the 2000s. The program was an extensive campaign "designed to eliminate violent opposition to the state by reinforcing the traditional Saudi interpretation of Islam" and "eliminate the intellectual support for Islamic extremism."[99] The Saudi leadership saw it as part of their efforts to strengthen the official narrative on Wahhabi Islam, and to counter what the Saudi elite mostly saw as the violent outcome of people misrepresenting or misinterpreting the ideas and intentions of Wahhabism. King Abdullah made his views clear in several speeches, including one as crown prince in 2003, when he said: "We should not allow a minority of deviant terrorists to target its [i.e., Islam's] image. The bullets that kill women and children, terrorize those secured in their safety and destroy innocent communities, do not come from rifles, but from deviant thoughts and misguided interpretations of our great religion and its noble message."[100] The PRAC program, as an outcome of views such as this, therefore was an attempt not at winning an ideological war among contending opinions, but rather sought to counter what the state saw as abnormal or deformed religious thinking and an abuse of religion.

The program, predominantly run from the Ministry of the Interior but with input from a range of state institutions, has a number of elements. The first is prevention, which targets children, young adults, and the public. It aims to provide a more moderate interpretation of the religion, backed by jurisprudence from mainstream clerics, and to counter the claims of unrecognized, often self-appointed scholars with more extremist views. The prevention campaign runs through several outlets, including activities at schools, support for moderate scholars to publish material, sponsored media programs, and other activities.[101] For young men, there are also activities provided to occupy their time more effectively and reduce the likelihood of them being attracted to radical ideas because they are bored or unemployed.[102]

The second tenet of the PRAC program is rehabilitation. The key activity within this is counseling, where clerics, scholars, and academics hold discussions and debates, normally with prisoners jailed for extremist activities who agree to the therapy.[103] Ideally, others, including psychologists and the militant's family members, are involved as well. It is run by four sub-committees within the Ministry of the Interior.[104] The counseling itself is conducted by the Religious Scholars Subcommittee, consisting of around 100 scholars who make contact with willing detainees, provide them with courses, and discuss religious ideas with them. Other subcommittees monitor the counseling and assess the security risk when considering if detainees are ready for release. On or nearing release from jail, counseled prisoners are also given help transitioning back into society and avoiding trouble in the future, and usually are monitored and required to maintain contact with the Security Subcommittee running the program. The Saudi government claims that the counseling program is very successful, with a success rate supposedly of 80–90 percent.[105] While this probably overstates the result, the program is useful at a couple of levels. First, it certainly has *some* effect on countering extremism, whatever the actual percentage rate of nonrecidivism. Second, the counseling process and the contact after release from prison lets the state assess the specific views and risks posed by an individual, and keep watch on them. In this way, the program is not just a means to deradicalize, important as that is, but also serves Saudi counterterrorism efforts.

The third aspect of the PRAC program is "aftercare," covering halfway accommodation for prisoners being released back into the community, reintegration programs for returnees from United States or foreign custody such as former inmates of Guantanamo Bay, and policies to avoid participants reoffending.[106] Such measures are designed to reinforce nonextremist views and practices, get people used to societal expectations and patterns after a time in custody, and keep participants from returning to radical groups or seeking out old friends and mentors who might then be able to reradicalize them. Again, this part of the program allows monitoring and assessment of those involved, and is also useful because it moves beyond a religious focus to bring in family members, old social networks, cultural practices, and other linkages and obligations that serve to deter participants from reoffending.[107]

ISLAMISM AND SAUDI SECURITY

The Saudi regime since the 1990s has faced new security threats and dynamics related to Islamism. This has included a confrontation with violent extremism during the AQAP insurgency against the Saudi state in the early to mid 2000s, as well as other threats from radical Islamism opposition figures, radicalized fighters returning from jihad abroad, and even the rise of societal opposition to the Al Saud that draws on Islam for its justification or legitimization. The Saudi government has responded in various ways, waging war directly with the most rejectionist and violent of groups, with "softer" counterterrorism means to counter and undermine extremist messages, and at times through arrests and other forms of repression. Some measures, especially the repression and arrests of prominent figures in the 1990s, were largely ineffective.

Yet, after 9/11, the Saudi government was often criticized for not doing enough to combat extremism. In the mid-2000s and beyond, this included criticism for their emphasis on softer forms of counterterrorism.[108] There was an assumption that if the Saudis were not emphasizing hard counterterrorism strategies and tactics, it was because they were secretly sympathetic to the extremists. Some may have been, at least in some specific cases. However, it is important to recall that the Saudi system itself, and the regime and elites at its summit, were themselves threatened by homegrown extremists, especially during the AQAP conflict of 2003–2005. They handled the task of countering AQAP and winning that conflict in a certain way and for certain reasons; a one-dimensional, violent suppression of such extremists, without wider counterterrorism and de-radicalization efforts, would probably have been unproductive. Had the state been seen simply as repressing or even killing those who disagreed with it, and especially if claims of torture or abuse had been more substantial, this would ultimately have undermined the state. It would have made the state's claim to be acting with religious endorsement ring hollow. It would have weakened the legitimacy of state institutions, not least of all the security and law enforcement apparatus. And it would have undermined the claims to authority of more moderate clerics.

Along similar lines, many of the more stringent observers of the country in the West typically point to underlying sources of Saudi support for terrorism, such as the funding for extremists that has come out of the Kingdom, the fiery rhetoric of some clerics, and the state's appointment from time to time of figures sympathetic to terrorism. Rather than damning the Saudi leadership, this highlights the conflicted position they are in, and their need to strike a delicate balance between, on the one hand, the key actors on who the regime rests for support and legitimacy, especially the Wahhabi clergy, and on the other hand more reformist forces within the country and external actors such as the United States, on which they also rely for regime and national security. This largely neutralizes the common question as to whether the Saudi regime is more or less secure as a result of its relationship with the Wahhabi clergy: the answer is that the state and regime would not exist without that relationship, and may not be able to maintain power without it, yet the royal-clerical dynamic requires an acutely sensitive compromise in policymaking that, if not balanced perfectly, itself becomes a security risk for the Al Saud.

The political leadership have tried to "contain, regulate, and mobilize" Wahhabism by placing a metaphorical circle around it as an ideology and around the clerics most prominent within it. The religious establishment were co-opted, for the most part very successfully, while those outside the circle are marginalized, sometimes repressed, and if need be, repressed violently. As a national security tactic, this has worked to the extent that the Al Saud and the political elite have stared down the threat from extremism, gaining substantial assistance from the clergy and without radicalizing many clerics or turning them into opposition against the royals and their main policies. Whether this tactic can continue to work in the future is less certain. In the coming years and decades, the Saudi regime will not only need to keep balancing the old relationships that have traditionally sustained its rule, but will also have to address a range of new dynamics and emerging threats. Saudi society, the political economy, the mechanics of royal rule, and the international environment are all likely to become still more complex in the years ahead.

NOTES

1. This observation is made routinely in the literature, but see for examples Thomas Hegghammer, *Jihad in Saudi Arabia: Violence and Pan-Islamism since 1979* (Cambridge: Cambridge University Press, 2010), 2 and Tim Niblock, *Saudi Arabia: Power, Legitimacy and Survival* (London: Routledge, 2006), 163.

2. Figures from Council on Foreign Relations, "Backgrounder: Saudi Arabia: Withdrawal of U.S. Forces," New York: Council on Foreign Relations, May 2, 2003, http://www.cfr.org/saudi-arabia/saudi-arabia-withdrawl-us-forces/p7739, accessed November 26, 2013, cited in Rachel Bronson, *Thicker Than Oil: America's Uneasy Partnership with Saudi Arabia* (New York: Oxford University Press, 2006), 235.

3. Niblock, *Saudi Arabia*, 4.

4. Ibid., 26.

5. Andrew Hammond, *The Islamic Utopia: The Illusion of Reform in Saudi Arabia* (London: Pluto Press, 2012), 38.

6. As discussed in Ibid., 50–56.

7. The survey is conducted regularly, but not all years include sampling of Saudi Arabians, thus the 2010 survey has been chosen as a recent one reflective of the mood of the 2000s, and prior to the Arab uprisings. On the survey see Shibley Telhami, *2010 Annual Arab Public Opinion Survey*, University of Maryland with Zogby International, http://www.brookings.edu/~/media/research/files/reports/2010/8/05%20arab%20opinion%20poll%20telhami/0805_arabic_opinion_poll_telhami.pdf, accessed November 25, 2013.

8. David Pollack, "Saudi Arabia by the Numbers," *Foreign Policy*, February 12, 2010, n.p., http://www.foreignpolicy.com/articles/2010/02/12/saudi_arabia_by_the_numbers, accessed November 26, 2013.

9. See *Arabs: What They Believe and What They Value Most* (Washington: Arab American Institute, 2002), 67 (Table XXIV), http://b.3cdn.net/aai/15b74344248440f677_xzm6yho0g.pdf, accessed November 26, 2013.

10. David Pollack, "What Do Saudis Want?" *Foreign Policy*, February 12, 2010, n.p., http://www.foreignpolicy.com/articles/2010/02/12/what_do_saudis_want, accessed November 26, 2013.

11. David E. Long, *Culture and Customs of Saudi Arabia* (Westport: Greenwood Press, 2005), 5.

12. Ibid., 5–16.

13. The Hijaz example is noted in Madawi Al-Rasheed, *A Most Masculine State: Gender, Politics, and Religion in Saudi Arabia* (Cambridge: Cambridge University Press, 2013), 12–14.

14. For some context on this, see Kelly J. Shannon, " 'I'm glad I'm not a Saudi woman': The First Gulf War and U.S. Encounters with Saudi Gender Relations," *Cambridge Review of International Affairs*, published online by Taylor and Francis October 12, 2012, http://www.tandfonline.com/doi/abs/10.1080/09557571.2012.678296#.Upan_uLpfwo, accessed November 28, 2013.

15. Joseph A. Kéchechian, *Legal and Political Reforms in Saudi Arabia* (London: Routledge, 2013), 178–182; and most recently, on protests in late 2013, see Ben Hubbard, "Saudi Women Rise Up, Quietly, and Slide into the Driver's Seat," *The New York Times*, October 26, 2013, http://www.nytimes.com/2013/10/27/world/middleeast/a-mostly-quiet-effort-to-put-saudi-women-in-drivers-seats.html?_r=0, accessed November 28, 2013.

16. Nimrod Raphaeli, "Demands for Reforms in Saudi Arabia," *Middle Eastern Studies*, 41, 4 (2005), 522; Kéchechian, *Legal and Political Reforms in Saudi Arabia*, 174–177.

17. As noted very widely, but see for example Madawi Al-Rasheed, "Saudi Arabia: Local and Regional Challenges," *Contemporary Arab Affairs*, 6, 1 (2013), 32–33.

18. Madawi Al-Rasheed, *A History of Saudi Arabia*, 2nd ed. (Cambridge: Cambridge University Press, 2010), 263.

19. Michaela Prokop, "The War of Ideas: Education in Saudi Arabia," in Paul Aarts and Gerd Nonneman (eds.), *Saudi Arabia in the Balance: Political Economy, Society, Foreign Affairs* (London: Hurst, 2005), 61.

20. Ibid., especially 63–70.

21. On the various wings of the royal family and the basis for their loyalties and variations, see Madawi Al-Rasheed, "Circles of Power: Royals and Society in Saudi Arabia," in Paul Aarts and Gerd Nonneman (eds.), *Saudi Arabia in the Balance: Political Economy, Society, Foreign Affairs* (London: Hurst, 2005), 199–211.

22. Ibid., 189.

23. Hegghammer, *Jihad in Saudi Arabia*, 1–2; Niblock, *Saudi Arabia*, 68–69; and Al-Rasheed, *A History of Saudi Arabia*, 138–143.

24. This point has been made extensively, but see for example Niblock, *Saudi Arabia*, 83–85.

25. Ibid., 77–78.

26. Roel Meijer, "The 'Cycle of Contention' and the Limits of Terrorism in Saudi Arabia," in Paul Aarts and Gerd Nonneman (eds.), *Saudi Arabia in the Balance: Political Economy, Society, Foreign Affairs* (London: Hurst, 2005), 295–298.

27. Mariam Mufti and Robert L. Lamb, *Religion and Militancy in Pakistan and Afghanistan: A Literature Review* (Washington: Center for Strategic and International Studies, June 2012), 24, http://csis.org/files/publication/120628_Mufti_ReligionMilitancy_Web.pdf, accessed November 29, 2013.

28. Ibid., 24.

29. See Stéphane Lacroix, *Awakening Islam: The Politics of Religious Dissent in Contemporary Saudi Arabia* (Cambridge: Harvard University Press, 2011), 109–118 but especially 113–114.

30. Ibid., 114.

31. Thomas Hegghammer and Stéphane Lacroix, "Rejectionist Islamism in Saudi Arabia: The Story of Juhayman al-'Utaybi Revisited," *International Journal of Middle East Studies*, 39, 1 (2007), 105.

32. International Crisis Group (ICG), *Saudi Arabia Backgrounder: Who Are the Islamists?* (Brussels: ICG Middle East Report N°31, 21 September 2004), 1–2.

33. Hegghammer and Lacroix, "Rejectionist Islamism in Saudi Arabia," 105.

34. On al-Albani and *ahl al-hadith* see Lacroix, *Awakening Islam*, 81–89.

35. What follows is based mostly on Hegghammer and Lacroix, "Rejectionist Islamism in Saudi Arabia," 105–106.

36. Ibid., 106.

37. Ibid.

38. Lacroix, *Awakening Islam*, 114–115.

39. These figures are from Hegghammer, *Jihad in Saudi Arabia*, 47.

40. Ibid.

41. Lacroix, *Awakening Islam*, 158–160.

42. Ibid., 163–164.

43. On these two figures—easily the two best-known *al-Sahwa* scholars in the 1980s and 1990s—see for example Guido Steinberg, "The Wahhabi Ulama and the Saudi State: 1745 to the Present," in Paul Aarts and Gerd Nonneman (eds.), *Saudi Arabia in the Balance: Political Economy, Society, Foreign Affairs* (London: Hurst, 2005), 30–32.

44. Toby Craig Jones, "Religious Revivalism and Its Challenge to the Saudi Regime," in Mohammed Ayoob and Hasan Kosebalaban (eds.), *Religion and Politics in Saudi Arabia: Wahhabism and the State* (Boulder: Lynne Rienner, 2009), 112–114.

45. Ibid.

46. Ibid., 113.

47. John R. Bradley, "Al Qaeda and the House of Saud: Eternal Enemies or Secret Bedfellows?," *The Washington Quarterly*, 28, 4 (2005), 145.

48. On this period and these jihads in Bosnia, Chechnya, Tajikistan and elsewhere, see for example Hegghammer, *Jihad in Saudi Arabia*, 48–58.

49. Ibid., 68–69.

50. Ibid., 72.

51. Ibid.

52. Ibid., 73.

53. Ibid.

54. Ibid., 72–73.

55. Niblock, *Saudi Arabia*, 163–164.

56. Hegghammer, *Jihad in Saudi Arabia*, 144.

57. Ibid., 145.

58. For background on the al-Shu'aybi school see Ibid., 83–98.

59. Ibid., 152.

60. Ibid.

61. Meijer, "The 'Cycle of Contention' and the Limits of Terrorism in Saudi Arabia," 278.

62. Hegghammer, *Jihad in Saudi Arabia*, 1.

63. Meijer, "The 'Cycle of Contention' and the Limits of Terrorism in Saudi Arabia," 278–279.

64. For background on al-Uyayri see Hegghammer, *Jihad in Saudi Arabia*, 118–122.

65. Ibid., 199–202.

66. Ibid., 201.

67. Meijer, "The 'Cycle of Contention' and the Limits of Terrorism in Saudi Arabia," 279.

68. Hegghammer, *Jihad in Saudi Arabia*, 128.

69. Meijer, "The 'Cycle of Contention' and the Limits of Terrorism in Saudi Arabia," 280.

70. What follows is from Hegghammer, *Jihad in Saudi Arabia*, 202–204.

71. Ibid., 203.

72. Ibid., 204.

73. Ibid., 205–206.

74. For an extensive list and details of attacks in the spring of 2004 see IntelCenter, *al-Qaeda in the Arabian Peninsula: Shotting, Hostage Taking, Kidnapping Wave—May/June 2004 (AQAP-SHK-WMJ04) v1.1* (Alexandria: IntelCenter/Tempest Publishing LLC, 2004), http://www.intelcenter.com/AQAP-SHK-PUB-v1-1.pdf, accessed November 9, 2013.

75. On the kidnapping and beheading of Johnson, see "Militants behead US hostage," *BBC News*, June 18, 2003, http://news.bbc.co.uk/2/hi/middle_east/3820495.stm, accessed November 9, 2013; and IntelCenter, *al-Qaeda in the Arabian Peninsula*, 19–24.

76. Hegghammer, *Jihad in Saudi Arabia*, 213.

77. This term is Hegghammer's; see Ibid., 213–217.

78. For an up-to-date list of AQAP activities and matters, see the collection of materials and the timeline published on the dedicated page "Al Qaeda in the Arabian Peninsula," on the website of *The New York Times*, http://topics.nytimes.com/top/reference/timestopics/organizations/a/al_qaeda_in_the_arabian_peninsula/, accessed December 9, 2013.

79. Hegghammer, *Jihad in Saudi Arabia*, 217–226.

80. Many scholars have used this term, differentiating between "hard" and "soft" counterterrorism tactics. See as examples Ibid., 218–221; also Christopher Boucek, "Saudi Arabia's 'Soft' Counterterrorism Strategy: Prevention, Rehabilitation, and Aftercare," *Carnegie Paper Number 97* (Washington: Middle East Program, Carnegie Endowment for International Peace, September 2008).

81. What follows here on the debate over jihad in Iraq versus Saudi Arabia is largely drawn from Hegghammer, *Jihad in Saudi Arabia*, 222–226.

82. Ibid., 223.

83. Ibid.

84. Bradley, "Al Qaeda and the House of Saud," 146.

85. For example Nawaf Obaid and Anthony Cordesman, *Saudi Militants in Iraq: Assessment and Kingdom's Response* (Washington: Center for Strategic and International Studies, 19 September 2005), http://csis.org/files/media/csis/pubs/050919_saudimiltantsiraq.pdf, accessed December 9, 2013. This is a reputable source, but the authors were writing in September 2005 before the Iraqi conflict reached its peak. They put the number of foreign fighters at 3,000 at that time, with Saudi nationals constituting 12 percent of them, or 350 people. Given that the 3,000 number was a cautious and conservative one, and extrapolated out to 2007 or 2008, it is highly likely that a total of over 1,000 Saudis eventually went to fight in Iraq.

86. Bradley, "Al Qaeda and the House of Saud," 145.

87. Hegghammer, *Jihad in Saudi Arabia*, 225.

88. Ibid.

89. As discussed in Obaid and Cordesman, *Saudi Militants in Iraq*, 13–16.

90. Hegghammer, *Jihad in Saudi Arabia*, 225.

91. Roel Maijer, "Saudi Arabia's Religious Counter-Terrorist Discourse," *Middle East Institute* website, February 15, 2012, n.p., http://www.mei.edu/content/saudi-arabia%E2%80%99s-religious-counter-terrorist-discourse, accessed December 9, 2013.

92. A. S. M. Ali Ashraf, "Transnational Cooperation on Anti-Terrorism: A Comparative Case Study of Saudi Arabia and Indonesia," *Perceptions*, XII, (Summer/Autumn 2007), 99–100.

93. For a more detailed list of Saudi activities with an international cooperation element, see Ibid., 108 (Table 2).

94. Ibid., 101.

95. Hegghammer, *Jihad in Saudi Arabia*, 124.

96. Ibid., 126–127.

97. Rachel Bronson, "Rethinking Religion: The Legacy of the U.S.-Saudi Relationship," *The Washington Quarterly*, 28, 4 (Autumn 2005), 126; Ali Ashraf, "Transnational Cooperation on Anti-Terrorism," 105–108.

98. *Hawala* involves the transfer of money without funds actually being moved, based on an honor system and personal networks among the intermediaries in the system, who keep an informal running tab of the total that each of them owes to or is owed by others. The system is often used by expatriate workers, who value its speed and low cost, but the absence of records means that its usefulness to terrorists and others is obvious.

99. Boucek, "Saudi Arabia's 'Soft' Counterterrorism Strategy," 3.

100. Speech by King Abdullah bin Abd al-Aziz, Crown Prince of Saudi Arabia, to the 2003 Organization of the Islamic Conference summit, Kuala Lumpur, Malaysia, 17–18 October 2003, quoted in Ali S. Awadh Asseri, *Combating Terrorism: Saudi Arabia's Role in the War on Terror* (Karachi: Oxford University Press, 2009), 86.

101. Asseri, *Combating Terrorism*, 88; Boucek, "Saudi Arabia's 'Soft' Counterterrorism Strategy," 8–10.

102. Boucek, "Saudi Arabia's 'Soft' Counterterrorism Strategy," 8.

103. On the counselling program see Ibid., 11–17.

104. On the subcommittees, see Asseri, *Combating Terrorism*, 88–91.

105. Boucek, "Saudi Arabia's 'Soft' Counterterrorism Strategy," 21.

106. Ibid., 17–21.

107. Ibid., 20–21.

108. For some comment on these, with very different bases behind the discussions, see Hegghammer, *Jihad in Saudi Arabia*, 218–221; and Bradley, "Al Qaeda and the House of Saud," especially 143–148.

CHAPTER 6

Emerging Strategic and Security Issues

Having laid out the security issues and dynamics that shape security, the question that naturally stems from this is where Saudi Arabia and its security dynamics currently stand, and where they might be headed. Above all, how stable is the Middle East and, within it, is Saudi Arabia? Which issues might most impact the Saudi regime and its complex state-society relationship in the coming years, and which are specific to Saudi Arabia and which are exogenous but likely to impact it? This chapter will look at several critical issues that currently confront, or may soon emerge to challenge, the Saudi royal dynasty, the state and its elite, and the country in general. While neither definite nor comprehensive, the discussion that follows encompasses some issues that now exist or for which there is mounting evidence. The aim is to provide some ideas and an exploration of possibilities, not a set of concrete predictions.

It would be easy to paint a bleak picture of the future. Indeed, many observers do exactly that: Saudi Arabia became a topical research area in the early-mid-1990s, and many assessments at that time were strongly negative in their prognoses. A 1994 book review noted this astutely: "There is a cottage industry forming to predict the impending fall of the House of Saud. . . . Of course, this all makes for much more dramatic reading than would a version that says the regime faces financial problems, as well as uncertainties stemming from succession, and that fairly substantial political changes will no doubt be needed in the coming decade . . . ."[1] This is as true now, in the 2010s, as it was back then. As this book has argued, Saudi Arabia *has* made political and economic changes, many of them very substantial. More reform is almost certain in the coming decade. The Saudi regime *could* fall—it has faced periods of particular unpopularity with its society, and it remains to the present day unpopular, even detested, by some of its people—but its past durability and its co-optive and repressive capacity suggest that, while a revolution is not impossible, the probability of it should not be overstated.

A final caveat concerns the distinctions between the interests of various actors and forces in the Saudi system, and the variations between those at the core of the system and those operating more distantly from central power. In discussing security, the question of *whose* stability and security is being discussed is a critical one. Something that improves the security of the royals may, simultaneously, have less importance for or even harm the security of society. The interests of the elite and of society converge on many matters of security, but not all, while other actors link into the system and share the elite's interest in stability, especially those co-opted into the extended patronage and social networks that the Al Saud uses to maintain their rule. The security of the state is important, since it dominates political organization and commands the allegiance of most ordinary Saudis, and if it were to collapse or fail, the impacts on Saudi society and the region would be colossal. Thus, the focus here is on regime and state stability—that is, the stability of the royal dynasty, other political elites, and state institutions—although not exclusively.

EMERGING DOMESTIC POLITICAL AND ECONOMIC ISSUES AND REGIME STABILITY

The Saudi political system is, paradoxically, a source of both stability and instability. The royal family provides an elite base to the regime and is a force for continuity, but it also polarizes those Saudis who hunger for more political change than the royals will permit. The networks that the royals have built around them, including the key symbiotic relationships, are a source of stability provided the royals can, and wish to, sustain the bargain. Even the relationship with the United States could be seen in this light, as something that aids security when it is managed discreetly, but is a security risk when it is too strong, is too overt, or seen as signifying U.S. dominance over the Kingdom. The rentier nature of the Saudi system then adds a seemingly stabilizing dynamic to the state-society relationship, letting the regime "buy" both support and the ability to repress those who will not be bought. Yet, several political economy issues are emerging that seem likely to pose future challenges for security and stability in Saudi Arabia: strains on the rentier bargain; the need for economic reforms; and pressures for political liberalization.

Strains on the Rentier Bargain

Since the first commercial volumes of Saudi oil were extracted from under the Kingdom's sands, hydrocarbon revenues have supported Al Saud rule.

Even before the age of oil, Ibn Saud solidified his rule, as leaders historically so often had, using rents such as trade and pilgrimage income. What changed in the late 1940s and especially the 1950s was not rentierism specifically but the sheer volume of rents available. Oil rents have given successive kings and elites the means to construct a modern state apparatus while both formally and informally co-opting, shaping, and if necessary repressing the population.

While rents are not the sole explanation for the durability of the regime, they have been immensely important. Saudi Arabia is a rentier state by any common definition, which traditionally has been whether the state receives at least 40 percent of its income from rents. In the Saudi case, while oil revenues fluctuate greatly year by year, they are typically over 80 percent of state revenue, usually more. In 2011, they were 92.5 percent. In 2009, when prices were suddenly at a low point, rents still delivered 85.2 percent of state revenue.[2] Even over 2000 to 2005, the figure was a little lower but above 80 percent, coming in at 80 to 85 percent in each of those years.[3]

The Saudi population is co-opted by rents in a variety of ways. For much of the population, state jobs are available in the public service or with state-owned firms. Saudis prefer this arrangement: in 2011, the government employed 998,138 people, 92.1 percent of them Saudi nationals and only 7.9 percent foreigners. In contrast, the private sector employed almost 7.8 million people, including 844,476 Saudis, but this was only 10.9 percent of total private sector employment, making foreign nationals 89.1 percent of the private sector workforce.[4] This stems in part from the generous terms and conditions of employment in the public sector: in 2011, Saudi nationals in the private sector were paid a minimum monthly wage of SR3,000 (US$800) versus a public sector wage for general positions that ranged from a minimum of SR3,750 (US$1,000) to some SR24,750 (US$6,599) per month.[5] Many Saudis also view the public sector as a more prestigious place to work. By all accounts, furthermore, the hours and complexity of the work is lower in the public sector than the private. The education and training systems also remain inadequate in preparing young Saudis to be globally competitive in the private sector.[6] All this means that the attempts to shift more Saudis into jobs currently performed by foreigners have not worked, despite this "Saudi-ization" policy dating back to the mid-1980s.[7] The most tempting conclusion from all of these indicators is that it reflects the co-optive role played by public sector employment, with the state deliberately creating many jobs for Saudis, and paying them very well, so that wealth is shared and seen to be shared with society.

The state also "buys" support and legitimacy, using rents in other ways. There is very little taxation of Saudi nationals, for example.[8] No personal income taxes in the usual sense are applied to Saudi nationals (although the state enforces the collection of zakat, or "alms," an Islamic donation required as a tenet of Islam, which is assessed at 2.5 percent per annum of a person's or entity's net income and assets). Otherwise, there are corporate income taxes, income taxes on foreign nationals, and a range of government fees and charges, but the overall tax obligations of Saudis are modest compared to taxpayers in OECD economies or even in other, nonoil states of the Middle East. Despite this low level of overall taxation, Saudi nationals enjoy a large welfare structure, including free education and healthcare funded by the state, and payments and cheap loans to help with the costs of marriage, building a house, or starting a business. There are also other generous subsidies, including on gasoline, electricity, and water.[9] The Saudi government spends around 10 percent of its GDP on subsidies, and is the highest spender in the region on education.[10] Such spending is a core mechanism of regime maintenance by the Saudi rulers: at the height of the Arab uprisings, in March 2011, King Abdullah announced a US$130 billion spending package,[11] a co-optive tactic triggered by regime fears of an uprising at home.

Such spending can be highly effective, but arguably is profligate; it is certainly a strain on the state's coffers. Such spending simply would not be possible without the tremendous oil wealth at the state's disposal. This wealth, however, has politically trapped the Al Saud. They have become reliant on using it to allay the need for substantive political concessions and reforms, and to postpone economic or other reforms that might be unpopular. This means that if rents fall suddenly, or shift into a permanent decline, the Al Saud will have to cut spending, borrow, or make new bargains with society. Cutting spending is politically unpalatable for the royals, and so in the past they have always chosen to borrow when rents fell. The Saudi budget was in deficit from the mid-1980s until the early 2000s due to low oil prices for nearly all of that period, and the cuts made were in project spending, not welfare or social spending.[12] The state borrowed much of the money needed to cover these budget deficits.[13]

If a future decline in oil income is large enough for long enough, or above all permanent, borrowing will not be a solution for the regime, in which case the Saudi rentier bargain—if it still exists when that time comes—will be unsustainable. The most likely scenario is that strains on the rentier bargain will increase year by year as rents decline, pushing the ruling elite to make reforms that in turn require concessions to specific elites and society more broadly. Whether this can be done in a stable way, if the entire rentier bargain has to be renegotiated or replaced, remains to be seen, but is unlikely given past attempts by the state to negotiate real, substantive reform.

Moreover, even if oil prices do not fall, the rentier bargain looks like being eroded, and perhaps destroyed outright, by population growth. High population growth rates have been an issue for nearly all the Middle East in recent decades, with the region's total population increasing almost sixfold from 1950 to 2005, with the annual growth rate rising from 2.5 percent in the 1950s and 1960s to 2.75 from the 1970s to the end of the millennium.[14] In Saudi Arabia, the increase was even more dramatic. Population grew from 3.2 million in 1950 to 24.57 million in 2005—with the growth rate reaching an astonishing

5.87 percent per annum[15]—while the working-age population jumped from 1.75 million to 14.8 million in the same period.[16] Economic growth and private sector development was nowhere near sufficient to employ all the additional job-seekers created by population growth. The pressure of population growth was accommodated, in economic terms, by a relative decline in income per capita. GDP per capita boomed in the 1970s, peaking in 1981 at US$17,543 (adjusted to 2011 dollars), then plummeting to US$5,841 in 1988 after oil prices collapsed, then slowly trending upward again in the 1990s; only with the 2003–2008 oil boom did GDP per capita rise again sharply.[17] In real terms, the 1981 GDP was surpassed only in 2008, when the figure hit US$18,065.[18] With the budget reliant on oil revenues, it followed a nearly identical pattern.[19]

This dramatic fluctuation in per capita and state income, including the seven-year decline and near-stagnation from the mid-1980s until the early-2000s, shows that rentier bargains are fragile. The Saudi state met its end of the bargain for many years, as mentioned, only by borrowing. Even then, the economy faced a significant and rising unemployment rate in the 1990s, including very high youth unemployment, with obvious risks for the regime.[20] Such a problem could easily emerge again, since population is still increasing at around 2.7 percent per year, and so doubling every 26 years. This would mean that, if rents remain stable in real terms, GDP per capita would drop from the 2011 figure of US$20,777 per person to US$9,147 by 2040. Oil prices may rise, of course, softening the impacts of population growth, but there is also a very real risk that oil wealth per capita will not keep up with population. In that case, the rentier bargain will either have to be restructured into a broad welfarist one as currently exists in Iran, Iraq, Algeria, and other oil economies with large populations, or it will have to be replaced completely, with grave risks for Al Saud rule, and for stability if the regime resists such dramatic reform. It is difficult to know *when* this might happen, but if the rentier bargain has to be reconstructed any time soon, the state remains unprepared and unwilling to offer major concessions to society. This would almost certainly be politically destabilizing for the Kingdom, and a security risk for the region and the international energy system.

Economic Risks and the Potential Security Impacts

The rentier bargain relies on the co-optive capability of the state being strong. Not only could population growth undermine the bargain, but overall rent income is, as mentioned, capricious. Instability and new security challenges could just as easily come about because of oil production or export volumes decreasing, which could happen for a couple of different reasons. Most obviously, oil may simply run out faster than expected. Some oil analysts fear that Saudi oil reserve figures are rubbery and inaccurate, and the Saudis do not publish detail on individual fields or the basis for their overall reserve estimates, making it very unclear what the lifespan and future output of key fields might be.[21] The largest field, Ghawar, has produced roughly half of Saudi output for over 30 years, so just knowing its prospects would illuminate the long-term prospects for Saudi production overall. There is some evidence that Ghawar may enter a production decline sooner than expected.[22] Regardless, the overall Saudi reserve figures are questionable because their methodology is kept secret and because they appear uncorrelated with production;[23] past increases in reserves have usually seemed to be the result of OPEC politics,[24] not scientifically based adjustment. If production were to unavoidably peak and decline any time soon, while the regime remains ill-prepared for a decline in rents, it would have a disastrous impact on stability, even threatening the survival of the regime if the decline in total revenue was steep.

Another problem is that Saudi domestic oil consumption is rising at a worrying pace, such that there is a growing risk of this cutting into the volumes available for export. This is the result of subsidies and other misguided policies that encourage the inefficient use and overconsumption of oil and gas.[25] As one paper put it, "[I]n Saudi Arabia in 2002, the after-tax price of gasoline was set at only US$0.19/l[iter]. These below-market prices result in the implicit subsidization of energy consumption. . . . As a result, energy consumption growth has been much faster than economic growth. In other words, generous subsidies for energy are responsible for implausibly high energy intensity," with the surprising but potentially disastrous possibility that the enormous rise in domestic consumption might "even turn net exporters into net importers."[26] Strange as it may seem, Saudi Arabia risks running out of exportable oil. A 2011 Chatham House report made similar arguments, suggesting that absent any changes to current trajectories of production and consumption, Saudi Arabia could run out of exportable oil by 2038.[27] In September 2012, a Citigroup report made headlines by assessing that the year might actually be as early as 2030.[28] Regardless, the possibility of oil exports ceasing or declining is a dire one for Saudi security. The economy, which in 2012 earned around US$311 billion from oil, remains completely unready for such an event. Even a more gradual decline in export volumes would add to pressure on the rentier bargain. At any rate, moreover, subsidies already cost the Saudi state dearly: oil for domestic use by power providers, for example, is priced at between US$5 and US$15 per barrel, a fraction of the market price, and overall, the Citigroup report estimated that about US$80 billion per year is lost through oil not being exported at market price.[29] For the regime, choosing to co-opt society through energy subsidies is a trade-off. While there are political benefits from subsidies, they come at the expense of export income and the politically support that that could bring.

Such future threats to Saudi stability are a reminder of the ongoing need for economic reform. The economic reforms made since 1999 have been significant, including incentives for private sector development, policies to attract foreign investment, commercial legal reforms, stock market reforms, and changes in the finance, insurance, and other sectors.[30] These were sufficient for Saudi Arabia to join the World Trade Organization in 2005. Still, there remains much to be done if some of the longer-term threats to economic and political stability are to be addressed. As already discussed, the population growth rate remains among the highest in the world, and without a drop in population, which is extremely unlikely, the only alternatives are to expand the private sector or to make Saudis more attractive to employers who might then employ them to replace foreign workers. However, the education system is not producing graduates with sufficient skills, creativity, or motivation to compete with foreign workers.[31] Some observers argue that there is also a rentier mentality or a *mudir* ("manager") syndrome, in which Saudis do not want to work in difficult, dirty, or less prestigious jobs, and instead expect that quality professional and managerial work will be offered by the state.[32] The *mudir* idea is controversial, but if at all accurate, is a sign of how difficult substantial reform will be.

Demographic and educational challenges exist alongside other long-term risks for stability. One is that the economy, for all the reforms since 1999, remains relatively closeted. Even though the state has sought new foreign investment, it also has a "negative list" of economic sectors where foreigners may not invest. There are 20 sectors or subsectors on the list, which in reality cover much of the economy. The list includes, for example, oil exploration and drilling, gas, telecommunications, insurance, power transmission, and several other areas.[33] Some of these are understandable, but many are either protectionist or economically nationalist in origin. Somewhat similarly, the state has promised much more privatization that it has been willing to deliver; the program stalled for a long time,[34] until the mid- and late-2000s. This was probably because of the unpopularity of privatization and the risk that it would undermine regime legitimacy. Many Saudis feel that services have declined in firms that have been sold, while others simply want the state to remain central in the economy.[35]

As a result, thus far reform has only focused on certain areas and types. Administrative changes, more efficient processes, and legal amendments to encourage business and trade have all been prominent, not deeper macroeconomic liberalization. This has boosted the Saudi ranking in indexes such as the World Bank's *Doing Business* report.[36] Such reforms are valuable in making business cheaper and easier to conduct, or giving greater clarity to firms about processes and regulations, but they have only minor impacts on the structure of the economy. Structural reform, such as floating the currency and allowing full global competition in most economic sectors, has barely been done, apart from the most basic adjustments. For the government, the reform question is a critical, and risky, one. Too little reform risks economic underperformance, which would carry political risks, yet economic reform that is too dramatic or rapid could be just as politically perilous. Some changes, especially liberalizing labor laws to unify wages and conditions for Saudis and non-Saudis, or raising new taxes such as personal income tax or a consumption tax, are simply out of the question politically while the rentier bargain dominates the political economy.

New Political Pressures and Regime Responses

A second realm in which reform pressures are likely in the future is in the political space. This is linked to the rentier dynamic too, because a regime's aim in enacting a rentier arrangement is in part to avoid democratic concessions or public accountability. One of the surprises for early theorists of rentierism was that, contrary to their predictions, the state was usually not able to become autonomous from society.[37] Even if oil wealth brought (and bought) considerable policy independence for leaders, they still faced an underlying threat of opposition. This always, to some extent, figured in their decision making. Despite the rentier bargains of the Gulf, popular demands for political reform, and among some groups other reform, are likely to increase in the coming years. This is the product of new technologies, media, and other sources of information, which better inform people about what is occurring elsewhere in the world and act as a means for social groups to coordinate their activities and spread their messages.[38] Additionally, economic change and reform is likely to create demands for political reform. If rents decrease or become more disaggregated, or if economic reform prompts businesspeople or other groups to become more vocal, this too will intensify the pressure for political reform.[39]

Even in rentier states that might be able to successfully co-opt or repress society, there is still the demonstration effect of change elsewhere. The clearest recent example of this was the 2011 Arab uprisings. These occurred primarily in the Arab republics, beginning in Tunisia and spreading to Egypt and then Libya, Yemen, and Syria. But the Gulf monarchies still felt threatened by them. Bahrain witnessed significant unrest in early 2011,[40] plus there were less dramatic but still notable protests in Oman, based on anger at corruption and unemployment, and among the Shia in Saudi Arabia.[41]

As a result, the Saudi regime offered new spending, as mentioned, and some modest political and social reforms. Women have been added to the Shura Council as voting members, and as of 2015, will be allowed to vote in municipal elections. To critics, these are token reforms, and certainly the Saudis have been the key force for conservatism and counterrevolution in the region since 2011.[42] Most likely, such reforms are designed to suggest a willingness to undertake reform, without the elite having to allow genuine political transformation. The Saudi regime will not offer true democratization or state accountability to society unless its very survival requires it, which for now is not the case. Separately, part of the regime's response has included financial, educational, and other co-optation for the Kingdom's Shia, and more widely, promises to crack down on corruption and other sources of popular ire.[43] Again, such steps have been notable, but have not required the regime to transfer real political power to society.

That the Saudi regime has acquiesced to societal pressure, and initiated reforms in response, has led some observers to suggest that deeper political reform is possible in the future. More likely, however, the regime will strive to avoid genuine political liberalization and especially democratization. Past practice has usually involved limited reform, combined with an emphasis on religion, stability, and nationalism, giving an impression of state responsiveness while promoting quietism and toleration of the regime by society. The regime will want, ideally, this strategy to be sustained. If a sufficient proportion of society comes to no longer accept the regime's word on reform and stability, however, or opposition reaches a critical mass, then more substantial change will probably be essential to the Al Saud's survival. Yet, for the moment, the evidence is scant and unconvincing that deep political liberalization or a democracy bargain is coming to Saudi Arabia. For all the opposition and dissatisfaction that the Al Saud faces, the regime remains sufficiently tolerated, capable, and legitimate, and its rents voluminous enough, not to have to make dramatic political concessions.[44]

Sectarian Issues and Saudi Security

Perhaps the most pressing sociopolitical concern for the regime at present is the question of sectarianism, and how best to manage the discontent among the Shia minority. As discussed in Chapter 2, this is no simple matter: it is a layered problem, linked to the location of the Shia in the east, the history of confessional conflict in the area that is now Saudi Arabia, worsened by regional politics and regime fears of Iranian incitement of sectarian tensions, and amplified by the Wahhabi clerics' harsh views toward the Shia. Shia identity is sustained and reinforced by their sense of uniqueness, the narratives articulated by many of their own clerics, and the solidarity created by strong family and social linkages among them. For the Saudi regime, there is a need to keep the Wahhabi elite on side and so to tolerate much of their anti-Shia rhetoric, while many elites are suspicious of the Shia anyway, worried about their loyalties to the state or their openness to Iranian influence.

The discrimination that the Shia have faced, and to a significant extent continue to face, is substantial.[45] While basic and private Shia religious conduct is not usually interrupted, bureaucratic hurdles are placed in the way of approvals for new mosques and other Shia establishments. Many Shia also claim that the judicial system is prejudicial. In the eastern province, Shia Jafari courts can hear matters such as those related to personal status, but elsewhere and for other matters, the Shia are subject to courts operating under Sunni Hanbali jurisprudence. The Shia are excluded from many areas of government employment, especially in sensitive, security institutions such as the Ministry of the Interior, the National

Guard, Defense, the police force, the diplomatic service, and others. The regime has attempted to improve the treatment of Shia since the unrest in the east began in 2011, funding initiatives such as scholarships for Shiites to study overseas, but this has only gone a small way toward addressing the grievances that so many Shia feel.[46] Contrariwise, offsetting this co-optation has been the repressive tactics of the state to repress the Shia unrest, especially from 2012 onward.[47]

Given the regime's long-term, nation-building and nationalism goals, as well as its main elite bargains, it is risky to let sectarian tensions continue or worsen. Yet, the regime, yet again, is faced with the need for a delicate balancing act: the clerics and conservative social forces will react negatively to policies that are too generous or inclusive to the Shia, while if the regime simply ignores Shia grievances, or bluntly tries to repress them, they risk a continuation or worsening of the unrest and violence that has already plagued the eastern province since 2011. The future of sectarian relations in Saudi Arabia depends on the state's ability to maintain this balance, and in turn how the Shia views and responds to that. This suggests three possible future trajectories. One is more of the same, where the Shia continue to receive some co-optive largesse, but not too much, while large numbers of them remain angry and maintain their protests. This may buy time for the regime to develop a better strategy, but is not a long-term solution to the Shia "question." It could also see matters deteriorate and sectarian violence increase. Along these lines, the second possibility is of a marked deterioration in relations, and much greater violence and instability. The Shia would have difficulty mounting a massive civil conflict against the state, given the resources, intelligence capabilities, and security assets it would bring to bear on such a revolt, but a dramatically worse and more violent insurrection in Shia areas cannot be discounted. A final possibility is that the regime and the Shia come to an arrangement that enhances rather than undermines security and the interests of both the state and the Shia. The Shia have many activists in their ranks who have agitated peacefully for reform, and in the same tradition as the Sunni, have petitioned for more resources, new infrastructure, and better employment prospects in state institutions, both in the early-mid-2000s[48] and again in the early 2010s.[49] The additional spending in the eastern province and on the Shia in recent years is a positive sign, which could potentially improve the living standards and social conditions of the Shia enough to also improve their ability to engage politically but peacefully with the state in new ways. Yet, there are also very negative signs on the prospects for this scenario, in particular that the Saudi regime has increasingly sectarianized the unrest in the eastern province, blaming matters on the Shia and obtaining Wahhabi rulings against the protests.[50]

NEW INTERNATIONAL RISKS AND OPPORTUNITIES

The Gulf strategic environment and security setting are all changing, and this is bringing new security concerns and opportunities to the region and to Saudi

Arabia. Both the dynamics of the Gulf region and global-level major power dynamics are in flux, and will confront Saudi Arabia with new security challenges in the coming years.

Security Challenges in the Gulf Region

Among Saudi Arabia's traditional friends on the Arab side of the Gulf, globalization and economic change are beginning to rewrite the basis and structure of power in the region. This was discussed in Chapter 4, but is worth reiterating here, since it has started a trajectory that is likely to have significant future impacts on Saudi Arabia's security environment, strategic reach, and long-term prospects relative to its Gulf neighbors. Briefly, Saudi Arabia has benefitted in the past from its military strength comparative to the smaller states of Bahrain, Kuwait, Oman, Qatar, and the UAE, but this is changing, as both economic power and soft power become more important in contrast to military power. Military strength still matters for regional power rivalries such as the Saudi-Iranian one, perhaps, but matters little for Riyadh's ability to exert influence over its smaller neighbors or in more subtle ways. The term *security* now has a broader meaning in the Gulf, and this is something with which the Saudi regime must come to terms. Changes in energy dynamics, especially oil prices, have also been important, as low prices in the late-1980s and 1990s prompted economic openings and reforms, which were then followed by high prices again from 2003 onward, which funded new initiatives and made several Gulf states crucial international investment, financial, transport, shipping, and tourism centers.[51] Some, like Dubai, became household names in the West by the early 2000s by virtue of this shift. This, too, has changed the Gulf setting for Saudi Arabia, making it more competitive in an economic sense and making the size of a state less relevant.

Beyond these dynamics, there are other important factors shaping the Gulf of the twenty-first century. One is the maturing of its leaderships. While much of the oil wealth from the price booms over 1974–1984 or so was wasted—spent on arms, portfolio investment, and 'white elephant' projects[52]—the boom of the 2000s saw the opposite. Gulf rulers spent the wealth in far more sensible ways, including in infrastructure, education, transport, the modernization of state-owned firms, and major events. Surplus rents were invested in long-term, diversified, risk-based investments.[53] While such spending may still be driven by regime maintenance and self-preservation desires, in preparation for a time when hydrocarbons are finally depleted, state policies nonetheless have been cleverer and more strategic in the 2000s oil boom compared to previous ones.[54] This is true of Saudi Arabia, just only the smaller Gulf states, although arguably the small states have so far carved for themselves more prominent nonenergy roles in the global economy than has Saudi Arabia.

Important also is that the Gulf states have become more activist. The smaller states have created very particular positions for themselves in the global economy, and used clever marketing to "brand" their states. Dubai built an international image around its airline, its tourism sector, and an image of being open, safe, and business friendly.[55] Qatar has also sought to do something similar, such as by using its airline and major cultural events to build its image,[56] and it has branded itself through sport as well, hosting events such as the 2006 Asian Games—and Qatar would be hosting the 2022 FIFA World Cup—and through cultural influence such as Al-Jazeera television channel, which reframed Arab media.[57] Qatar has also adopted a unique and independent foreign policy, taking active and ambitious roles in international forums and in initiatives such as the NATO-led military operation in Libya in 2011 during the uprising there against Muammar Qaddafi.[58] Saudi Arabia has acted very similarly in the foreign policy realm, trying to take on a greater regional role. It has been active in Arab-Israeli affairs (as noted with the example of the 2002 and 2007 Saudi peace plan[59]) and with regional economic initiatives. It has also been more ambitious in its rivalry with Iran and in offsetting Iranian reach, as a recent example by supplying and assisting the opposition forces in Syria in the current civil war there.[60] However, it has not been as successful in taking on the economic roles, and gaining the soft power, that the UAE and Qatar have achieved.

For Saudi Arabia, all of the above has security dimensions. The small Arab Gulf states can no longer be influenced as extensively, or in the same way, as in the past. Regional bodies such as the Gulf Cooperation Council (GCC) have broadened their scope to meet both the security needs, and increasingly economic ones as well. The failure of initiatives such as a single GCC currency suggest that the smaller states are willing to resist Saudi Arabia, especially where they are concerned about ceding too much power to their larger neighbor.[61] The sheer physical and demographic size of Saudi Arabia is less impressive to its neighbors than once was the case. Even its power in the oil market has declined, in line with its inability to set prices anymore and by the rise of new state powers such as Qatar as global gas actors. As some of these smaller GCC states become international actors in their own right, gaining influence as economic actors, soft power centers, and even in their strategic links with the United States and other major powers, their strategic relationships with Saudi Arabia will become less and less crucial to them.

There are several implications for Saudi Arabia. One is that, in the security realm, they cannot rely on having the same influence in the Gulf subregion and over their smaller allies as they once had. They will almost certainly see these small states more willing to challenge them, and more able to pursue their own international policy outcomes where they disagree with Riyadh's. Some such divisions are already apparent, for example, between Saudi Arabia and Qatar over their support for anti-Asad rebel forces in Syria.[62] A second implication of the changing nature of Gulf power is that Saudi Arabia will want and need to find ways to compete with the soft power of the smaller states. It has already tried direct competition in some case, as with its funding the Dubai-based satellite television channel Al-Arabiya, set up in large part to compete with Al-Jazeera.[63] For the time being, it is less able to compete in other areas. In tourism, perhaps most obviously, the Kingdom has long welcomed pilgrims, and sometimes business and expatriate visitors, and while this has delivered it some soft power, it has not built the same economic structure and international goodwill that states such as Dubai have gained a large-scale, liberalized leisure tourism industry.[64] For the same reason—that of its strong cultural conservatism and unique Wahhabi clerical influence over social as well as religious policies, Saudi Arabia will probably never be able to carve a niche in cultural, sporting, or artistic events, given its strict visa rules, gender divisions, and the perceptions held of it in the outside world. Likewise, Saudi Arabian Airlines is not about to become a serious competitor to Emirates, Etihad, or Qatar Airways. While the Saudis may be able to compete in some areas—shipping, transport, perhaps also higher education, media, and information technology—it is not about to become a household name alongside Dubai.

Such challenges are emerging and expanding even as the Kingdom's more traditional security challenges still remain in place and as complex as ever. The future of much of the region is in flux. In Iraq, the security situation had appeared to improve after 2008 and stabilize from 2010 to 2012, but security conditions in 2013 and 2014 have worsened to again rival the worst years of the mid-2000s.[65] If Iraq deteriorates further into a new civil war, or even has sustained levels of violence comparable to 2004–2008 civil conflict, this would have significant impacts on Saudi Arabia. It could see Saudi Islamists again try to take up arms and go to Iraq, again attacking Iraqi government forces and trying to destabilize it, or perhaps this time fighting Shiites or Kurds rather than focusing on U.S. forces. Such radicalization would have a negative impact on sectarian relations and stability in Saudi Arabia in the longer term, or could see another confrontation between the Saudi security services and Islamic extremists. Just as confronting for Saudi security would be a situation where instability in Iraq merged with that in Syria, and perhaps spread into Lebanon. In such a case, Saudi Arabia would be left as the main conservative Sunni force in the region, fighting a broad and extended proxy conflict with Iran over the future of a large part of the northern Middle East. Some reporting is already raising this specter: " 'The battlefields [of Iraq and Syria] are merging,' Martin Kobler, the UN's outgoing envoy to Iraq, told the Security Council on July 16th. Indeed, the Iraqi government is so concerned about Sunni fighters coming over from Syria that it is physically separating itself from its war-torn neighbour by digging deeper trenches and higher berms along the border."[66] Finally, on this note, renewed conflict in Iraq would worsen what is already an intense Saudi-Iranian rivalry in Syria. Both states would feel as if they were engaged in a battle for their fundamental security—indeed, they probably would be—and in a future competition over Iraq, they would involve themselves and seek influence far more assertively than they did in the past.

Iran is of great strategic interest to Riyadh, especially the future of U.S.-Iranian relations and Iran's future role in the Gulf; in fact, the two dynamics are interlinked from Riyadh's perspective. For the Saudis, Iran is a strategic rival and threat to stability in the Gulf, a point the Saudis make with reference to Iran's quantitative military capacity, the Islamic Revolutionary Guard Corps' (IRGC) former meddling in the region, and not least of all, Iran's nuclear program, which the Saudis see as a core threat to the strategic balance in the Gulf. Prince Turki al-Faisal, the former intelligence chief of Saudi Arabia, provided a colorful insight into the Saudi thinking in December 2013 when he noted that "the game of hegemony toward the Arab countries [by Iran] is not acceptable . . . we won't accept to wear Iranian clothes."[67]

Much has come to depend on the U.S.-Iranian rapprochement that appears to have begun as a result of the November 2013 Geneva agreement on Iran's nuclear program. Although the deal is only an interim, six month one, the Saudis have been vocal in their opposition to it, concerned that it marks a clear strategic win for Iran, and implying that much of the victory comes at Saudi Arabia's expense. In particular, the agreement was seen as delivering legitimacy to the Iranian leadership and their claims to regional power status, and as giving them relief from economic sanctions at a time when their economy was weakening relative to the economic power of Saudi Arabia, Qatar, and other Gulf states engaged in the proxy conflict in Syria. The deal, in other words, looked to Riyadh like it would deliver Iran a boost in its rivalry with Saudi Arabia, and became a key source of the increased tension between Washington and Riyadh in the latter part of 2013.

Also important and closely linked to Saudi-Iranian rivalry is the question of what the outcome of the civil war in Syria will ultimately be. It was still undecided at the time of this writing (early 2014). The impact on Saudi security and regional influence is already substantial. If Bashar al-Asad's forces militarily defeat the insurgency against them, the fact that they did so with Iranian support and as an Iranian ally in the Arab world will be an enormous blow to the Saudis' regional influence and image. It will send the message that the Saudis were outmaneuvered by Iran, and suggest that their oil wealth may be able to buy some influence but cannot guarantee Riyadh the regional outcomes it wants. It may even undermine the Saudi claim to be a global middle power, which they argue across economic, strategic, and cultural lines. Conversely, if the opposition forces eventually defeat the Syrian government and remove Bashar al-Asad from power, it will add weight to the Saudi claims of regional leadership and dent Iran's aspirations in the Middle East and back in the Gulf. Given the complexity of the conflict to Middle Eastern politics, there will almost-certainly be other impacts from the conflict, potentially including on the U.S. role in the region, the Israeli-Palestinian conflict, Qatar's attempts at regional influence, or the prospects for particular states such as Lebanon. Regardless, the impacts on the rivalry between Tehran and Riyadh are likely to be intense and sustained.

External Powers, Old and New

The other new dynamic that Saudi Arabia will have to deal with in future years is an ongoing relationship with a United States that is in gradual relative decline, and a rise in the influence of new powers such as China and India. In the strategic realm, the United States is likely to remain the dominant outside power in the Gulf for a long time yet—probably for two or three more decades—since China is focused on its commercial and energy linkages in the Gulf, rather than showing an interest in becoming a military power. The shift in global power is something that the entire region must address, but in the case of Saudi Arabia, addressing it is complex given the importance and sensitivity of its relationship with Washington.

The U.S. relationship is still crucial to Riyadh in several respects. For Saudi Arabia, the United States is already in place as its main arms supplier through until at least 2030, with the scope for future sale of arms potentially worth as much as US$60 billion out to 2030.[68] The Saudis began exercising the agreement in late 2011, with purchases and contracts worth about $30 billion.[69] The nature of these contracts is also important, because it includes platforms, upgrades, and equipment that is unique to the United States or in which the United States offers particular quality, and where the Saudis and their GCC allies have been trying to enhance their capability. The sales will also improve their interoperability with U.S. forces. It is difficult to imagine where the Saudis would find comparable alternative platforms and equipment, and there is no evidence of the United States withdrawing from the region or abandoning their current security interests such that they would not supply such arms to the Saudis.

The United States and Saudi Arabia share a great many strategic concerns and so they are likely to remain in a security relationship—even one that fluctuates in importance and is tested from time to time—for many years yet. The United States will retain a long-term interest in Iraqi stability, for example, as will Saudi Arabia. The United States will remain concerned about Iran's regional role and nuclear program, even if the Geneva agreement ushers in a period of improved U.S.-Iranian relations, and so will want to ensure that the GCC states have a qualitative military capacity to offset Iran's quantitative one. Not least of all, Islamic extremism and terrorism will remain a core security concern for the United States, with the Saudis central to regional counterterrorism and deradicalization efforts.

However, the U.S.-Saudi relationship, which only a few years ago seemed to be regaining warmth and strength, in 2013 returned to being tenser. This is a sign that, apart from some shared strategic and security concerns, the two states ultimately share very little in common and have markedly different strategic cultures and security perspectives. In 2013, it began to appear as though Washington and Riyadh disagreed on almost every major Middle Eastern dynamic that was shaping the strategic environment. The Saudis wanted the United States to do much more to help resolve the Israeli-Palestinian conflict, with senior Saudi figures publicly stating their frustration.[70] Washington and Riyadh, as mentioned, had greatly divergent views on the Geneva agreement with Iran and the desirability of its approach, with the Saudis maddened that the United States pursued the Geneva agreement even though it was contrary to Riyadh's strategic interests. They have also differed strongly on Syria, with Riyadh favoring U.S. airstrikes on Bashar al-Asad's forces after it was alleged that they used chemical weapons against civilians in August 2013. The Saudi frustration over U.S. policy on Syria was probably the reason why Riyadh declined a rotating UN Security Council seat in October 2013. Their statement on this said: "Allowing the ruling regime in Syria to kill and burn its people by the chemical weapons, while the world stands idly, without applying deterrent sanctions against the Damascus regime, is also irrefutable evidence and proof of the inability of the Security Council to carry out its duties and responsibilities."[71] While this primarily criticized Russia and China, it also included implicit censure of the United States, after the Saudis had called several times on the United States to act more decisively. Whether or not the Saudi view was realistic, it nonetheless impacted how they saw the United States and on their relationship with Washington.

The U.S.-Saudi tensions probably reflect a fear by the Saudis that the United States is gradually shifting away from them and paying decreasing attention to Riyadh's security interests and perspectives.[72] The United States and Iran were close allies prior to the 1978–1979 Iranian revolution, and there is a fear among some Saudi foreign policy elites that the and that this could happen again, not just at the expense of U.S.-Saudi relations but even prejudicing Saudi security by favoring Iran's. A lot would be required to allow this to happen—it would take years, probably a generation, for U.S.-Iran relations to shift so profoundly—but it remains an underlying anxiety for some key Saudi elites.

Such anxieties are probably on firmer ground in terms of oil and energy security. In that respect, there indeed are significant changes underway with implications for how vital Saudi Arabia will be for U.S. energy security in the future. The declining U.S. reliance on oil for its economic growth, and especially the more recent and sudden emergence of U.S. unconventional oil and gas,[73] stand to make the Saudis far less important in U.S. eyes.[74] This is not likely to annul the relationship, since the United States will continue to share several security interests with Riyadh and will still need to import a substantial amount of oil, including from the Middle

East.[75] Still, the changing global energy system will impact Saudi perceptions of, and relations with, the United States, all the more so if the United States eventually becomes a net energy exporter.[76]

Changing U.S. energy demand might also mean that oil exporters such as Saudi Arabia look to new markets, especially in Asia. Some of the scenarios for the future of the Gulf predict that the GCC states will become much stronger and more diversified economies as a result of expanding trade and investment with China and other emerging Asian economies.[77] An approximately threefold increase in Chinese GDP is projected over 2010 to 2020,[78] consistent with China's recent growth rates of around 7 percent per annum. This would drive enormous increases in Chinese demand for energy, some sources assessing that demand could jump 500 percent or more over 2005 to 2030.[79] This will also mean new competition for the Middle East in manufacturing, but that issue is more likely to affect the poorer, more diversified Arab republics than the GCC.[80] For the Arab Gulf oil states, the rise of China will almost certainly prove a long-term windfall.

What is less clear about the rise of China, India, and other new economic powers is the degree to which they will become strategic actors in the Middle East and the Gulf, and how positive or negative that might be for Saudi security. Some sources are quite convinced of some sort of new strategic role for these states, if primarily for economic reasons:

> Rising powers—notably India and China—are also likely to seek some role in the Gulf security system, although probably as part of a multilateral framework, for reasons of cost as well as diplomacy. Their own interest in protecting shipping links with the Gulf will grow as their trade with the region expands. They are also likely to be increasingly keen to project their own power overseas. It is notable ... that both China and India deployed ships to counter piracy off the coast of Somalia in late 2008, following attacks by pirates on Chinese and Indian vessels.[81]

China has played other political and diplomatic roles in the Middle East, for example in peacekeeping, contributing forces to the United Nations Interim Force in Lebanon, and through an increased aid program to the region.[82] These are minor roles in the larger scheme of major power politics in the Middle East, however, probably intended primarily as symbolic gestures of support for regional peace and stability rather than the start of a strategic interventionist approach. Trade and economic concerns remain paramount to China and India, at least for the time being. This has kept Chinese-Saudi ties quite solid in recent years. The two states established diplomatic relations in 1990, but prior to that were already trading with each other, and the relationship was further developed in the mid-late-2000s by increased trade and high-level political visits.[83] As the trade relationship grew in value in the 2000s, so too did Saudi investment in China. Yet, at the military level, ties are very modest. Apart from a large Saudi missile purchase from China in the late 1980s,[84] the arms trade between the two is modest, and the United States dominates Saudi arms purchases.

The longer term challenge for the Saudis, then, is above all about how to maintain an appropriate balance between their strong and necessary U.S. relationship—necessary above all for strategic and military reasons—while also managing ties with emerging powers but especially China, for now mostly in the trade and investment realms but longer-term potentially with Beijing being a power with strategic reach to the Gulf. The Kingdom has long had a policy of looking toward Asia for new and diversified trade and investment opportunities, but otherwise the Saudi-Chinese relationship has been dominated by the trade in oil, and oil will probably continue to dominate the relationship for the coming years. In the event that China and the United States develop tensions or come to blows, however, the Saudis would be placed in an awkward position, needing to maintain a strategic relationship (of convenience) with one and a predominantly economic relationship with the other. Matters with India are far simpler, where the relationship is based almost exclusively on trade and expatriate labor.[85] Since the prospects are strong of a closer U.S.-India relationship in the future, not least of all to offset greater Chinese strategic reach, the Saudis will also have an easier time balancing their ties with India and the United States.

This will not stop the Saudis from looking to new sources of diplomatic influence. If Saudi oil income remains high, its long-term wealth will sustain its middle power role and encourage it in that role. The Saudi regional role since the Arab uprisings began and its rivalry with Iran are both evidence that Riyadh is willing to take on a more activist international role when it supports their interests. The Saudis may look toward wider bilateral ties as a way of playing a stronger international role, including with Europe and with states in the Indian Ocean region. They may also try to be more active in international forums, but they are a member-state in few regional or selective ones. They are in the Group of 20 (G20), as its only Arab member-state, and the G20's influence has increased dramatically since the 2008 financial crisis and the decline in influence of the Group of Eight. But whether Saudi Arabia would seek a greater role in the G20, and whether the G20 would welcome such a role, is debatable: Saudi Arabia is in the G20 largely because it is wealthy, a member of OPEC, and representative of a large global Arab and Muslim Middle Eastern population.[86] To date Riyadh has viewed the G20 not as an outlet for diplomatic influence so much as a path to new economic opportunities.

The only other arena where the Saudis might seek a greater role is the GCC, but as already discussed, their capacity to do so is constrained and challenged by the rising roles of some smaller member-states. Member-states collaborate through the GCC on security to some extent, especially in security coordination and the integration of some shared systems, but their primary security relationships are with the United States. The December 2013 decision by the GCC to form a joint military command[87] is important in improving the quality of their defense, but is also a sign of the limits to such cooperation, given that the

GCC members have taken until 2013 to agree to such a step, and as the GCC rapid deployment force still remains so modest in size.

As a result, the Saudis are likely to continue seeing the GCC more in economic terms. Whether the GCC is the vehicle for this is, however, debatable. The failure of the single Gulf currency was a reminder of problems that can impede initiatives for deep change by the GCC states. They also failed, at their 2012 summit in Riyadh, to agree on a Saudi proposal to integrate their economies.[88] This would have included much closer economic, political, and military co-ordination, and the creation of a new management body for the Council, replacing its secretariat, based in Riyadh. Only Bahrain was supportive of the plan, and the other states probably opposed to the new powers that the Saudis would gain under the proposal.[89] If the GCC is not an effective mechanism for economic or strategic initiatives, therefore, then one of the challenges that Riyadh will face in the future is to find new multilateral bodies through which to pursue its interests.

EXISTING, EMERGING, AND POTENTIAL UNCONVENTIONAL AND ASYMMETRIC THREATS

Beyond traditional threats from domestic instability and international security, Saudi Arabia is also likely to faces several new, emerging threats, including unorthodox and asymmetrical ones. Terrorism and Islamic extremism is perhaps the most obvious and important, as discussed at length in Chapter 5. The focus here is on some other issues, including food security, water security, climate change, and population pressures. These have a growing profile in international security debates, and the risks they potentially pose are significant.

Assessing environmental threats, not least of all climate change, is acutely difficult. The predictions of what climate change might mean vary so wildly, and the associated calculations and modeling are so complex and at times controversial that while climate change is a clear risk, the specifics of that risk often prove harder to confirm. However, some broad issues from climate change, with implications for Saudi security, are obvious. The first of these is that the Saudi approach to economic growth, energy use, and the rationing of other resources is not sustainable.[90] Hydrocarbon use, electricity subsidy and consumption rates, water desalinization and usage levels, and other environmentally sensitive measures are all a problem for Saudi Arabia (and to similar extents the other GCC states). The population growth rates in the GCC, including Saudi Arabia very glaringly, is a problem too: absent some action to reduce environmental impacts per capita, a future population of Saudi Arabia of around 50 million by 2040 or thereabouts is simply unsustainable. Saudi carbon emissions are among the highest in the world, in part because it is a modestly sized, wealthy population spread over a large territory—but also, crucially, because there is no policy to address carbon emissions and, in fact, subsidies of petroleum products, electricity, and the like lead to wasteful practices and excessive energy consumption. Saudi Arabia is ranked 18th globally for greenhouse gas emissions, but on a per capita basis is 11th.[91]

The possible impacts of climate change are severe for Saudi Arabia and its region. At current rates of projected twenty-first century global warming, the Persian Gulf waters are estimated to rise between 0.09 meters and 0.88 meters,[92] which could have marked impacts on coastal cities and towns given that many are only a few meters above sea level. Climate change of this sort would have an effect also on the Gulf waters themselves. It would create higher water temperatures and salinity, above already warm and salty levels because so much of its water recirculates within the Gulf. The Arabian Peninsula's land space, and the ability of humans to use it, would also be impacted. If global average temperatures were to rise between 1.8 degrees Centigrade and 3.6 degrees Centigrade by 2070 as some predictions suggest, this would have a catastrophic impact on land use: underground nonrenewable water aquifers would be depleted even faster than at present (and they are already being exploited at six times the rate of replenishment).[93] Even some of the nomadic herding that occurs at present in Saudi Arabia would no longer be possible. Finally, whatever the direct impacts on the Kingdom, climate change will probably create problems elsewhere in the Middle East that will impact on stability and thus on Saudi security. As examples, an increase in refugee and people movements, regional unrest or conflict, and higher crime rates would all flow on to impact Saudi regional relations, economic prospects, and overall security.

The Saudi regime has done little to minimize the risks of climate change, and they view population growth as a risk because of unemployment, not climate change, and thus something to be managed through job creation and social spending rather than being linked to climate policy. Saudi Arabia's conservative leadership and bureaucratic politics mean that change is slow, including the recognition of new threats or risks and action to counter them.[94] The Saudis have not been active in international forums and processes. They only signed on to the Kyoto Protocol very late, for example, and even then as a non-Annex 1 party (meaning Riyadh had no reduction target and mostly was encouraged to reduce emissions through energy efficiency and switching under the Clean Development Mechanism). Prior to that, it opposed the Protocols energetically.[95] Subsequently, it has been strenuous in opposing new post-Kyoto mechanisms, citing the economic impacts on it of any carbon emission reduction policies.[96] It follows a line, shared by many OPEC member-states, that carbon reduction schemes will lower world demand for oil and other hydrocarbons, harming energy exporters such as Saudi Arabia. This "discrimination" argument has also seen it supported by the smaller GCC states, other oil producers, and during the 2001–2009 George W. Bush administration, by the United States.[97]

In the longer term, if even some of the more conservative estimates about the impacts of global warming prove correct, the Saudis will want and need to act quickly against climate change if they are to minimize its impacts. By that stage it may be too late to avoid many of them. The Arabian Peninsula desert and Gulf and Red Sea marine environments are all highly delicate and susceptible to changes in temperature, precipitation, and in the case of marine areas, to increased salinity. The Gulf, in particular, has unique corals and sea life that has adjusted to what is already a very salty, hot underwater environment. On land, the ecosystem is equally delicate and the climate already extremely hot and dry. This all makes Saudi concerns about carbon emission reduction strategies seem, at the very least, ill-considered. Just how much of a security threat climate change will eventually be remains uncertain, of course, but Saudi opposition to any substantial international action seems shortsighted and imprudent. Even if the Saudi regime is starting to acknowledge the risks of climate change and talk about the need to address it,[98] they are yet to act emphatically on it, and are unlikely to welcome a major global initiative that would threaten their oil and gas income.

On top of the risks of climate change, Saudi Arabia long had in place policies that created environmental problems, which still affect the Kingdom. The emphasis on food self-sufficiency and the development of a water-intensive agricultural sector, for example, was a case of what one observer has called "in effect, exporting water."[99] The Saudi policy from the 1970s to the early 2000s of actively developing their agricultural sector was an example: "During the 1980s, Saudi Arabia became the sixth-largest wheat exporter in the world (with production reaching nearly five million tons in the early 1990s) courtesy of nonrenewable ground water provided through inefficient irrigation systems."[100] Agricultural subsidization was reduced as of the mid-2000s, mostly the result of the leadership redefining food security as security of food access rather than self-sufficiency, while coming to the realization that much agricultural output was simply never going to be profitable on a truly competitive basis. Saudi Arabia is expected to produce no wheat at all by 2016, as one example of how agriculture is being reorganized.[101] This agricultural focus was money poorly spent; an enormous waste and diversion of scarce water resources into unviable projects.

The issue of climate change and agriculture links into the other unconventional security risks that Saudi Arabia may find itself facing in the future: water security and population pressures. Although the Saudis have abandoned most of their water-intense agricultural production, there is every risk that a "freshwater shortage will be the Gulf states' critical environmental stress for the foreseeable future, exacerbated by a burgeoning population and the economic expansion to sustain it."[102] For the Saudis and other GCC states, the answer has been to construct desalinization plants. Desalinized water accounts for about half of Saudi Arabia's drinking water, with another 40 percent coming from nonrenewable groundwater and the remaining 10 percent from surface water in more mountainous parts of the country.

This makes them deeply reliant on desalinized water. The Gulf monarchies overall operate around half the world's desalinization plants, and Saudi Arabia leads the Gulf: its "Saline Water Conversion Company (SWCC) is the largest desalinated-water company in the world, producing approximately 3 million cubic meters per day and 5,000 megawatts of power, representing 50 percent of the kingdom's drinking water and 20 percent of its power generation."[103] However, desalinization is not sustainable. It is enormously expensive, costing around US$0.50–US$0.60 per cubic meter to produce (compared to a cost of around US$0.08 per cubic meter to treat water for consumption in the United States). Saudi water is heavily subsidized by the easy and cheap availability of hydrocarbons that provide the energy needed for desalinization. It is also heavily subsidized in the final price charged to consumers, which is a distortionary policy that does nothing to control demand or reduce waste.[104] A 2010 article, stressing the need for reform of water pricing, noted that "Saudi Arabia has some of the lowest consumer prices for water in the world . . . [J]ust five major cities in the world charge less than the Saudi municipal authorities for a cubic metre of water."[105] It then noted that "the average monthly water bill [is] less than SAR1.00 (US$0.27)," a remarkably low figure suggesting that the government is only recovering perhaps one or two percent of its costs to supply this water.[106]

The main challenge in reforming water prices is the same as that, already discussed, for reforming any other state subsidization. Whatever the environmental vulnerability or budgetary pressures caused by water subsidies, the regime will always be focused on the more immediate risks of political dissatisfaction and threats to regime legitimacy that might come from reducing subsidies. The rentier bargain is simply too strong a motivator against reform. Alternative measures to cut waste, meanwhile, are not likely to have much impact.[107] As a result, subsidies are likely to remain and inefficient water use to continue.

One of the ways in which the Saudis, and other Gulf states, are trying to offset future food security risks is through the purchase of foreign agricultural land. This agricultural investment—"land grabbing" to its critics[108]—has been substantial and in some quarters very contentious. The Saudis have placed considerable resources into land purchases abroad: according to one report in 2013, Saudi companies were involved in purchasing over one million hectares' worth of land in recent years, in particular in Pakistan, Sudan, Argentina, and Ethiopia. This makes them far from the largest such global investor; however, there are plans by several large Saudi firms to spend billions on further acquisitions out to 2020,[109] which would make them more prominent in international agricultural land investments.

While this appears to help address the problem of future Saudi food security, its critics claim that it brings a range of problems and creates security problems for both investing economies and the poorer ones they target. For labor markets, it takes Saudi jobs offshore, and in most cases, turns farm owners into farm laborers in the countries where the investments are made. It can create negative environmental impacts in target countries, and add to the costs of shipping food when it is sent back to the investing country. To some critics, it is even a form of neocolonialism, in which a wealthy state buys its own food security at the expense of a weaker, poorer state's food security, often damaging local communities in the process. Such arguments claim longer-term negative impacts for the investor, as well, if such investment creates tensions between the investor and recipient state, something possible in cases where such investment adds to food insecurity in the target country.[110] This is all the more likely given the prominence of government firms and sovereign wealth funds in such investments: accurately or not, critics and people in recipient states often view the investor as an arm of the state where they are based. Yet to states such as Saudi Arabia, such risks will probably continue to appear worth taking. The Saudi regime was spooked by the high commodity prices of 2008 and again in 2011, and they have extremely limited capacity to develop the agricultural sector back home. The food price surges in 2008 and 2011 were an especially sharp reminder to Arab regimes about the political risks from food prices; in poorer states the prices either caused strain on state budgets because of subsidies, or protests in cases where consumer prices had to be raised, while in wealthier economies like Saudi Arabia there was still considerable popular disquiet about the cost of basic necessities.[111]

One final dynamic, linked to food, water, and the environment, is population growth and demographic pressure. This was mentioned earlier in the course of discussing unemployment pressures and the risks of this for stability, as well as highlighting how population pressures can hamper the success or failure of economic diversification schemes and national employment programs. It is worth reiterating, however, that demography is a broader political economy issue, with other potential security implications.

Demographic change and differences among Saudis of various ages can create intergenerational tensions, stemming from the lower opportunities available to one generation versus their parents', or even just a perception of such unfairness. Some Saudis are worse off than they would have been a generation ago, because of the disparities of wealth across the country, and others are less well off than average, such as the Shia and some Sunnis from more remote areas or lacking the right connections or support.[112] But there is a further sense among some young Saudis of *relative* deprivation, whereby even if they will admit that they are not poor or especially badly off, they complain that they lack the same educational and employment opportunities that the previous generation was given. Therefore, even though on average they may be better educated or more traveled than their parents were at the same age, many young Saudis are often pessimistic when asked about the future, especially about relative economic conditions and opportunities.[113] This may also extend into dissatisfaction with the older generation, which sometimes manifests in the workplace. Younger Saudis educated abroad are often resentful toward, or critical of, the traditional management and leadership style of older Saudis, while these older Saudi managers often disparage young Saudis' work ethics and attitudes.[114] While such tensions are difficult to generalize about, and certainly impossible to quantify, they exist, and pose risks. They create institutional weaknesses and mistrust and shape and intensify youth grievances. This can and does flow on to a mistrust of government as well, lessening confidence in the state and its institutions in cases where, for example, *wasta* ("intermediation," the use of connections) is perceived by a young Saudi as being socially exclusionary, unfair, and, in effect, a type of corruption.[115]

If young Saudi men are aggrieved and disappointed with older Saudis at the summit of businesses and state institutions—and the political system, for that matter—it is even more so for young Saudi women. The exclusion of women from public office and an enormous range of senior roles, and the social restrictions placed on them, have long been a source of resentment for many of them.[116] Some female entrepreneurs and academics have become more prominent, and demanded greater participation for women in public and commercial roles, but the prospects for substantial change are inhibited by the influence of the Wahhabi clerics and the regime's need to keep religious and other conservative forces onside.[117] Yet, Saudi women have a strong claim that they are underutilized: they are some 56–57 percent of university students, but only 20 percent of the Saudi overseas scholarship students.[118] Only about 17 percent of them are in the job market, compared with three-quarters of men.[119] And they have a high unemployment rate, by some measures 35 percent or more,[120] due more to discrimination, and limits on their employment options, than to any shortcomings in their skill or motivation.

To underutilize such a large share of half the population is a negative for economic growth and development, and ultimately for social harmony, stability, and security. It deprives the economy of skilled workers, which by reputation at least are often better workers than the men; as one Saudi employer commented: "[Saudi women] have a low level of attrition, a better attention to detail, a willingness to perform and a productivity about twice that of Saudi men."[121] It is also planting seeds of dissatisfaction among women. While women lack the power to change the system, they can still mount opposition to existing policies and practices, and have begun to do so.[122] They are an important component in the legitimacy of the state and for support for the Al Saud, and so cannot be completely ignored, even if the Wahhabi elite seem to the royals to be a more important source of legitimacy. The question is not why there is female resentment about their economic and social opportunities, but rather why this resentment is not a great deal stronger and deeper. In the future, the Saudi government may be forced into making a distinct choice of whether to keep placating conservative clerics, or to give women greater employment opportunities and enhance economic development.

Demography is important in one final aspect: that of labor markets, and how the large number of expatriates in the Kingdom links to and impacts cultural and national identity. Expatriates are a minority of the overall population in Saudi Arabia, being around one-quarter of the population of nearly 28 million, but they are a majority of the labor force, around 60 percent.[123] This creates a dual labor market and a socioeconomic stratification between Saudis and various expatriate groups. It is also a potential security issue. Many of the poorer expatriate laborers live near or below the poverty line, a substantial number are exploited or mistreated, and a great many have a negative view of their host culture and society. These workers, as a result, lack "human security,"[124] something that has potential implications for Saudi security. Most commonly and simply, it is a key cause of negative press about Saudi Arabia and other host countries.[125] More deeply, it also creates labor market insecurity and cultural insecurity among Saudis. Labor market security is an issue because when a foreign worker is relatively itinerant and uncommitted to the host economy, they are much less likely to share their knowledge or skills, and more likely to leave suddenly. In the absence of a transfer of skills to the Saudi national workforce, a reliance on expatriates is also a security risk because it leaves the economy vulnerable to greater shocks or recession if the foreign worker population departs suddenly. In a serious political crisis or regional conflict, a great many workers flee, taking with them their labor skills and experience. Even if they return, the immediate economic impacts of their departure can be substantial. At the same time, many Saudis worry about the reliance on foreign workers, especially that it is damaging to national identity and culture. Many Saudis see their corporate cultures as often being essentially foreign, where an overwhelming majority of employees are foreign—which in the commercial realm is the case with most firms—and they worry, too, that Saudi identities are being unduly influenced or heterogenized by the influences of a large expatriate population. While this may seem very negative, such a view is often found. If it becomes widely enough held in the future, it could come to shape political views.

CONCLUSION

If Saudi Arabia has faced considerable threats to its stability in the past, it is likely to face just as significant ones in the years ahead. While the regime's rule is resilient and seemingly durable, and it has stared down threats from external foes, internal unrest, and terrorism in the past, there is no guarantee that it will be able to do so in the future. The dynamics under which the Kingdom's royal family and political elite operate are changing, and will continue to do so. Some of the challenges identified in this chapter are the ones that will shape stability, and perhaps confront the regime's very emphatically, in the future, although it is always difficult to predict exactly which issues will arise and with what degree of seriousness.

The origins of these threats vary. Some are the product of the Saudi political system and the ruling bargain that has sustained the Al Saud for around a century, such as their reliance for survival on the Wahhabi clerical elite, key business and tribal figures, and an external protector. The regime is also responsible for the endurance of the rentier dynamic, and despite many positives for them from that dynamic, there are plenty of problems and risks inherent in it too. Other threats arise from external sources; the Saudis can respond to regional changes and challenges to their security, but can only shape or preempt such changes and challenges to a limited extent. Still other threats are emerging ones, such as the risk of climate change, intergenerational struggles and tensions, and depleting water and other natural resources, where the Saudi government faces difficult decisions about how to respond to risks that may seem far into the future or, to some, are not even matters worth worrying about anyway.

The dynamics outlined in this book are important and imperative ones, reflecting the size and prominence of Saudi Arabia in international economics and security. The Kingdom is a key Sunni Arab actor in the Middle East, at the moment arguably the main Sunni Arab power, given Egypt's political instability during and since the 2011 uprising that overthrew Husni Mubarak. Saudi Arabia's rivalry with Iran is important, not just for the Gulf but in the wider region, as the Syrian civil war since 2012 has demonstrated. As the world's largest oil producer and exporter—at least for the time being—Saudi Arabia occupies a crucial position in the global economic order and the world's energy system, and its approach to economic policy, foreign relations, and climate change are all framed and influenced by the dominance of oil in its political economy. In the Gulf, it both leads and follows the smaller Gulf states; leading on strategic and military issues and as a traditional diplomatic actor, but following, in many ways, when it comes to globalization, economic reform, and carving a position in the international economic order. For all the reasons outlined in this book—from energy, to Islam, to regional power rivalries, to emerging international security issues—Saudi Arabia is an important international middle power and a key state within the Middle East region. This will not change for the foreseeable future, and in fact there is every possibility that its importance in the coming years will be even greater than it has been in the past.

NOTES

1. Review of Said K. Aburish, *The Rise, Corruption, and Coming Fall of the House of Saud* (London: Bloomsbury, 1994), reviewed by William B. Quandt, *Foreign Affairs*, 74, 5 (September-October 1995), pp. 178–179.

2. Research and Statistics Department, Saudi Arabian Monetary Agency (SAMA), *Forty-Eighth Annual Report* (Riyadh: Saudi Arabian Monetary Agency, August 2012), 90, 92 (Table 8.5).

3. See Tim Niblock with Monica Malik, *The Political Economy of Saudi Arabia* (London: Routledge, 2007), 179 (Table 6.2).

4. All the employment statistics here are from data in SAMA, *Forty-Eighth Annual Report*, 183 (Table 18.5), 185 (Table 18.7).

5. Ibid., 184, 188.

6. Niblock with Malik, *The Political Economy of Saudi Arabia*, 208–210.

7. Ibid., 139–141.

8. On taxation in Saudi Arabia see for example the document KPMG, *2013 – Thinking Beyond Borders – Saudi Arabia*, KPMG, 2013, http://www.kpmg.com/Global/en/Issues AndInsights/ArticlesPublications/thinking-beyond-borders/Documents/saudi-arabia-2013.pdf, accessed December 13, 2013; and the webpage HSBC Bank, *Tax Navigator: Going to Saudi Arabia*, HSBC Expat, n.d., http://www.expat.hsbc.com/1/2/hsbc-expat/expat-experience/ expat-finances/global-tax-navigator#!/arriving/SA, accessed December 13, 2013.

9. "Subsidies 'Distort' Saudi Arabia Economy Says Economy Minister," *Financial Times* (London), May 7, 2013, http://www.ft.com/cms/s/0/f474cf28-b717-11e2-841e-00144feabdc0 .html#axzz2nIoDUh4N, accessed December 13, 2013.

10. See Middle East and Central Asia Department, International Monetary Fund, *Energy Subsidies in the Middle East and North Africa: Lessons for Reform* (Washington: International Monetary Fund, March 28, 2013), http://www.imf.org/external/np/fad/subsidies/pdf/ menanote.pdf, accessed December 13, 2013.

11. "Amid Protests, Saudi King Raises Benefits but Strengthens Security," *The New York Times*, March 18, 2011, http://www.nytimes.com/2011/03/19/world/middleeast/19 saudi.html, accessed December 13, 2013.

12. Niblock with Malik, *The Political Economy of Saudi Arabia*, 113–116, especially 114 (Table 4.7).

13. Clement M. Henry and Robert Springborg, *Globalization and the Politics of Development in the Middle East* (Cambridge: Cambridge University Press, 2001), 179–180.

14. Paul Rivlin, *Arab Economies in the Twenty-First Century* (Cambridge: Cambridge University Press, 2001), 9–11.

15. Ibid., 219.

16. Ibid.

17. The GDP per capita in current US$ figures are derived from data accessed via the "Download Data" tab on the webpage *Data: Saudi Arabia* (Washington: The World Bank, n.d.), n.p., http://data.worldbank.org/country/saudi-arabia, accessed December 13, 2013.

18. Ibid.

19. Rivlin, *Arab Economies in the Twenty-First Century*, 231 (Figure 10.2).

20. Niblock with Malik, *The Political Economy of Saudi Arabia*, 141.

21. Matthew R. Simmons, *Twilight in the Desert: The Coming Oil Shock and the World Economy* (Hoboken: John Wiley & Sons, 2005), 69–70.

22. Ibid., 155–179.

23. An interesting table of numbers, which shows the lack of correlation between Saudi production and claimed reserves, is in Peter W. Wilson and Douglas F. Graham, *Saudi Arabia: The Coming Storm* (Armonk: M. E. Sharpe, 1994), 207 (Table 5.8).

24. Simmons, *Twilight in the Desert*, 269–275.

25. This is widely discussed by observers of the Saudi political economy, such as in Steffen Hertog and Giacomo Luciani, "Energy and Sustainability Policies in the Gulf States," in David Held and Kristian Ulrichsen (eds.), *The Transformation of the Gulf: Politics, Economics and the*

Global Order (London: Routledge, 2012), 236–257. See also Yousef Alyousef and Paul Stevens, "The Cost of Domestic Energy Prices to Saudi Arabia," *Energy Policy*, 39, (2011), 6900–6905; and Dermot Gately, Nourah Al-Yousef and Hamad M.H. Al-Sheikh, "The Rapid Growth of Domestic Oil Consumption in Saudi Arabia and the Opportunity Cost of Oil Exports Foregone," *Energy Policy*, 47, (2012), 57–68.

26. Mohsen Mehrara, "Energy Consumption and Economic Growth: The Case of Oil Exporting Countries," *Energy Policy*, 35 (2007), 2944.

27. Glada Lahn and Paul Stevens, *Burning Oil to Keep Cool: The Hidden Energy Crisis in Saudi Arabia* (London: The Royal Institute of International Affairs, 2011), 2 (Figure 1).

28. Ayesha Daya and Dana El Baltaji, "Saudi Arabia May Become Oil Importer by 2030, Citigroup Says," *Bloomberg*, September 4, 2012, n.p., http://www.bloomberg.com/news/ 2012-09-04/saudi-arabia-may-become-oil-importer-by-2030-citigroup-says-1-.html, accessed December 13, 2013.

29. As reported in Ibid., n.p.

30. On these see for example Niblock with Malik, *The Political Economy of Saudi Arabia...*, 200–230; and Monica Malik and Tim Niblock, "Saudi Arabia's Economy: The Challenge of Reform," in Paul Aarts and Gerd Nonneman (eds.), *Saudi Arabia in the Balance: Political Economy, Society, Foreign Affairs* (London: Hurst, 2005), 85–110.

31. Niblock with Malik, *The Political Economy of Saudi Arabia*, 208–209.

32. The term is used and discussed in a couple of pieces, most notably Daryl Champion, *The Paradoxical Kingdom: Saudi Arabia and the Momentum of Reform* (New York: Columbia University Press, 2003), 200–202.

33. For the full list see the brochure *Answering Your Investment Needs: A Detailed Guide to Investing in Saudi Arabia*, Saudi Arabian General Investment Authority, n.d., https:// www.sagia.gov.sa/Documents/Wizard/Investment%20guide.pdf, accessed December 13, 2013.

34. Niblock with Malik, *The Political Economy of Saudi Arabia*, 111–112, 146–147.

35. See the examples offered in Abdul Aziz Aluwaisheg, "When Privatization Goes Wrong," *Arab News*, September 15, 2013, http://www.arabnews.com/news/464657, accessed December 13, 2013.

36. World Bank, *Doing Business 2014: Understanding Regulations for Small and Medium-Size Enterprises* (Washington, DC: World Bank Group, 2013). See for example page 16 (Table 1.4), which shows how substantial certain reforms have been, especially those to business processes and regulations, and the details on page 221.

37. This is discussed in Matthew Gray, "A Theory of 'Late Rentierism' in the Arab States of the Gulf," *Center for International and Regional Studies Occasional Paper No. 7* (Doha: Georgetown University School of Foreign Service in Qatar, 2011), especially 10, 14–16.

38. Much scholarship exists on this line of argument; see for example as a couple of recent works: N. Janardhan, "New Media: In Search of Equilibrium," in Mary Ann Tétreault, Gwenn Okruhlik, and Andrzej Kapiszewski (eds.), *Political Change in the Arab Gulf States: Stuck in Transition* (Boulder: Lynne Rienner, 2011), 225–245; and Rex Brynen, Pete W. Moore, Bassel F. Salloukh, and Marie-Joëlle Zahar, *Beyond the Arab Spring: Authoritarianism & Democratization in the Arab World* (Boulder: Lynne Rienner, 2012), especially 233–256 on new media but also 191–212 on political change in the rentier states. There are many more: there are several entire books written on, for example, the impact in the Middle East of Al-Jazeera television or new communications tools such as Facebook and Twitter.

39. Brynen et al., *Beyond the Arab Spring*, 205–208.

40. On the 2011 Bahrain uprising see "Popular Protests in North Africa and the Middle East (III): The Bahrain Revolt," *MENA Report No. 105* (Brussels: International Crisis Group, April 6, 2011), http://www.crisisgroup.org/~/media/Files/Middle%20East%20North %20Africa/Iran%20Gulf/Bahrain/105-%20Popular%20Protests%20in%20North%20Africa %20and%20the%20Middle%20East%20-III-The%20Bahrain%20Revolt.pdf, accessed December 16, 2013.

41. Frederic Wehrey, *The Forgotten Uprising in Eastern Saudi Arabia* (Washington: Carnegie Endowment for International Peace, 2013).

42. Mehran Kamrava, "The Arab Spring and the Saudi-Led Counterrevolution," *Orbis*, 56, 1 (2012), 96–104.

43. Marina Ottaway and Marwan Muasher, "Arab Monarchies: Change for Reform, Yet Unmet," *Carnegie Middle East Paper* (Washington: Carnegie Endowment for International Peace, December 2011), 16–17.

44. For some good arguments on this see for example F. Gregory Gause III, "Kings for All Seasons: How the Middle East's Monarchies Survived the Arab Spring," *Brookings Doha Center Analysis Paper Number 8* (Doha: The Brookings Institution, September 2013), http:// www.brookings.edu/research/papers/2013/09/24-resilience-arab-monarchies-gause, accessed December 13, 2013.

45. What follows on anti-Shia conduct and discrimination is from Andrew Hammond, *The Islamic Utopia: The Illusion of Reform in Saudi Arabia* (London: Pluto Press, 2012), 26–30, 86–90; "The Shiite Question in Saudi Arabia," *Middle East Report N°45* (Brussels: International Crisis Group, September 19, 2005), 9–12, http://www.crisisgroup.org/~/ media/Files/Middle%20East%20North%20Africa/Iran%20Gulf/Saudi%20Arabia/The%20Shiite %20Question%20in%20Saudi%20Arabia.pdf, accessed December 16, 2013; and Wehrey, *The Forgotten Uprising in Eastern Saudi Arabia*, 4–6, 11–12.

46. Wehrey, *The Forgotten Uprising in Eastern Saudi Arabia*, 12–13.

47. Ibid., 14–16.

48. Jerzy Zdanowski, "The Saudi Shi'a and Political Reform in Saudi Arabia," in Mary Ann Tétreault, Gwenn Okruhlik, and Andrzej Kapiszewski (eds.), *Political Change in the Arab Gulf States: Stuck in Transition* (Boulder: Lynne Rienner, 2011), 145–147.

49. Wehrey, *The Forgotten Uprising in Eastern Saudi Arabia*, 18.

50. Ibid., 13–14.

51. Florence Eid, "The new face of Arab investment," in John Nugée and Paola Subacchi (eds.), *The Gulf Region: A New Hub of Global Financial Power* (London: Royal Institute of International Affairs, 2008), 69–80.

52. Gray, "A Theory of "Late Rentierism" in the Arab States of the Gulf," 21–22.

53. Ibid., 21–22, 28–30, and 34–35; and Fred H. Lawson, "The Persian Gulf In the Contemporary International Economy," in Mehran Kamrava (ed.), *The Political Economy of the Persian Gulf* (London: Hurst, 2012), 13–38.

54. This is a key argument in Suzanne Maloney, "The Gulf 's Renewed Oil Wealth: Getting It Right This Time?," *Survival*, 50, 6 (2008), 129–150.

55. As examples of the reforms in Dubai, including to this end, see Christopher M. Davidson, *Dubai: The Vulnerability of Success* (London: Hurst, 2008), 99–135.

56. See Matthew Gray, *Qatar: Politics and the Challenges of Development* (Boulder: Lynne Rienner, 2013), 159–184; Mehran Kamrava, *Qatar: Small State, Big Politics* (Ithaca: Cornell University Press, 2013), 53–68.

57. Gray, *Qatar*, pp. 166–170; Kamrava, *Qatar*, pp. 72–78.

58. Gray, *Qatar*, pp. 207–210.

59. On this see for example Joseph Kostiner, "Saudi Arabia and the Arab–Israeli Peace Process: The Fluctuation of Regional Coordination," *British Journal of Middle Eastern Studies*, 36, 3 (December 2009), 417–429.

60. This is discussed in "Syria's Metastasising Conflicts," *Middle East Report N° 143* (Brussels: International Crisis Group, 27 June 2013), pp. 1, 4, 7–8, 13–14, and 23–24.

61. Majed Al-Maymoni, "UAE Pulls out of GCC Monetary Union Plan," *Saudi Gazette*, May 21, 2009, http://www.saudigazette.com.sa/index.cfm?method=home.regcon&content id=2009052138554, accessed December 17, 2013.

62. Mariam Karouny, "Saudi Edges Qatar to Control Syrian Rebel Support," *Reuters*, May 31, 2013, http://www.reuters.com/article/2013/05/31/us-syria-crisis-saudi-insight-idUSBRE9 4U0ZV20130531, accessed December 16, 2013; and David B. Ottaway, "The Saudi-Qatari Clash over Syria," *The National Interest*, July 2, 2013, http://nationalinterest.org/commentary/ the-saudi-qatari-clash-over-syria-8685, accessed December 2013.

63. Noted in, for example: Marwan M. Kraidy, "Hypermedia and Governance in Saudi Arabia," *Annenberg School for Communication Departmental Papers* (Philadelphia: University of Pennsylvania, 2006); and Marc Lynch, *Voice of the New Arab Public: Iraq, Al-Jazeera, and Middle East Politics Today* (New York: Columbia University Press, 2006), 43–45.

64. See on this Aryn Baker, "Saudi Arabia to Tourists: We Are Just Not That into You," *Time*, March 22, 2013.

65. See for example "Strife in Iraq: Worse and Worse," *The Economist*, May 25, 2013; Duraid Adnan, "Execution-Style Killings in Iraq Raise Fears of Return to Sectarian Violence" *The Washington Post*, November 27, 2013, http://www.nytimes.com/2013/11/28/world/mid-dleeast/a-grim-day-for-civilians-in-iraq-as-executions-spike.html, accessed December 16, 2013; Interview with Marian Fantappie, "Explaining the Political Factors behind the Increasing Violence in Iraq," *International Crisis Group website*, October 4, 2013, http:// www.crisisgroup.org/en/publication-type/interviews/2013/fantappie-explaining-the-political -factors-behind-the-increasing-violence-in-iraq.aspx, accessed December 13, 2013.

66. "Violence in Iraq: The Nightmare Returns," *Pomegranate* (*The Economist* blog), July 17, 2013, http://www.economist.com/blogs/pomegranate/2013/07/violence-iraq, accessed December 16, 2013.

67. Quote in Steven Erlanger, "Saudi Prince Criticizes Obama Administration, Citing Indecision in Mideast," *The New York Times*, December 15, 2013, http://www.nytimes.com/ 2013/12/16/world/middleeast/saudi-prince-accuses-obama-of-indecision-on-middle-east.html? src=recg&_r=2&, accessed December 16, 2013.

68. "U.S. Announces $60 Billion Arms Sale for Saudi Arabia," *Reuters*, October 20, 2010, http://www.reuters.com/article/2010/10/20/us-usa-saudi-arms-idUSTRE69J4ML20101020, access August 16, 2013.

69. Mark Landler and Steven Lee Myers, "With $30 Billion Arms Deal, U.S. Bolsters Saudi Ties," *The New York Times*, December 29, 2011, http://www.nytimes.com/2011/12/ 30/world/middleeast/with-30-billion-arms-deal-united-states-bolsters-ties-to-saudi-arabia.html, accessed August 16, 2013.

70. Erlanger, "Saudi Prince Criticizes Obama Administration, Citing Indecision in Mideast," n.p.

71. Robert F. Worth, "Saudi Arabia Rejects U.N. Security Council Seat in Protest Move," *The New York Times*, October 18, 2013, http://www.nytimes.com/2013/10/19/world/middle east/saudi-arabia-rejects-security-council-seat.html, accessed December 17, 2013.

72. Robert F. Worth, "U.S. and Saudis in Growing Rift as Power Shifts," *The New York Times*, November 25, 2013, http://www.nytimes.com/2013/11/26/world/middleeast/us-and -saudis-in-growing-rift-as-power-shifts.html, accessed December 17, 2013.

73. On US unconventional oil see as background Leonardo Maugeri, "The Shale Oil Boom: A U.S. Phenomenon," *Discussion Paper #2013-05* (Cambridge: Belfer Center for Science and International Affairs, Harvard University, June 2013).

74. Worth, "U.S. and Saudis in Growing Rift as Power Shifts," n.p.

75. Maugeri, "The Shale Oil Boom: A U.S. Phenomenon," 25–28.

76. Ibid., 27.

77. See as an example Economist Intelligence Unit, *The GCC in 2020: Outlook for the Gulf and the Global Economy* (London: Economist Intelligence Unit, March 2009), 4–6, http:// graphics.eiu.com/marketing/pdf/Gulf2020.pdf, accessed December 17, 2013.

78. Economist Intelligence Unit, *The GCC in 2020*, 5–6.

79. For example Geoffrey Kemp, *The East Moves West: India, China, and Asia's Growing Presence in the Middle East* (Washington: Brookings Institution Press, 2010), 6–9.

80. This is part of the assessment in Miria Pigato, *Strengthening China's and India's Trade and Investment Ties to the Middle East and North Africa* (Washington: The World Bank, 2009), especially 11–20.

81. Economist Intelligence Unit, *The GCC in 2020*, 7.

82. Kemp, *The East Moves West*, 5–6.

83. Ibid., 80–82.

84. Ibid., 83–84.

85. Ibid., 37–41.

86. Sven Behrendt, "The G20 and Saudi Arabia's Changing Foreign Policy Agenda," Carnegie Endowment for International Peace website, September 21, 2009, http://carnegieen dowment.org/2009/09/21/g20-and-saudi-arabia-s-changing-foreign-policy-agenda/xrz, accessed December 17, 2013.

87. "GCC Approves Joint Military Command," *Saudi Gazette*, December 12, 2013, http:// www.saudigazette.com.sa/index.cfm?method=home.regcon&contentid=20131212189348, accessed December 17, 2013.

88. Angus McDowell, "Gulf Arabs Delay Talk of Union at Riyadh Meeting," *Reuters*, May 14, 2012, http://www.reuters.com/article/2012/05/14/us-gulf-union-idUSBRE84D0MH 20120514, accessed December 17, 2013.

89. Ibid.

90. Mari Luomi, *The Gulf Monarchies and Climate Change: Abu Dhabi and Qatar in an Era of Natural Unsustainability* (London: Hurst, 2012), 9–31, especially 9–10.

91. Ibid., 66 (Table 8).

92. Figures cited in Dennis Kumetat, "Climate Change in the Persian Gulf – Regional Security, Sustainability Strategies and Research Needs," Paper for the Conference: *Climate Change, Social Stress and Violent Conflict*, Hamburg, Germany, November 19–20, 2009, 2, http://personal.lse.ac.uk/ kumetat/pdfs/Kumetat,_Climate_change_in_the_Persian_Gulf.pdf, access December 17, 2013.

93. Ibid., 2–3. For a more technical analysis see also Shakhawat Chowdhury and Muhammad Al-Zahrani, "Implications of Climate Change on Water Resources in Saudi Arabia," *Arabian Journal for Science and Engineering*, 38, 8 (August 2013), 1959–1971.

94. Kumetat, "Climate change in the Persian Gulf," 8–9.

95. Joanna Depledge, "Striving for No: Saudi Arabia in the Climate Change Regime," *Global Environmental Politics*, 8, 4 (November 2008), 11–12.

96. Ibid., 12–16, also cited in Kumetat, "Climate Change in the Persian Gulf," 10.

97. Luomi, *The Gulf Monarchies and Climate Change*, 203–205.

98. Humeyra Pamuk, "Saudi Arabia Sees Need to Act on Climate Change," *Reuters*, December 5, 2012, http://www.reuters.com/article/2012/12/05/us-climate-talks-saudi-idU SBRE8B41B820121205, accessed December 17, 2013.

99. James A. Russell, "Environmental Security and Regional Stability in the Persian Gulf," *Middle East Policy*, 16, 4 (Winter 2009), 92.

100. Ibid.

101. David Rosenberg, "Food and the Arab Spring," Global Research in International Affairs Center website, October 27, 2013 http://www.gloria-center.org/2011/10/food-and -the-arab-spring/, accessed December 18, 2013.

102. Russell, "Environmental Security and Regional Stability in the Persian Gulf," 93.

103. Ibid., 92.

104. Luomi, *The Gulf Monarchies and Climate Change*, 26–27.

105. "Pressure Grows for Saudi Tariff Reform," *Global Water Intelligence*, 11, 10 (October 2010), 14.

106. Ibid.

107. Luomi, *The Gulf Monarchies and Climate Change*, 43–44.

108. "Buying Farmland Abroad: Outsourcing's Third Wave," *The Economist*, May 21, 2009, http://www.economist.com/node/13692889, accessed December 18, 2013.

109. See Joseph Holden and Margarethe Pagel, *Transnational Land Acquisitions: What Are the Drivers, Levels, and Destinations, of Recent Transnational Land Acquisitions?* (Nathan Associates/ EPS-PEAKS, 2013), 23–25, 44, http://partnerplatform.org/?azrv33t9, accessed December 18, 2013.

110. "Buying Farmland Abroad," n.p.; and Sue Branford, "The Great Global Land Grab," in Marcin Gerwin (ed.), *Food and Democracy: Introduction to Food Sovereignty* (Kraków: Alliance of Associations Polish Green Network, 2011), 81–82.

111. See Marco Lagi, Karla Z. Bertrand and Yaneer Bar-Yam, *The Food Crises and Political Instability in North Africa and the Middle East*, August 15, 2011, http://papers.ssrn.com/sol3/ papers.cfm?abstract_id=1910031, accessed December 18, 2013.

112. Kristian Coates Ulrichsen, *Insecure Gulf: The End of Certainty and the Transition to the Post-Oil Era* (London: Hurst & Company, 2011), 88.

113. Mai Yamani, *Changed Identities: The Challenge of the New Generation in Saudi Arabia* (London: Royal Institute of International Affairs, 2000), 72–76.

114. Ibid., 87–89.

115. Ibid., 88–89, although this is a region-wide problem not unique to Saudi Arabia.

116. Madawi Al-Rasheed, *A History of Saudi Arabia*, 2nd Edn (Cambridge: Cambridge University Press, 2010), 268–269.

117. Ibid., 269.

118. Saudi Arabia Ministry of Higher Education, *Women in Higher Education: Saudi Initiatives & Achievements* (Riyadh: Deputyship for Planning & Information, Ministry of Higher Education, 2010), 1.

119. Katy Watson, "Winning the Case for Women in Work: Saudi Arabia's Steps to Reform," *BBC News*, December 13, 2012, http://www.bbc.co.uk/news/business-20697030, accessed December 18, 2013.

120. Natalie Robehmed, "Saudi Startup Finding Women Jobs Acquired For $16M," *Forbes*, September 10, 2013, http://www.forbes.com/sites/natalierobehmed/2013/09/10/a-saudi-startup-finding-women-jobs-acquired-for-16m/, accessed December 18, 2013.

121. A Saudi grocery store manager, quoted in Ben Hubbard, "In Taking Jobs, Women Take on a Saudi Taboo," *The New York Times*, December 2, 2013, http://www.nytimes.com/2013/12/03/world/middleeast/saudi-women-make-small-but-significant-strides-in-the-work-force.html?_r=0, accessed December 18, 2013.

122. Sean Foley, *The Arab Gulf States: Beyond Oil and Islam* (Boulder: Lynne Rienner, 2010), 167–210; Al-Rasheed, *A History of Saudi Arabia*, 268–270.

123. Ulrichsen, *Insecure Gulf*, 89.

124. Ibid., 90.

125. Ibid., 89–90.

APPENDIX A

Biographies

ABD AL-AZIZ BIN ABD AL-RAHMAN AL SAUD (ALSO REFERRED TO AS IBN SAUD)

Abd al-Aziz bin Abd al-Rahman Al Saud, commonly referred to as Ibn Saud, was the founder and first king of the modern nation-state of Saudi Arabia. Born in 1876 in Riyadh, he was exiled along with most of the Al Saud family after the collapse of the second Saudi emirate. He was politically crafty and calculating, having to remove his father and some brothers as a political threat before he could begin the process of reestablishing Saudi rule. In 1902, he began the reconquest of what is now Saudi Arabia, capturing Riyadh that year and, gradually, nearly all of what is now Saudi Arabia over the period to the mid-1920s.

The formation of the Kingdom of Saudi Arabia was proclaimed by Ibn Saud in 1932, and he was king of that nation-state until his death in 1953. Ibn Saud's rule was in some ways very traditional, and he demonstrated strong political cunning in managing both elite relationships and in cementing his rule over conquered areas. He also began investing in the institutions and infrastructure of a modern state; a task made much easier once oil started to be exported in sizeable quantities in the late 1940s.

Ibn Saud had at least 22 wives—probably many more—who bore him at least 45 sons, of whom 36 survived into adulthood and had children of their own. He married for a range of reasons, including to cement alliances and to exert his authority in conquered areas, although he was very fond of several wives. As a result of these marriages, the Al Saud dynasty is a large one with a broad range of wings and lines—not to mention the cadet branches of the family, which make it enormous. This has created considerable political complexity, and enormous resources have been spent to co-opt key figures in the family, less during Ibn Saud's lifetime and more as oil wealth has become so massive.

Ibn Saud died in 1953 of a heart attack, with power passing to his son Saud.

Further information: There are a range of biographies published on Ibn Saud as well as on aspects of his rule such as the conquest of the Hijaz and his use of the Ikhwan. See also the general histories of modern Saudi Arabia, which spend considerable time on Ibn Saud and his era, including Madawi Al-Rasheed, *A History of Saudi Arabia*, 2nd ed. (Cambridge: Cambridge University Press, 2010), pp. 37–101 and Alexei Vassiliev, *The History of Saudi Arabia* (New York: New York University Press, 2000), pp. 210–353.

KING FAISAL

Faisal (or Faysal) bin Abd al-Aziz Al Saud (1906–1975) was king of Saudi Arabia from 1964 to 1975. Long as aspirant to the throne, he was a rival with Saud, who ruled 1953–1964 and who was eventually forced to abdicate.

Faisal's rule was noteworthy in several respects. In contrast with Saud, he was an able manager, handling the country's finances astutely and using oil money to fund economic development and modernization. In the foreign policy realm, his pro-Palestinian views were popular with Saudis, as were his pan-Islamist ideas in some circles. He was well regarded by the United States, which also approved of his strong anti-Communist views and his rivalry with Egyptian president Gamal Abd al-Nasser, although relations were strained over the Palestinian issue and U.S. support for Israel.

He married four times, including to women from key families. He educated his children well—many of them at top U.S. universities—setting them up for key roles in the Kingdom.

He was assassinated by a nephew in 1975.

Further information: There are a couple of recent biographies on Faisal, but the best is Alexei Vassiliev, *King Faisal: Personality, Faith and Times* (London: Saqi, 2013). There are also a range of books covering Saudi Arabia under Faisal, including the outstanding piece on Saudi modernization: Sarah Yizraeli, *Politics and Society in Saudi Arabia: The Crucial Years of Development, 1960–1982* (London: Hurst/New York: Oxford University Press, 2012).

KING ABDULLAH BIN ABDUL-AZIZ AL SAUD

Abdullah bin Abdul-Aziz Al Saud, born 1924, is king of Saudi Arabia at this writing (February 2014). He ascended the throne in 2005 after the death of Fahd, although the latter's incapacitation as of 1996 meant that Abdullah had played a key role in royal affairs and governance since that time.

Abdullah was well groomed for the role of king. He has held a range of political and administrative appointments since the 1950s, including being commander of the Saudi Arabian National Guard (1963–2010), second deputy prime minister (1975–1982), first deputy prime minister (1982–2005), and of course crown prince as of 1982 as well as prince regent as of 1996.

Abdullah has a reputation of being a comparative moderate in the royal family. His political reforms since becoming king suggest this to be the case, too, although some reforms may be the result of opposition pressure for reform, which has been strong since the early 1990s and was a critical issue when he assumed full power in 2005, as the Kingdom faced a confrontation with Islamic extremists, secular demands for social and other reforms, and the need to guarantee long-term development and stability. Regardless of the intent, his initiatives have been notable: the creation of key economic cities, the establishment of new institutions of higher education, and the expansion and modernization of infrastructure in the country. His political, administrative, and judicial reforms have also been notable, some probably stemming from his more moderate views and others from societal pressures, including the post 2011 Arab uprisings.

Further information: The only biography on Abdullah is the brief and hagiographic: S. Rob Sobhani, *King Abdullah of Saudi Arabia: A Leader of Consequence* (Washington: Caspian Publishing, 2009). Given Abdullah's prominent role in Saudi Arabia not just since 2005, but extending back to the 1980s, most modern histories and political studies of Saudi Arabia cover Abdullah in some depth; an accessible scholarly work is Tim Niblock, *Saudi Arabia: Power, Legitimacy and Survival* (London: Routledge, 2006); a good more popular one is Robert Lacey, *Inside the Kingdom: Kings, Clerics, Modernists, Terrorists and the Struggle for Saudi Arabia* (London: Hutchinson, 2009).

SALMAN BIN ABD AL-AZIZ AL SAUD (HEIR APPARENT AS AT EARLY 2014)

Salman bin Abd al-Aziz Al Saud, born 1935, is the crown prince of Saudi Arabia and minister of defense.

Appointed crown prince after the death of his brother Nayef, he has considerable political experience, including as mayor of Riyadh (1950–1955), governor of Riyadh (1962–2011), and as of November 2011, minister of defense. He also performs a range of other social and charitable roles.

He is thought to be fairly conservative, given that his education and experience has been almost exclusively inside Saudi Arabia, and as a result of some public statements and affiliations.

His health is thought by some to be poor or in decline.

Further information: The only biography on Salman is a very obscure work, published on demand: Lambert M. Surhone, *Salman Bin Abdulaziz Al-Saud*

(Beau-Bassin: Betascript Publishing, 2011). Otherwise, modern histories and
political analyses of Saudi Arabia include some, if limited, discussion of Salman,
as do some of the works on the city of Riyadh, where Salman was prominent as
mayor and then governor for so long. His website includes some speech and
lecture transcripts, and some other information: see http://www.sultanbinsalman
.sa/en/Pages/default.aspx.

Chronology

Early 1700s	Ottoman control established in Hijaz (1517) and later al-Hasa; Al Saud family under Muhammad (?–1765, r. 1727–1765) in control of parts of Najd
1744	Alliance formed between Muhammad ibn Abd al-Wahhab (1703–1792) Muhammad Al Saud, head of the Al Saud family; this alliance created the *first Saudi state* or *first Saudi emirate* of 1744–1818
1773	Saudi conquest of Riyadh
1784	Saudi conquest of al-Hasa
1801	Saudi move into Iraq; attack on Karbala' and massacre of Shiites there
1803	Assassination of Abd al-Aziz, head of the Al Saud dynasty, in response to the massacre in Karbala
	Saudi conquest of Mecca in the Hijaz, the holiest city in Islam
1804	Saudi conquest of Medina
1811	Egyptian expeditionary force sent to recapture Mecca and Medina
1818	Egyptian force captures the Saudi capital Dir'iyya, bring the first Saudi state to an end
1818–1824	Key Al Saud figures in exile; most taken to Egypt after the conquest of Dir'iyya, some fleeing elsewhere
1824	Turki Al Saud returns from exile, bases himself in Riyadh, and in so doing creates the *second Saudi state* or *second Saudi emirate*
1830	Saudi conquest of al-Hasa
1834	Family rivalry leads to Turki being assassinated by a cousin, Mishari
	Turki's son Faysal manages to wrestle power back from Mishari

1836	Formation of the Rashidi emirate, based in Ha'il; lasted to 1921
1837–1843	Faysal captured by Egyptian forces and sent to Cairo for his refusal to pay tribute; Egyptians appoint another Saudi as ruler
1865	Death of Faysal; his son Abdullah assumes power
1865–1887	Period of intense intra-Saudi rivalry between Abdullah (until 1871), Saud, and Abd al-Rahman, with others drawn in as well
1871	Ottomans push back into the region, seizing al-Hasa and Asir
1887	Rashidis attack Riyadh, turning it into a client city/area
1891	Battle of Mulayda, near Riyadh, between Saudi and Rashidi forces brings the second Saudi state to an end
1893–1902	Key Saudi figures in exile in Kuwait, including Abd al-Aziz (Ibn Saud), later the founder of the modern state of Saudi Arabia
1902	Abd al-Aziz bin Abd al-Rahman Al Saud (also known as Ibn Saud) leaves Kuwait, conquers Riyadh, executes the Rashidi governor in Riyadh, and declares himself ruler; in effect this is the start of the *third Saudi state* and the formation of modern Saudi Arabia
1902–1921	Period of conflict between the Saudis and Rashidis
1904	Saudi conquest of Abha (a key town in 'Asir, in the southwest)
1906	Saudi conquest of Qasim, pushing the Rashidis back toward their main base of Ha'il
1913	Saudi conquest of al-Hasa
	Ottoman-Saudi Treaty, technically leaving al-Hasa as Ottoman but in reality giving Ibn Saud control over it
	Saudi agreement with the Shia leadership in al-Hasa, promising religious freedom in exchange for political allegiance; quickly breached by the Saudi leader
1915	Anglo-Saudi Treaty, recognizing Ibn Saud's control of Najd and al-Hasa; British agree to provide arms and finance to Ibn Saud as well
1916–1924	Saudi rivalry with Sharif Hussein of Mecca, who in 1916 had declared himself king of the Arabs
1921	Saudi conquest of Ha'il, signifying the end of the Rashidi emirate
1922	Saudi conquest of 'Asir
1924	Saudi conquest of Ta'if, in effect also the conquest of Hijaz
1925	Final Saudi conquest of Hijaz, including of the port city of Jedda and the holy city of Medina
1926	Ibn Saud declares himself "King of the Hijaz;" on top of being "Emir of Najd" this signified his control over much of what is modern Saudi Arabia
1927	Treaty of Jedda between the British and Ibn Saud gave British agreement to the borders of the area that Ibn Saud then controlled, and ensured him independence from London

1927–1930	Ikhwan revolt again Ibn Saud: the Ikhwan wanted to expand into Iraq, Transjordan, Kuwait and perhaps even further, which would have brought Ibn Saud into direct conflict with the British, who controlled these areas
1928	Ibn Saud meeting with the *'ulema* in Riyadh; the *'ulema* endorse Ibn Saud's rule, one of the first cases of the royal-*'ulema* bargain that remains in place to the present day
1929	Battle of Sabilla, 30–31 March, in which over 500 Ikhwan were killed; the last main battle of the Ikhwan revolt
1932	Declaration of the foundation of the Kingdom of Saudi Arabia
1933	The first Saudi oil concession with Standard Oil of California
1933–1934	Saudi war with Yemen; let to the borders that then endured through the twentieth century
1935	Oil drilling in Saudi Arabia begins
1939	First export of Saudi oil
1942	First U.S. diplomatic mission in Saudi Arabia, when a U.S. diplomat was sent to Jedda, mostly to work on oil issues
1945	Ibn Saud meeting with U.S. president Franklin D. Roosevelt on February 14 on the USS *Quincy*
1949	First U.S. military adviser arrives in Saudi Arabia Saudi oil production surpasses 500,000 bbls/day
1950	Trans-Arabian Pipeline (TAP) begins operation
1953	Ibn Saud dies (November 9); his son Saud succeeds him as king
1954	Saudi oil production surpasses 1,000,000 bbls/day
1958	Another of Ibn Saud's sons, Faisal, and the key rival with Saud for the throne, gains much greater power after family intervention
1962	Faisal presents a Ten Point Program for economic reform and development
1964	Saud forced to abdicate; Faisal becomes king (November 2)
1967	Arab-Israeli "Six Day War," including the Israeli conquest of the West Bank and Gaza Strip; this would be a key problem for regional stability, and an irritant for U.S.-Saudi relations under Faisal
1972	Saudi Arabia takes part ownership of ARAMCO
1973–1974	Arab oil embargo on the United States after its support for Israel in the 1973 Arab-Israeli War; massive increases in oil prices
1975	Faisal assassinated by a nephew, angered at the modernization of the Kingdom and the earlier repression of protestors against this modernization and social change, Khalid becomes king (March 25)
1978–1979	Iranian revolution, with the overthrow of Shah Muhammad Reza Pahlavi and the seizure of power by key clerics led by Ayatollah Ruhollah Khomeini; this radically altered the strategic dynamic in the Gulf
1979	Siege of the Grand Mosque in Mecca

1979–1989	Soviet war in Afghanistan; a significant number of Saudis went to fight against the Soviets and were radicalized and emboldened as a result
1980	Shia riots in the Eastern Province
	Saudi Arabia takes full control of ARAMCO
1981	Gulf Cooperation Council established, with Saudi dominance of the body
1982	Khaled dies; Fahd becomes king (June 13)
1986	Oil prices plummet; the following year Saudi Arabia runs its first modern budget deficit
1990–1991	Gulf War, after the August 2, 1990 Iraqi occupation of Kuwait
1991	Key petitions by both moderates-reformists and Islamists
1992	Saudi *Basic Law* passed
	A Consultative Assembly established
1993	Consultative Assembly begins meeting; expanded to 60 members
1994	Osama bin Laden stripped of Saudi citizenship because of his opposition activities
1995	Significant bombing in Riyadh; a sign of growing violence among opposition Islamist forces
	Fahd incapacitated by a stroke; Crown Prince Abdullah takes over day-to-day duties of the king
1996	Key attacks by Saudi extremists, including the Khobar Towers bombing and the Riyadh bombing of a U.S. military facility
2001	9/11 terrorist attacks in the United States
2003	U.S.-led Iraq War; removal of the Saddam Hussein regime
	Suicide bombing in a compound in Riyadh kills 35
	Key Saudi intellectual figures sign a petition calling for political reform
2003–2005	Key phase of the al-Qa'eda in the Arabian Peninsula (AQAP) conflict with the Saudi state
2004–2008	Period of oil price boom
2005	Fahd dies; Abdullah becomes king (August 1)
	Saudi Arabia joins the World Trade Organisation (WTO)
	Consultative Assembly expanded to 150 members
	Local council elections held, with half of all positions open to competitive electoral processes; only registered adult males over 21 allowed to vote
2007	Committee of Allegiance formed to appoint successors to the throne
2008	Oil prices peak at over US$148/bbl (in June)
2010	Agreement reached on a US$60 billion arms deal with Saudi Arabia, the largest arms sale agreement in U.S. history
2011	Arab uprisings, sometimes called the "Arab Spring," begin in Tunisia (late 2010) then spread to Egypt, Bahrain, Libya and elsewhere in early 2011

Saudis intervene in Bahrain by sending security forces to help suppress the significant uprising there

King Abdullah announces a massive spending program of some US$130 billion, in response to the Arab uprisings, including some protests in Saudi Arabia

Prince Nayef appointed crown prince after Sultan dies

2011–   Shia uprising in the Eastern Province of Saudi Arabia; regime attempts at its suppression as of 2012 are only of limited success

2012–   Syrian civil war sees the Saudis become major suppliers to some more moderate opposition elements

2012   Prince Salman appointed crown prince after Nayef dies

2013   Thirty women appointed to the Consultative Assembly, the first time women have been given this role

Saudi Arabia turns down a UN Security Council non-permanent seat, supposedly because of the international failure to act on Syria

Saudi relations with the United States increasingly strained throughout the year, especially as the Saudis voice more public concerns over U.S. policy toward Syria

Glossary

Advice and Reform Committee (ARC) — A comparatively radical opposition group to the Saudi royal family, operating in exile, and active in the 1990s.

Al-Aqsa Intifada — The popular name for the uprising by Palestinians in the occupied territories of the West Bank and the Gaza Strip, usually dated as September 29, 2000 through to late 2005.

Allegiance Council — Formed in 2007, the Allegiance Council is responsible for selecting successors to the throne of Saudi Arabia. It has 28 members (as at the end of 2013), consisting of Ibn Saud's sons if still alive and not incapacitated, otherwise a grandson joins it instead.

Al-Qa'eda — Literally "the base." A violent extremist Sunni network dedicated to overthrowing the Saudi regime, evicting Western military forces and much else of the Western presence from the Muslim world, and reestablishing an Islamic caliphate (a single leader of the Sunni Muslim community worldwide).

Al-Qa'eda in the Arabian Peninsula (AQAP) — The main Al-Qa'eda splinter group operating in Saudi Arabia and Yemen in the 2000s and 2010s, responsible for a number of terrorist attacks and violent confrontations with Saudi security forces.

Al-Sahwa — Meaning "awakening." A powerful Islamic revivalist movement in Saudi Arabia from the mid-twentieth century, especially vocal in later decades. It effectively collapsed in the mid-1990s but was succeeded by other groups.

Al Saud — The name of the ruling family dynasty in Saudi Arabia, with "Al" meaning "the line of" and "Saud," more precisely "Suʿud," being the dynastic name.

ARAMCO (later Saudi ARAMCO) — The Saudi state-owned oil company. It began life as a U.S.-owned firm, but was nationalized in the 1970s. It now controls oil and gas reserves, exploration, and extraction in the Kingdom.

Bida' — Literally "innovation." The term is used by some religious scholars and leaders, including the Saudi Wahhabi clerics, as a negative term for practices and customs that crept into Muslims' conduct over time.

Committee for the Defense of Legitimate Rights (CDLR) — A Saudi dissident group that called for a stricter application of Islamic law in Saudi Arabia and the protection of human rights. Formed in 1993, it went into exile in London in the mid-1990s, and was superseded by other groups in the 2000s.

Committee for the Propagation of Virtue and the Prevention of Vice (CPVPV) — See *Mutawwa'*.

Dir'iyya — The town from which the Saudi ruling family originated, located to the northwest of Riyadh; the capital of the first Saudi state over 1744–1818.

Fatwa (pl. *fatāwa*) — A religious opinion or edict issued by experts in *shari'a* (Islamic law).

Gulf Cooperation Council (GCC) — A sub-regional bloc with both trade and security roles, the GCC was formed in 1981 and consists of Saudi Arabia, Bahrain, Kuwait, Oman, Qatar, and the United Arab Emirates.

Hasa — Or "al-Hasa." A region in the east of Saudi Arabia, now part of the Eastern Province. The majority of Saudi Arabia's Shia population are located in this area.

Hijaz — A region in the west of Saudi Arabia, conquered by Ibn Saud in 1924. Jedda is its main trading city and most populous city, but Mecca and Medina, the two holiest cities in Islam, are also located in the Hijaz.

Ikhwan — The plural of "brothers," referring to a religious tribal force that was the main supporting militia for Ibn Saud during his expansion and creation of modern Saudi Arabia in the early decades of the twentieth century.

Islam — Literally "submission." Islam is a major monotheistic religion that emerged in the Arabian Peninsula, in what is today Saudi Arabia, in the early seventh century. Adherents believe in the oneness of *Allah* (God); the finality and purity of the Qur'an, in Arabic, as God's word and final revelation; andwhile Islam recognizes many prophets from the Jewish and Christian tradition that the Prophet Muhammad (570–632) was the last and greatest of the prophets. It has around 1.6 billion adherents worldwide, identifying with a number of sects and, within those, with different jurisprudential schools and variants.

Jihad — Translates literally as "struggle," but also means, and is often emphasized as, "holy war." It is a duty of Muslims to confront opponents of or threats to Islam; this can be in a military sense, but also nonviolent forms of spiritual struggle, including within oneself.

Majlis — Literally "a sitting place." It may be used to refer to a council, legislature, or other body that meets and acts as a consultative or decision-making institution. It also has a separate meaning, which appears in the Saudi context, as a gathering of people with a leader or senior figure, where the latter can negotiate with or co-opt the former.

Majlis al-Shura — A common term for a legislative political body such as a national parliament or chamber of review. The Saudi Consultative Assembly uses this term in Arabic. Separately, the term can also refer to an advisory body that elects and/or advises the Caliph in an Islamic governance system.

Mecca — A city in eastern Saudi Arabia, in the Hijaz. The holiest city in Islam, the birthplace of the Prophet Muhammad, and the place where he began his ministry. Muslims face in the direction of Mecca for prayer, and it is the location for the Muslim Hajj, or pilgrimage.

Mujahideen — Literally "strugglers" or "jihadists," the term is used to describe those engaging in *jihad*. It is most commonly used to apply to those engaging in radical or violent confrontation with the enemies of Islam.

Mutawwaʿ (pl. *Mutawwaʿeen*) — Originally referring to informal religious advisers, the is now used for the Saudi "religious police." They are responsible for enforcing Islamic laws and practices and have sometimes been controversial in so doing.

Najd — The inland region in central Saudi Arabia from where the Al Saud emerged. The Saudi capital, Riyadh, is located in Najd.

Organization of the Petroleum Exporting Countries (OPEC) — Formed in 1960, and now consisting of 12 member states, OPEC is an oil exporter cartel established to coordinate oil policies and prices and ensure a stable income from oil. Saudi Arabia was a founding member.

Ottoman Empire — A Turkic empire founded in 1299 and, from 1453 to 1918, a major power. It was at its peak in the sixteenth and seventeenth centuries. It controlled much of the Middle East at various times, including coastal parts of what is now Saudi Arabia.

Prevention, Rehabilitation and Aftercare Program (PRAC) — A structured program of measures to counter Islamic extremism in Saudi Arabia, established after the violent confrontations between Islamic extremists and the Saudi government in the early-2000s. It claims a success rate of 80–90 percent.

Rashidi emirate — A dynasty in the north of modern Saudi Arabia, the Rashidis were a powerful rival to the Al Saud from the mid-nineteenth century until their conquest by the Saudis in 1921.

Rentier State (also *Rentierism*) — A state which derives a substantial proportion of its income from "rents," most commonly oil or gas royalties but also other payments that are the result of natural assets. Rentier states are often assumed by scholars to be co-optive, needing little or no taxation and facing little pressure for democratization. Saudi Arabia is often described as a rentier state.

Salafist — The term for the *salafi* movement within Sunni Islam, a strict, literalist movement seeking to copy the earliest adherents to Islam, who it considers

to be the ideal model of Muslim conduct and belief. The Wahhabi movement
is sometimes treated by scholars as *salafi*, although despite some shared charac-
teristics, *salafists* are more widespread.

Saudi Arabian National Guard (SANG) — A land-based military branch in
Saudi Arabia, reporting through its own minister to the king, thus also serving
as a type of royal guard. Traditionally drawn from tribal groups, including
some *Ikhwan* descendants, it was modernized in the 1980s and 1990s.

Saudi National Security Council (SNSC) — The coordinating body for Saudi
national security, intelligence, and high-level foreign relations. Founded by
King Abdullah in 2005, and consisting of key ministers, it formalized and
modernized decision making on security, while keeping these decisions under
Al Saud control.

Shari'a — The body of religious law and codes of moral conduct in Islam. *Shari'a*
is based on the Qur'an, the traditions and sayings of the Prophet Muhammad,
and jurisprudence based on precedent, interpretation, and debate.

Shia (adj. *Shiite*) — The second-largest sect in Islam, which broke with Sunni
Islam over the question of succession to the Prophet Muhammad. Shiites
believe that Ali, the Prophet's cousin and son-in-law, was his rightful successor
and that subsequent succession should follow this line. Iran, Iraq, Bahrain, and
Azerbaijan are majority Shia, but there are Shia populations in much of the
Muslim world.

Shura — Meaning "consultation." It is a principle of traditional leadership in the
Arab Muslim world, where local leaders would consult with key people in the
community, and the basis for some Muslim claims of a compatibility between
Islam and democracy.

Sudairi — The term for the children, especially the sons, of Hassa bint Ahmed Al
Sudairi (1900–1969), one of Ibn Saud's favorite wives. The "Sudairi Seven"
refers to the group of seven full brothers of this line, who were extremely
powerful in twentieth century Saudi Arabia; King Fahd, as well as princes
Nayef, Sultan, Salman, and others, were/are among the Seven.

Sunni — The largest sect within Islam; some 85 percent or more of the world's
Muslims are Sunni. It is often described as the most orthodox sect. It accepts
leaders who are not from the Prophet Muhammad's bloodline. Saudi Arabia
is majority Sunni, but with a Shia minority of some 10–15 percent of the
population.

Tawhid — Literally "oneness," in Islamic doctrine it is the term used for "monotheism," and is at the absolute core of Muslim belief and the declaration of
faith.

'ulema (sing. *'alim*) — Refers to Muslim legal scholars who are experts in Islamic
jurisprudence. Some Muslims reserve the term for the more highly educated
scholars, while others extend it to less prominent or more local clerics as well.
In Saudi Arabia, Islamic courts draw judges from the ranks of the *'ulema.*

Wahhabi — A very conservative, revivalist movement in Islam, which emerged under the prominent figure Muhammad ibn Abd al-Wahhab (1703–1792) and which gained power and reach through al-Wahhab's 1744 alliance with the Al Saud dynasty's head, Abdullah (?–1765). Many adherents reject the term *Wahhabi*, preferring to use either *salafi* or *muwahhid* (meaning "unitarian").

Zakat — The practice of giving alms or donations to charity; a basic tenet of Islam. It is usually set at 2.5 percent of the value of assets per year. It is meant to only be applied to those who can afford it, who are encouraged to voluntarily pay more than the minimum.

Bibliography

Aburish, Saïd K. *The Rise, Corruption, and Coming Fall of the House of Saud*. London: Bloomsbury, 1994.

Alasfoor, Reyadh. *The Gulf Cooperation Council: Its Nature and Achievements. A Political Analysis of Regional Integration of the GCC States, 1979–2004*. Lund: Lund University, 2007.

Ali, Abbas J. *Business and Management Environment in Saudi Arabia*. Abingdon: Routledge, 2009.

Allen, Charles. *God's Terrorists: The Wahhabi Cult and the Hidden Roots of Modern Jihad*. London: Little, Brown, 2006.

Al-Rasheed, Madawi. *A Most Masculine State: Gender, Politics, and Religion in Saudi Arabia*. Cambridge: Cambridge University Press, 2013a.

Al-Rasheed, Madawi. "Saudi Arabia: Local and Regional Challenges." *Contemporary Arab Affairs* 6, no. 1 (2013b): 28–40.

Al-Rasheed, Madawi. *A History of Saudi Arabia*. Cambridge: Cambridge University Press, 2010, 2nd ed.

Al-Rasheed, Madawi. *Contesting the Saudi State: Islamic Voices from a New Generation*. Cambridge: Cambridge University Press, 2007.

Al-Rasheed, Madawi. "Saudi Arabia: The Challenge of the US Invasion of Iraq." In *The Iraq War: Causes and Consequences*, edited by Rick Fawn and Raymond Hinnesbusch. Boulder: Lynne Rienner, 2006: 153–161

Al-Rasheed, Madawi. "Circles of Power: Royals and Society in Saudi Arabia." In *Saudi Arabia in the Balance: Political Economy, Society, Foreign Affairs*, edited by Paul Aarts and Gerd Nonneman. London: Hurst & Company, 2005: 185–213.

Alyousef, Yousef, and Paul Stevens. "The Cost of Domestic Energy Prices to Saudi Arabia." *Energy Policy* 39 (2011): 6900–6905.

Amnesty International. *Amnesty International Annual Report 2012*. London: Amnesty International Ltd, 2012. http://files.amnesty.org/air12/air_2012_full_en.pdf.

Anscombe, Frederick F. *The Ottoman Gulf: The Creation of Kuwait, Saudi Arabia, and Qatar*. New York: Columbia University Press, 1997.

Antoniades, Alexis. "The Gulf Cooperation Council Monetary Union." In *The Political Economy of the Persian Gulf,* edited by Mehran Kamrava. London: Hurst & Company, 2012: 173–191.

Arab American Institute. *Arabs: What They Believe and What They Value Most.* Washington, DC: Arab American Institute, 2002. http://b.3cdn.net/aai/15b74344248440f677 _xzm6yho0g.pdf.

Ashraf, A. S. M. Ali. "Transnational Cooperation on Anti-Terrorism: A Comparative Case Study of Saudi Arabia and Indonesia." *Perceptions* XII (2007): 91–121.

Asseri, Ali S. Awadh. *Combating Terrorism: Saudi Arabia's Role in the War on Terror.* Karachi: Oxford University Press, 2009.

Bachar, Shmuel, Shmuel Bar, Rachel Machtiger, and Yair Minzili. "Establishment Ulama and Radicalism in Egypt, Saudi Arabia, and Jordan." *Center on Islam, Democracy, and the Future of the Muslim World, Research Monographs on the Muslim World, Series No. 1, Paper No. 4* (Washington, DC: Hudson Institute, 2006).

Bahgat, Gawdat. "Saudi Arabia and the Arab-Israeli Peace Process." *Middle East Policy* 14, no. 3 (2007): 49–59.

Bensahel, Nora, and Daniel L. Byman. "Introduction." In *The Future Security Environment in the Middle East: Conflict, Stability, and Political Change,* edited by Nora Bensahel and Daniel L. Byman. Santa Monica: RAND Corporation, 2004: 1–14.

Bill, James A., and Robert Springborg. *Politics in the Middle East.* Glenview: Scott, Foresman and Company, 1990, 3rd ed.

Blanchard, Christopher M., Kenneth Katzman, Carol Migdalovitz, and Jeremy M. Sharp. *Iraq: Regional Perspectives and U.S. Policy.* Washington, DC: Congressional Research Service Report to Congress, 2009.

Bodansky, Yossef. *Bin Laden: The Man Who Declared War on America.* New York: Random House, 2001.

Boucek, Christopher. "Saudi Arabia's 'Soft' Counterterrorism Strategy: Prevention, Rehabilitation, and Aftercare." *Carnegie Paper Number 97* (Washington, DC: Middle East Program, Carnegie Endowment for International Peace, 2008).

BP. *BP Statistical Review of World Energy 2013.* London: BP, 2013. http://www.bp.com/en/ global/corporate/about-bp/statistical-review-of-world-energy-2013.html.

Bradley, John R. "Al Qaeda and the House of Saud: Eternal Enemies or Secret Bedfellows?" *The Washington Quarterly* 28, no. 4 (2005): 139–152.

Bronson, Rachel. *Thicker Than Oil: America's Uneasy Partnership with Saudi Arabia.* New York: Oxford University Press, 2006.

Bronson, Rachel. "Rethinking Religion: The Legacy of the U.S.-Saudi Relationship." *The Washington Quarterly* 28, no. 4 (2005): 121–137.

Brynen, Rex, Pete W. Moore, Bassel F. Salloukh, and Marie-Joëlle Zahar. *Beyond the Arab Spring: Authoritarianism & Democratization in the Arab World.* Boulder: Lynne Rienner, 2012.

Byman, Daniel L. "Regional Consequences of Internal Turmoil in Iraq." In *International Politics of the Persian Gulf,* edited by Mehran Kamrava. New York: Syracuse University Press, 2011: 144–168.

Central Intelligence Agency. *CIA World Fact Book 2013–14.* Washington, DC: Central Intelligence Agency, 2013. https://www.cia.gov/library/publications/the-world-factbook/geos/ sa.html.

Champion, Daryl. *The Paradoxical Kingdom: Saudi Arabia and the Momentum of Reform.* New York: Columbia University Press, 2003.

Clatanoff, William C., Christopher Parlin, Robert Jordan, Charles Kestenbaum, and Jean-Francois Seznec. "Symposium: Saudi Arabia's Accession to the WTO: Is a 'Revolution' Brewing?" *Middle East Policy* 13, no. 1 (2006): 1–23.

Coll, Steve. *The Bin Ladens: Oil, Money, Terrorism and the Secret Saudi World.* London: Penguin, 2008.

Commins, David. *The Gulf States: A Modern History.* London: I. B. Taurus, 2012.

Commins, David. *The Wahhabi Mission and Saudi Arabia.* London: I. B. Taurus, 2009.

Cordesman, Anthony H. *Saudi Arabia: National Security in a Troubled Region.* Santa Barbara: ABC-CLIO/Center for Strategic and International Studies, 2009.

Cordesman, Anthony H. *Saudi Arabia Enters the Twenty-First Century: The Military and International Security Dimensions.* Westport: Praeger, 2003.

Cordesman, Anthony H., and Bryan Gold. *The Gulf Military Balance. Volume I: The Conventional and Asymmetric Dimensions.* Washington, DC: Center for Strategic & International Studies, 2013.

Cordesman, Anthony H., and Nawaf Obaid. *Saudi Internal Security: A Risk Assessment.* Washington, DC: Center for Strategic and International Studies, 2009.

Cronin, Stephanie. "Tribes, Coups and Princes: Building a Modern Army in Saudi Arabia." *Middle Eastern Studies* 49, no. 1 (2013): 2–28.

Davidson, Christopher M. *Dubai: The Vulnerability of Success.* London: Hurst & Company, 2008.

DeLong-Bas, Natana J. *Wahhabi Islam: From Revival and Reform to Global Jihad.* Oxford: Oxford University Press, 2004.

Eljelly, Abuzar M. A. "Ownership and Firm Performance: The Experience of Saudi Arabia's Emerging Economy." *International Business & Economics Research Journal* 8, no. 8 (2009): 25–34.

Feinstein, Andrew. *The Shadow World: Inside the Global Arms Trade.* New York: Picador, 2011.

Freedom House. *Freedom of the Press* 2012. Washington, DC: Freedom House, 2012. http://www.freedomhouse.org/report/freedom-press/2012/Saudi-Arabia.

Gately, Dermot, Nourah Al-Yousef, and Hamad M. H. Al-Sheikh. "The Rapid Growth of Domestic Oil Consumption in Saudi Arabia and the Opportunity Cost of Oil Exports Foregone." *Energy Policy* 47 (2012): 57–68.

Gause III, F. Gregory. "Kings for All Seasons: How the Middle East's Monarchies Survived the Arab Spring." *Brookings Doha Center Analysis Paper Number 8* (Doha: The Brookings Institution, September 2013). http://www.brookings.edu/research/papers/2013/09/24 -resilience-arab-monarchies-gause.

Gause III, F. Gregory. *The International Relations of the Persian Gulf.* Cambridge: Cambridge University Press, 2010.

Gause III, F. Gregory. "Saudi Arabia: Desert Storm and After." In *The Middle East after Iraq's Invasion of Kuwait,* edited by Robert O. Freedman. Gainesville: University Press of Florida, 1993: 207–234.

Gray, Matthew. *Qatar: Politics and the Challenges of Development.* Boulder: Lynne Rienner, 2013.

Gray, Matthew. *A Theory of "Late Rentierism" in the Arab States of the Gulf.* Doha: Center for International and Regional Studies, Georgetown University, School of Foreign Service in Qatar, 2011.

Greenberg, Maurice R., William F. Wechsler, and Lee S. Wolosky. *Terrorist Financing: Report of an Independent Task Force Sponsored by the Council on Foreign Relations.* New York: Council on Foreign Relations, 2002.

Hammond, Andrew. *The Islamic Utopia: The Illusion of Reform in Saudi Arabia.* London: Pluto Press, 2012.

Hegghammer, Thomas. *Jihad in Saudi Arabia: Violence and Pan-Islamism since 1979.* Cambridge: Cambridge University Press, 2010.

Hegghammer, Thomas, and Stéphane Lacroix. "Rejectionist Islamism in Saudi Arabia: The Story of Juhayman Al-'Utaybi Revisited." *International Journal of Middle East Studies* 39, no. 1 (2007): 103–122.

Helms, Christine Moss. *The Cohesion of Saudi Arabia: Evolution of Political Identity.* London: Croom Helm, 1981.

Henry, Clement M., and Robert Springborg. *Globalization and the Politics of Development in the Middle East.* Cambridge: Cambridge University Press, 2001.

Hertog, Steffen. "Defying the Resource Curse: Explaining Successful State-Owned Enterprises in Rentier States." *World Politics* 62, no. 2 (2010a): 261–301.

Hertog, Steffen. *Princes, Brokers, and Bureaucrats: Oil and the State in Saudi Arabia.* Ithaca: Cornell University Press, 2010b.

Hertog, Steffen, and Giacomo Luciani. "Energy and Sustainability Policies in the Gulf States." In *The Transformation of the Gulf: Politics, Economics and the Global Order,* edited by David Held and Kristian Ulrichsen. London: Routledge, 2012: 236–257.

Hiro, Dilip. *Desert Shield to Desert Storm: The Second Gulf War.* London: Paladin, 1992.

Hiro, Dilip. *The Longest War: The Iran-Iraq Military Conflict.* London: Paladin, 1990.

Ibrahim, Fouad. *The Shi'is of Saudi Arabia.* London: Saqi Books, 2006.

IntelCenter. 2004. "Al-Qaeda in the Arabian Peninsula: Shotting, Hostage Taking, Kidnapping Wave—May/June 2004." (*AQAP-SHK-WMJ04*) V1.1 (Alexandria: IntelCenter/Tempest Publishing LLC). http://www.intelcenter.com/AQAP-SHK-PUB-v1-1.pdf.

International Crisis Group (ICG). *Saudi Arabia Backgrounder: Who Are the Islamists?* Brussels: ICG Middle East Report N°31, 2004.

International Crisis Group (ICG). *The Shiite Question in Saudi Arabia.* Brussels: ICG Middle East Report N°45, 2005.

International Crisis Group (ICG). *Popular Protests in North Africa and the Middle East (III): The Bahrain Revolt.* Brussels: ICG MENA Report N°105, 2011.

International Institute for Strategic Studies (IISS). *The Military Balance 2014.* London: International Institute for Strategic Studies/Routledge, 114:1.

International Monetary Fund (IMF). *Energy Subsidies in the Middle East and North Africa: Lessons for Reform.* Washington, DC: Middle East and Central Asia Department, IMF, 2013. http://www.imf.org/external/np/fad/subsidies/pdf/menanote.pdf.

Janardhan, N. "New Media: In Search of Equilibrium." In *Political Change in the Arab Gulf States: Stuck in Transition,* edited by Mary Ann Tétreault, Gwenn Okruhlik, and Andrzej Kapiszewski. Boulder: Lynne Rienner, 2011: 225–245.

Jones, Toby Craig. "Saudi-Iraq Relations: Devolving Chaos or Acrimonious Stability?" In *Iraq, Its Neighbors, and the United States: Competition, Crisis, and the Reordering of Power,* edited by Henri Barkey, Scott B. Lasensky, and Phebe Marr. Washington, DC: United States Institute of Peace, 2011: 99–118.

Jones, Toby Craig. "Religious Revivalism and Its Challenge to the Saudi Regime." In *Religion and Politics in Saudi Arabia: Wahhabism and the State,* edited by Mohammed Ayoob and Hasan Kosebalaban. Boulder: Lynne Rienner, 2009: 109–120.

Kamrava, Mehran. *Qatar: Small State, Big Politics.* Ithaca: Cornell University Press, 2013.

Kamrava, Mehran. "The Arab Spring and the Saudi-Led Counterrevolution." *Orbis* 56, no. 1 (2012): 96–104.

Kéchechian, Joseph A. *Legal and Political Reforms in Sa'udi Arabia*. Abingdon: Routledge, 2013.

Kéchechian, Joseph A. *Power and Succession in Arab Monarchies: A Reference Handbook*. Boulder: Lynne Rienner, 2008.

Kerr, Malcolm H. *The Arab Cold War: Gamal 'Abd al-Nasir and His Rivals, 1958–1970*. London: Oxford University Press, 1971, 3rd ed.

Kobayashi, Yoshikazu. *Corporate Strategies of Saudi Aramco*. Houston: James A. Baker III Institute for Public Policy and Japan Petroleum Energy Center, 2007.

Kostiner, Joseph. "GCC Perceptions of Collective Security in the Post-Saddam Era." In *International Politics of the Persian Gulf*, edited by Mehran Kamrava. New York: Syracuse University Press, 2011: 94–119.

Kostiner, Joseph. "Saudi Arabia and the Arab–Israeli Peace Process: The Fluctuation of Regional Coordination." *British Journal of Middle Eastern Studies* 36, no. 3 (2009): 417–429.

Kostiner, Joseph. *The Making of Saudi Arabia, 1916–1936: From Chieftaincy to Monarchical State*. New York: Oxford University Press, 1993.

Kostiner, Joseph. "Transforming Dualities: Tribe and State Formation in Saudi Arabia." In *Tribes and State Formation in the Middle East*, edited by Philip S. Khoury and Joseph Kostiner. Berkeley: University of California Press, 1990: 226–251.

KPMG. *2013—Thinking Beyond Borders—Saudi Arabia*. Amstelveen, Netherlands: KPMG, 2013. http://www.kpmg.com/Global/en/IssuesAndInsights/ArticlesPublications/thinking-beyond-borders/Documents/saudi-arabia-2013.pdf.

Lacey, Robert. *Inside the Kingdom: Kings, Clerics, Modernists, Terrorists and the Struggle for Saudi Arabia*. London: Hutchinson, 2009.

Lacey, Robert. *The Kingdom*. London: Fontana, 1982.

Lacroix, Stéphane. *Awakening Islam: The Politics of Religious Dissent in Contemporary Saudi Arabia*. Cambridge: Harvard University Press, 2011.

Lacroix, Stéphane. "Islamo-Liberal Politics in Saudi Arabia." In *Saudi Arabia in the Balance: Political Economy, Society, Foreign Affairs*, edited by Paul Aarts and Gerd Nonneman. London: Hurst & Company, 2005: 35–56.

Lahn, Glada, and Paul Stevens. *Burning Oil to Keep Cool: The Hidden Energy Crisis in Saudi Arabia*. London: The Royal Institute of International Affairs, 2011.

Lees, Brian. *A Handbook of the Al Sa'ud Ruling Family of Saudi Arabia*. London: Royal Genealogies, 1980.

Legrenzi, Matteo. *The GCC and the International Relations of the Gulf: Diplomacy, Security and Economic Coordination in a Changing Middle East*. London: I. B. Taurus, 2011a.

Legrenzi, Matteo. "Gulf Cooperation Council Diplomatic Coordination: The Limited Role of Institutionalization." In *Industrialization in the Gulf: A Socioeconomic Revolution*, edited by Jean-François Seznec and Mimi Kirk. Abingdon: Routledge, 2011b: 103–122.

Long, David E. *Culture and Customs of Saudi Arabia*. Westport: Greenwood Press, 2005.

Long, David E. *The Kingdom of Saudi Arabia*. Gainesville: University of Florida Press, 1997.

Mackey, Sandra. *The Saudis: Inside the Desert Kingdom*. New York: Norton, 2002, 2nd ed.

McMillan, Joseph. "Saudi Arabia and Iraq: Oil, Religion, and the Enduring Rivalry." *United States Institute of Peace Special Report 157* (Washington, DC: United States Institute of Peace, 2006).

Maley, William. *The Afghanistan Wars.* Basingstoke: Palgrave Macmillian, 2002.

Malik, Monica, and Tim Niblock. "Saudi Arabia's Economy: The Challenge of Reform." In *Saudi Arabia in the Balance: Political Economy, Society, Foreign Affairs,* edited by Paul Aarts and Gerd Nonneman. London: Hurst, 2005: 85–110.

Mehrara, Mohsen. "Energy Consumption and Economic Growth: The Case of Oil Exporting Countries." *Energy Policy* 35, no. 5 (2007): 2939–2945.

Meijer, Roel. "The 'Cycle of Contention' and the Limits of Terrorism in Saudi Arabia." In *Saudi Arabia in the Balance: Political Economy, Society, Foreign Affairs,* edited by Paul Aarts and Gerd Nonneman. London: Hurst, 2005: 271–311.

Momani, Bessma, and Matteo Legrenzi. "Introduction: The Geo-Economic Power of the Gulf." In *Shifting Geo-Economic Power of the Gulf: Oil, Finance and Institutions,* edited by Matteo Legrenzi and Bessma Momani. Farhman: Ashgate, 2011: 1–6.

Mufti, Mariam, and Robert L. Lamb. *Religion and Militancy in Pakistan and Afghanistan: A Literature Review.* Washington, DC: Center for Strategic and International Studies, 2012. http://csis.org/files/publication/120628_Mufti_ReligionMilitancy_Web.pdf.

National Commission on Terrorist Attacks Upon the United States (The 9/11 Commission). *Monograph on Terrorist Financing: Staff Report to the Commission.* Washington, DC: National Commission on Terrorist Attacks Upon the United States, 2004. http://govinfo.library.unt.edu/911/staff_statements/911_TerrFin_Monograph.pdf.

Nevo, Joseph. "Religion and National Identity in Saudi Arabia." *Middle Eastern Studies* 34, no. 3 (1998): 34–53.

Niblock, Tim. *Saudi Arabia: Power, Legitimacy and Survival.* London: Routledge, 2006.

Niblock, Tim, with Monica Malik. *The Political Economy of Saudi Arabia.* London: Routledge, 2007.

Nuruzzaman, Mohammed. "Politics, Economics and Saudi Military Intervention in Bahrain." *Journal of Contemporary Asia* 43, no. 2 (2013): 363–378.

Obaid, Nawaf, and Anthony Cordesman. *Saudi Militants in Iraq: Assessment and Kingdom's Response.* Washington, DC: Center for Strategic and International Studies, 2005. http://csis.org/files/media/csis/pubs/050919_saudimiltantsiraq.pdf.

Okruhlik, Gwenn. "State Power, Religious Privilege, and Myths About Political Reform." In *Religion and Politics in Saudi Arabia: Wahhabism and the State,* edited by Mohammed Ayoob and Hasan Kosebalaban. Boulder: Lynne Rienner, 2009: 91–107.

O'Reilly, Marc J. "Omanibalancing: Oman Confronts an Uncertain Future." *The Middle East Journal* 52, no. 1 (1998): 70–84.

Ottaway, Marina, and Marwan Muasher. "Arab Monarchies: Change for Reform, Yet Unmet." *Carnegie Middle East Paper* (Washington, DC: Carnegie Endowment for International Peace, December 2011).

Pelletierre, Stephen C. *The Iran-Iraq War: Chaos in a Vacuum.* New York: Praeger, 1992.

Philby, Harry St. John. *Arabian Jubilee.* London: Hale, 1952.

Prokop, Michaela. "The War of Ideas: Education in Saudi Arabia." In *Saudi Arabia in the Balance: Political Economy, Society, Foreign Affairs,* edited by Paul Aarts and Gerd Nonneman. London: Hurst, 2005: 57–81.

Puckett, Rebecca, Joshua Abel, and Sara Keefe. *Exploring the U.S.-GCC Relationship: A Discussion of Trade, Investment, and Commercial Opportunities.* Washington, DC: Elliott School of International Affairs, The George Washington University, 2008. http://elliott.gwu.edu/assets/docs/acad/itip/us_gcc_itip_capstone.pdf.

Quandt, William B. "Review of: Said K. Aburish. The Rise, Corruption, and Coming Fall of the House of Saud. London: Bloomsbury, 1994." *Foreign Affairs* 74, no. 5 (1995): 178–179.

Raphaeli, Nimrod. "Demands for Reforms in Saudi Arabia." *Middle Eastern Studies* 41, no. 4 (2005): 517–532.

Rivlin, Paul. *Arab Economies in the Twenty-First Century.* Cambridge: Cambridge University Press, 2001.

Sadowski, Yahya M. *Scuds or Butter? The Political Economy of Arms Control in the Middle East.* Washington, DC: The Brookings Institution, 1993.

Safran, Nadav. *Saudi Arabia: The Ceaseless Quest for Security.* Ithaca: Cornell University Press, 1988.

Salmoni, Barak A., Bryce Loidolt, and Madeleine Wells. *Regime and Periphery in Northern Yemen: The Houthi Conflict.* Santa Monica: RAND Corporation, 2010.

Saudi Arabian General Investment Authority (SAGIA). *Answering Your Investment Needs: A Detailed Guide to Investing in Saudi Arabia.* Riyadh: SAGIA, no date. https://www .sagia.gov.sa/Documents/Wizard/Investment%20guide.pdf

Saudi Arabian Monetary Agency (SAMA). *Forty-Eighth Annual Report.* Riyadh: Research and Statistics Department, Saudi Arabian Monetary Agency, 2012.

Shannon, Kelly J. "'I'm glad I'm not a Saudi woman': The First Gulf War and US encounters with Saudi gender relations." *Cambridge Review of International Affairs* (published online by Taylor and Francis, October 12, 2012). http://www.tandfonline.com/doi/abs/ 10.1080/09557571.2012.678296#.Upan_uLpfwo.

Sick, Gary. "The United States and the Persian Gulf in the Twentieth Century." In *The Persian Gulf in History,* edited by Lawrence G. Potter. New York: Palgrave Macmillan, 2009: 295–310.

Simmons, Matthew R. *Twilight in the Desert: The Coming Oil Shock and the World Economy.* Hoboken: John Wiley & Sons, 2005.

Steinberg, Guido. "The Wahhabi Ulema and the Saudi State: 1745 to the Present." In *Saudi Arabia in the Balance: Political Economy, Society, Foreign Affairs,* edited by Paul Aarts and Gerd Nonneman. London: Hurst & Company, 2005: 11–34.

Stockholm International Peace Research Institute (SIPRI). *SIPRI Fact Sheet: Military Spending and Arms Procurement in the Gulf States.* Stockholm: SIPRI, 2010. http://books .sipri.org/files/FS/SIPRIFS1010.pdf.

Teitelbaum, Joshua. *Saudi Arabia and the New Strategic Landscape.* Stanford: Hoover Institution Press, 2010.

Teitelbaum, Joshua. *The Rise and Fall of the Hashemite Kingdom of Arabia.* London: Hurst, 2001.

Telhami, Shibley. *2010 Annual Arab Public Opinion Survey.* College Park, MD: University of Maryland with Zogby International, 2010. http://www.brookings.edu/~/media/research/ files/reports/2010/8/05%20arab%20opinion%20poll%20telhami/0805_arabic_opinion _poll_telhami.pdf.

Tripp, Charles. *A History of Iraq.* Cambridge: Cambridge University Press, 2007, 3rd ed.

Trofimov, Yaroslav. *The Siege of Mecca: The Forgotten Uprising in Islam's Holiest Shrine.* London: Allen Lane, 2007.

Vassiliev, Alexei. *King Faisal: Personality, Faith and Times.* London: Saqi, 2013.

Vassiliev, Alexei. *The History of Saudi Arabia.* New York: New York University Press, 2000.

Wehrey, Frederic. *The Forgotten Uprising in Eastern Saudi Arabia.* Washington, DC: Carnegie Endowment for International Peace, 2013.

Wehrey, Frederic, Theodore W. Karasik, Alireza Nader, Jeremy J. Ghez, Lydia Hansell, and Robert A. Guffey. *Saudi-Iranian Relations since the Fall of Saddam: Rivalry, Cooperation, and Implications for U.S. Policy.* Santa Monica: RAND Corporation, 2009.

Wilson, Peter W., and Douglas F. Graham. *Saudi Arabia: The Coming Storm.* New York: M. E. Sharpe, 1994.

World Bank. *Doing Business 2014: Understanding Regulations for Small and Medium-Size Enterprises.* Washington, DC: World Bank Group, 2013.

World Bank. *Data: Saudi Arabia.* Washington, DC: The World Bank, no date. http:// data.worldbank.org/country/saudi-arabia.

Yizraeli, Sarah. *Politics and Society in Saudi Arabia: The Crucial Years of Development, 1960–1982.* New York: Columbia University Press, 2012.

Index

Abdullah Peace Plan: (2002), 75–76, 94, 156; Re-approval and re-issue of (2007), 76; U.S. response to, 76

Abu Musa island, 91, 102

Afghanistan: mujahideen, 22–23, 64, 121; relations with Saudi Arabia, 22–23, 64–65, 121–22, 126, 133; Saudi aid to anti-Soviet mujahideen, 22, 64; Saudi volunteer fighters in, 23, 24, 64, 69, 121–22, 123, 128–29, 132 (during Soviet war), 133 (during U.S. war); Soviet invasion and war in, 22–23, 24, 64, 120, 121, 123, 128–29; U.S. invasion and war, 78, 126, 127, 128, 133. *See also* Taliban

Agriculture, 35, 165. *See also* Land use

Air Defense Force, Royal Saudi, 39, 40

Air Force: Royal Saudi, 39, 40, 42*table*, 63, 64, 65–66; AWACS sale by the U.S. (1982), 64; comparison of military power across Gulf states, 42*table*; history, 40, 63; platforms, 40, 63; size, 39; U.S. Air Force, 68, 125. *See also* Air Defense Force; Dhahran air field

Al al-Sheikh family, 47

Al Khalifa dynasty/family (Bahrain), 41, 77, 90, 93–94, 96–97, 99

Al Rashid, Muhammad, 5. *See also* Rashidi emirate

Al Sabah dynasty/family (Kuwait), 5, 99. *See also* Kuwait

Al Saud, Abd al-Aziz (ruler 1765–1803), 3–4

Al Saud, Abd al-Aziz bin Abd al-Rahman (1876–1953; king 1932–1953; also known as Ibn Saud), 1, 5–9, 9–14, 15, 17, 25, 30, 31–32, 35–36, 39, 41, 45, 47, 48–49, 50, 56n75, 59–61, 99, 119, 134, 147; descendants, 17, 25, 30, 31–34; exile, 5, 6, 99; founder of third Saudi state, 1, 5–10, 39, 45, 50, 119; marriages and wives, 10, 26n28, 32; political tactics and pattern of rule, 5–14 passim, 35–36, 41, 119, 134, 147; sons of Ibn Saud as successors as king, 17, 25, 30, 31–32

Al Saud, Abd al-Rahman (late 19th century ruler), 5

Al Saud, Abdullah (king 2005–), 10, 24–25, 30–31, 32–33, 36, 37–38, 39, 43, 46, 51, 72, 74, 75–76, 78, 116, 119, 136, 148; as commander of SANG, 43; as crown prince/crown regent, 24–25, 74; as "Custodian of the Two Holy Mosques," 116; as a reformist, 24–25, 30–31, 32–33, 36, 37–38, 46, 51; response to the Arab uprisings (2011–), 148; response to Islamic extremism, 136

Al Saud, Abdullah (ruler 1814–1818), 4

About the Author

MATTHEW GRAY is associate professor at the Centre for Arab and Islamic Studies, at The Australian National University, Canberra, Australia. Prior to taking up this position in 2005, he spent many years in trade promotion and military intelligence roles with the Australian government. He is the author of *Qatar: Politics and the Challenges of Development* (2013), *Conspiracy Theories in the Arab World: Sources and Politics* (2010), and numerous journal articles, book chapters, and papers on Middle Eastern and particularly Persian Gulf politics, political economy, and international relations.